Yankee Publishing Incorporated
Dublin, New Hampshire
First Edition
Copyright ©1985 by Yankee Publishing Incorporated

Library of Congress Catalog Card Number: 84-51677
ISBN: 0-89909-060-5

GOOD NEIGHBORS U
COOKBOOK

YANKEE MAGAZINE'S

GOOD NEIGHBORS U.S.A. COOKBOOK

Edited by Clarissa M. Silitch

Designed by Margo Letourneau

YANKEE® BOOKS

A division of Yankee Publishing Incorporated
Dublin, New Hampshire

CONTENTS

EDITOR'S NOTE

That *Yankee* Magazine readers appreciate good food has been clear from the very start. Over the half century since its inception in 1935, *Yankee* has given its readers countless food ideas, and readers have replied in kind. Thanks to this energetic symbiotic culinary collaboration, Yankee has published many fine cookbooks — notably *Favorite New England Recipes, The Country Innkeepers' Cookbook, The Yankee Church Supper Cookbook, Great New England Recipes,* and *The Best Recipes from New England Inns* — all with a distinctly New England flavor. But when Yankee Books held a Recipe Contest in 1981-1982, (announced in the October 1981 issue of *Yankee* Magazine), we were amazed at the volume of recipes that poured in from *every* American state. Many of the letters we received asked *why* we only published recipes from New Englanders. Why didn't we have a book of recipes from *Yankee* readers nationwide?

We too wondered why we didn't, and resolved to see what could be done about it. Letters requesting original recipes were forthwith sent out to readers all over the country (New England included, of course!). The response to these mailings was so enthusiastic that we decided to publish the *Good Neighbors U.S.A. Cookbook.*

Meanwhile, another sort of contest initiated by *Yankee* magazine was in full swing — the "Cookbook of the Month" contest for cookbooks privately published by volunteer groups. So many excellent cookbooks were entered, that *Yankee* was hard put to decide upon just one a month. At the suggestion of Susan Mahnke, *Yankee* Food Editor, I wrote a number of these groups asking if they would make the recipes in their cookbooks available for possible inclusion in our new project — the *Good Neighbors USA Cookbook.* They kindly complied. See pages 306-307 for a list of these cookbooks and the recipes from them that appear in this book.

Seven superb cooks with editorial experience agreed to help us in compiling this book. Each had to select for testing up to a hundred recipes per chapter from the thousands of recipes available, evaluate recipe test reports, test the recipes herself if necessary, and finally, present us with the forty or fifty she considered most outstanding. Yankee wishes to thank Jeanette Perron (Soups, Appetizers, and Hors d'Oeuvres); Ann Skelly (Chicken and Turkey); Moira Burnham (Meats and Meat Casseroles); Veronica Marinaro (Fish and Seafood, also Vegetables and Vegetable Casseroles); Linda Bensinger (Breads and Breadstuffs); Carla Kardt (Pies and Desserts); and Bonnie Berrett (Cakes, Cookies, and Candy). The remaining two chapters were compiled by myself.

Yankee has a unique, but oddly effective method of testing recipes, depending on about fifty cooks domiciled in the Monadnock Region. These experts range from *bona fide* gourmet cooks to those renowned for home-cooking and pot-luck suppers; they choose recipes that appeal to their personal tastes to try out on family or friends, reserving a smidgin for Yankee staff members to sample. The cooks then fill out a report, describing the recipe they have tested, suggesting changes, if any, and telling us the reactions of those to whom it was served.

Thus, in the *Good Neighbors U.S.A. Cookbook* you'll find recipes of gourmet quality along with the family-style fare. No recipe requires special equipment or expertise, and the directions are clear and concise. This is a stimulating collection that reflects the taste and tables of America. Already — unpublished as it is at this writing — I myself have used and re-used many of the recipes. We think you will too!

Clarissa M. Silitch, Editor

DEDICATION

Yankee wishes to thank all the wonderful cooks
and cookbooks who have contributed their recipes and
expertise to make this book possible.

CHAPTER ONE

Hors d'Oeuvres, Appetizers, and Soups

Good beginnings usually set the tone for what is to follow. A somewhat different, attractive, and carefully made hors d'oeuvre, appetizer, or soup augurs well for the balance of the meal. Anticipation will be heightened, and the occasion will be enhanced. All of the recipes in this chapter have been selected on the basis of such criteria. Most are unique; all are attractive, tempting, and, of course, *good*.

Sometimes the beginnings given here can be the whole presentation, as in the case of hearty soups or stews for lunch or supper, or the hors d'oeuvres served at a cocktail party.

The first half of the chapter is devoted to cocktail spreads and dips and hors d'oeuvres and appetizers. Next come the soups — cream soups first, followed by seafood soups and chowders, and finally by an assortment of miscellaneous soups that fit neither of the first two categories. Check the index if you are looking for a particular sort of soup.

SPREADS AND DIPS

Chick Pea Dip

A somewhat different and easy hummus, kissed with a refreshing hint of mint.

two 15-ounce cans chick peas
⅓ cup fresh lemon juice
½ cup sesame seed oil
3 garlic cloves, crushed
1 tablespoon snipped fresh mint

⅛ teaspoon salt
(Tabasco to taste)
2 tablespoons olive oil
toasted pita bread wedges, or
   crackers

Drain liquid from chick peas; reserve ¼ cup liquid. Place chick peas, lemon juice, and reserved liquid into blender container and cover. Puree, scraping sides of container frequently with spatula until smooth. Transfer mixture to medium size bowl; stir in sesame seed oil, garlic, mint, and salt. Cover and refrigerate for at least 6 hours. Taste and adjust seasonings. Add a few drops of Tabasco if you like — but please taste as you go. Form well in center, and pour olive oil into well. Serve at room temperature with pita bread or crackers. Makes about 2 cups.

Terry West
Philadelphia, PA

Crab Dip

This one is elegant. Use it for a special occasion — or make one up.

8 ounces cream cheese
1 tablespoon milk
6½-ounce can flaked crab meat
   (remove any membrane)
2 tablespoons chopped onion
½ teaspoon prepared horseradish

¼ teaspoon salt
dash pepper
dash Tabasco
½ cup sliced almonds, toasted
2 tablespoons melted butter or
   cooking oil

Blend all ingredients except almonds and melted butter or cooking oil. Place in a 1-pint baking dish. To toast almonds, spread on cookie sheet and drizzle with melted butter or oil. Brown in oven at 400°F. for about 5 minutes — watch carefully, as they can scorch quickly. Sprinkle almonds over dip. Just before serving, heat in 375°F. oven for 15 minutes. Makes almost 2 cups.

Nancy Sieverts
Princeton, NJ

Fruit Dip

A wonderful idea for summer patio parties.

8-ounce package cream cheese
½ cup brown sugar, packed
⅓ cup confectioner's sugar
3 tablespoons milk
1 teaspoon vanilla

cut-up fresh fruit — pineapple and
    melon chunks, apple quarters,
    and seedless grapes
whole strawberries and mint leaves
    for garnish

Beat together first five ingredients until creamy. Put in pretty bowl and serve with platter of fruit. Garnish as suggested, and provide toothpicks for dipping. Makes 1 cup.

Jean Brownlee
Victorville, CA

Brouder's Guacamole

Both cool and peppery — an excellent guacamole.

1 ripe avocado
½ tomato, chopped
1 small scallion, chopped
2 Tuscany peppers (jarred),
    chopped

1 teaspoon juice from peppers
juice from ¼ lemon
salt and pepper to taste
tortilla chips

Mash meat of avocado. Stir in next six ingredients. Chill. Serve with tortilla chips. Makes about 1 cup.

Judith B. Harrington
Auburndale, MA

Sour Cream Florentine Dip

Crunchy, colorful, and good. Can be served with crackers, too.

10-ounce package frozen chopped
    spinach
1 cup sour cream
1 cup mayonnaise
1 small onion, chopped

8-ounce can water chestnuts,
    chopped
2¾-ounce box Knorr's vegetable
    soup
round or French loaf

Cook spinach and drain thoroughly. Combine with other ingredients, and refrigerate for a couple of hours. Hollow out round loaf of bread, stuff center with dip, and slice. (Use a good solid loaf with a hard crust.) Or cut loaf of French bread into small pieces for dipping. Serves 6-8.

Kathleen H. Beatrice
Lynchburg, VA

Sweet Vegetable Dip

A surprising sweet-sour taste and lovely light golden color.

3 eggs, lightly beaten
3 tablespoons white vinegar
3 tablespoons sugar
1 tablespoon butter

1 tablespoon minced dry or fresh
    onion
8-ounce package cream cheese
(chopped green pepper)

Blend eggs, vinegar, and sugar and cook over medium heat until thick, stirring constantly. Remove from heat and add butter, onion, cream cheese cut into small pieces, and optional green pepper. Stir until cheese is melted and dip is smooth. If cheese does not melt, put dip on low heat for a few minutes. Refrigerate until ½ hour before ready to use. Serve with raw vegetables for dipping. Makes about 1¾ cups.

E. D. Brown
Jordan, NY

Caviar Pie

Romanoff caviar is recommended for this deluxe party spread. Double the amount of caviar if you really love it. Chances are that the plate will be scraped clean, but if you are lucky enough to have some left over, enjoy as baked-potato topping or sandwich spread.

3 eggs
12 ounces cream cheese
3 tablespoons mayonnaise

2 or 3 pearl onions, minced very
    fine
3½ ounces lumpfish caviar

Hardboil eggs. Rinse under cold water. Chop yolks; set aside. Chop whites; set aside. Blend cream cheese with mayonnaise. Spread in 9-inch glass pie plate or 8x11-inch dish. Sprinkle yolks over cheese, then layer on minced onions, caviar, and chopped egg whites. Serve with melba toast, homemade (see below) or packaged. Serves about 20.

Melba Toast:

1 loaf good extra-thin white bread — Pepperidge Farm for example

Remove crusts; roll each piece flat with rolling pin and cut in half. Toast in oven on ungreased cookie sheets at 400°F. until golden brown, about 6-8 minutes. Cool.

Nancy Sieverts
Princeton, NJ

Cheddar Cheese-Ale Spread

Cheesy — with a nice bite!

6 cups shredded Cheddar cheese
3-ounce package cream cheese
4 tablespoons butter, softened
¾ cup beer or ale

1 teaspoon dry mustard
¼ teaspoon crushed red pepper
flakes

Beat cheeses and butter with electric mixer until smooth. Gradually beat in ale, mustard, and red pepper. Keep refrigerated. Makes about 6 cups.

Bonnie Berrett
Jaffrey, NH

Easy Chicken Liver Pâté I

Looks and tastes very grand, but a snap to make. It may be frozen. Don't give friends small loaves of it for Christmas unless you are willing to make an annual habit of it. Good for lunch or supper, too.

1 medium onion, quartered
1 large clove garlic, minced
2 eggs
1 pound chicken livers
¼ cup flour
1 teaspoon salt

¼ cup butter
½ teaspoon allspice
½ teaspoon ginger
1 teaspoon white pepper
1 cup heavy cream

Preheat oven to 325°F. Blend onion, garlic, and eggs at high speed for 1 minute. Add livers, one or two at a time, and blend. Add flour, salt, butter, spices, and cream. Blend 2 more minutes. Turn into well-greased 1-quart baking dish or two miniature loaf pans (5½ x 3¾ x 2½ inches). Cover with foil. Put dish or loaf pans in larger pan, and add hot water to halfway up sides. Bake for 3 hours for quart size; check at 1½ hours for miniatures. Cool without foil. Cover again and refrigerate. Serve with crackers or small bread rounds. Makes 1 large loaf or 2 small loaves.

Bern Potter Haines
Moorestown, NJ

Chicken Liver Pâté II

Easy, richly flavorful pâté that can be stored in refrigerator up to 3 days.

oil
1½ envelopes plain gelatin
2½ tablespoons lemon juice
1 pound trimmed chicken livers
1 medium onion, chopped
1 medium tart apple, peeled, cored,
    and chopped

½ cup beef broth
2 tablespoons chopped shallots
1 cup butter, cut into pieces
¼ cup cream sherry
1 teaspoon salt
¼ teaspoon dry mustard
dash Tabasco

Oil 5-cup mold or 5 crockery custard cups. In small bowl, soften gelatin in lemon juice. In saucepan, combine livers, onion, apple, beef broth, and shallots. Bring to boil over medium heat. Reduce heat, and simmer about 5 minutes. Add gelatin mixture and mix well. Remove from heat and add butter, a little at a time, blending well. Stir in sherry, salt, mustard, and Tabasco. Transfer mixture to blender, and puree until smooth. Let stand 15 minutes. Pour into mold or custard cups, cover, and chill overnight.

Barbara Wicks-Calnan
Andover, MA

Pâté Mold

This lively braunschweiger-cream cheese spread encased in beef aspic makes a spectacular hors d'oeuvre plate. Serve with crisp crackers.

1 envelope plain gelatin
2 tablespoons water
10½-ounce can beef consommé
1 pound braunschweiger liverwurst
8-ounce package cream cheese,
    softened

3 tablespoons dried onion flakes
1½ teaspoons Dijon mustard
2 tablespoons parsley
(black-olive slivers)

Soften gelatin in water, add consommé, and heat until well blended. Rinse 3-cup mold with cold water, drain, and pour in consommé mixture to cover bottom. Chill until gelatin has set. Reserve remaining consommé mixture. With hands or food processor, mix braunschweiger and cream cheese until well blended. Mix in onion flakes, mustard, and parsley. When consommé in mold has set, place pâté in mold, keeping mixture away from sides of mold. Reheat consommé mixture, add optional black-olive slivers, and pour into mold around pâté. Chill until set. When ready to serve, place mold in warm water for a moment or two, then place plate on top of mold and invert mold, so that aspic comes out of mold onto plate. Serves 10-12.

Elinor Sherman
Peterborough, NH

Molded Shrimp Spread

Bright and rich and smooth! Doubles as a rich luncheon salad.

10½-ounce can tomato soup
8-ounce package cream cheese
1 envelope unflavored gelatin
¼ cup water
½ cup chopped onion
½ cup chopped celery

2 tablespoons fresh snipped parsley
1 cup mayonnaise
1 pound cooked shrimp, chopped
lettuce
parsley sprigs

Pour tomato soup over cream cheese, and heat slowly in saucepan, mashing cheese while heating. When cheese is completely melted, remove from heat. Add gelatin mixed with water. Stir. Add onion, celery, parsley, and mayonnaise. Add chopped shrimp, mix thoroughly, and pour into 6-cup mold. Refrigerate until set. Unmold onto bed of lettuce and garnish with parsley sprigs. Serves 12-16.

Rachel Benoit
Manchester, NH

HORS D'OEUVRES AND APPETIZERS

Asparagus Pokes

Asparagus tips baked tender in delicate cheesy rolls sprinkled with sesame seed. You can use half the asparagus with the same amount of dough for heftier pokes.

¾ cup flour
1 cup grated sharp Cheddar cheese
¼ cup butter, softened

40-50 two-inch fresh asparagus
    tips, cooked slightly
sesame seeds
paprika

Knead flour, cheese, and butter into soft dough. Pat thin. Roll around asparagus tips, and then roll in sesame seeds. Bake for 15 minutes at 400°F. on ungreased cookie sheet. Sprinkle with paprika. Makes 40-50.

Martha Sharp Oyler
Anderson, IN

French-Fried Cauliflower

A good hors d'oeuvre to serve hot with drinks or cold as an appetizer for a picnic. The optional Worcestershire sauce adds a little bite.

1 large head cauliflower	2 tablespoons olive oil
4 tablespoons flour	(2 teaspoons Worcestershire sauce)
2 eggs, lightly beaten	½ teaspoon salt

Soak cauliflower in cold salted water, top downward, for 30-45 minutes. Drain and break into florets. In boiling salted water cook florets 15 minutes. Drain carefully and cool. Combine flour, eggs, olive oil, optional Worcestershire sauce, and salt to make a batter. Dip florets in batter and fry a few at a time in hot oil until golden brown. Drain on brown paper. Serves 8.

Elsie Stupinsky
Bernardsville, NJ

Exotic Canapés

Sharp, with unexpected flavors — great to serve with wine. The spread mixture may be prepared in advance and frozen until needed.

1 cup grated sharp Cheddar cheese	½ teaspoon curry powder
1 cup chopped black olives	dash salt and pepper
2 tablespoons mayonnaise	6 English-muffin halves, toasted
1 medium onion, grated	lightly

Combine cheese, olives, mayonnaise, onion, curry, salt, and pepper and mix well. Spread muffin halves with mixture. Place under broiler 4 minutes. Cut in quarters, and serve piping hot. Serves 24.

Marge Moran
Garden City, NY

Cocktail Gouda

Dare to be different — this one is! Eat each slice of pastry-wrapped cheese with a crisp slice of apple.

½-pound round Gouda cheese	2 apples, cored, sliced, and chilled
1 package frozen crescent rolls	

Remove wax or other covering from Gouda cheese. Separate crescent-roll triangles and stretch them a little. Wrap triangles around whole cheese, stretching as you go to fit, moistening seams and top to seal. Place on baking sheet and bake in 375°F. oven until dough begins to brown and cheese is soft but not liquid — about 15 minutes. Place immediately on serving dish, and ring with cold, unpeeled apple slices. Serves 6-8.

Fran Blakeney
Concord, NH

Chinese Chicken Wings

The fresh ginger root adds zing and chinoiserie.

12 chicken wings
⅓ cup soy sauce
⅓ cup honey

⅓ cup water
1 teaspoon grated fresh ginger root

Cut chicken wings at joints and discard wing tips. Place wings in baking dish in single layer. Combine soy sauce, honey, and water and pour over wings. Sprinkle with ginger root and cover dish. Bake at 300°F. for 1 hour. Uncover and bake 1 hour more, turning wings every 15 minutes. Makes 12.

Bonnie Berrett
Jaffrey, NH

Sesame Chicken Drummettes

Crisp, nutty little chicken morsels. To create "drummettes," sever wing joints, and use only the larger halves.

3½ pounds chicken wings
2 tablespoons sesame seeds
¾ cup bread crumbs
1 teaspoon paprika

½ teaspoon salt
¼ cup heavy cream
⅓ cup butter

Prepare drummettes from wings. Toast sesame seeds in small non-stick or lightly greased skillet over medium heat, shake pan constantly, and watch carefully for burning. Combine toasted seeds, bread crumbs, paprika, and salt in shallow dish. Dip chicken pieces in cream, then roll in crumb mixture. Refrigerate 1 hour. Put butter in 9x13-inch baking dish and melt in oven while oven preheats to 375°F. Remove dish from oven, add drummettes, and turn to coat evenly with melted butter. Bake 40-45 minutes, drain on paper, and serve hot or cold. Makes 15-20.

Jean Brownlee
Victorville, CA

Curried Chicken Balls

Lively and so interesting. Serve with toothpicks.

4¾-ounce can Underwood chicken spread
¼ cup chopped chutney
1 teaspoon curry powder

dash salt
dab mayonnaise
⅔ cup finely chopped almonds, toasted

Combine the first four ingredients, and moisten very lightly with mayonnaise — just enough to hold mixture together. Roll into ½-inch balls (about the size of marbles). Roll in chopped toasted almonds. Refrigerate to set. Makes about 24 balls.

Mrs. M.W. Sullivan
Boston, MA

The stuffed egg is ubiquitous. But here are some interesting variations on the theme.

Cidered Eggs

A slightly pickled kind of deviled egg. You can also serve these eggs un*stuffed, whole or divided, as an appetizer or side dish.*

¾ cup apple cider, or apple juice
¼ cup white vinegar
3 slices onion
¾ teaspoon salt
½ teaspoon whole pickling spice

½ clove garlic
6 hardboiled eggs, shelled
3 tablespoons mayonnaise
pinch dry mustard
paprika

Combine all ingredients except eggs, mayonnaise, mustard, and paprika in saucepan; bring to a boil. Reduce heat; simmer 5 minutes. Pour over eggs in sealable container. Cover container, and refrigerate 12-18 hours, turning eggs occasionally to pickle evenly. Remove eggs from liquid and drain. Cut eggs in half, remove yolks, and mash them with mayonnaise and mustard, adding more mayonnaise if mixture is too dry. Stuff whites with yolk mixture and sprinkle with paprika. Makes 12 stuffed egg halves.

Jojo Flye
Traverse City, MI

Carey's Deviled Eggs

A truly savory way to go with stuffed eggs.

6 hardboiled eggs
2 tablespoons mayonnaise
2 teaspoons mustard with
  horseradish
½ teaspoon sugar
2 tablespoons drained sweet pickle
  relish

¼ teaspoon cider vinegar
½ teaspoon garlic salt
pinch celery seed
dash black pepper
good dash nutmeg
green olives, sliced thin
paprika

Shell eggs and slice in half. Separate yolks and mash until creamy with no lumps. Add all other ingredients except olives and paprika, and mix well. Stuff whites with yolk mixture, and garnish with sliced olives and paprika. Makes 12 stuffed egg halves.

Carey Moss
Arlington, VA

Smoked Turkey Eggs

Yet another innovative variation on the deviled-egg theme.

8 hardboiled eggs, shelled and
  halved
4 ounces ground smoked turkey
⅛ teaspoon sage

1 teaspoon grated onion
dash Tabasco
creamy French dressing
minced fresh parsley

Remove yolks carefully from each egg half and mash in medium-sized bowl. Stir in turkey, sage, onion, and Tabasco. Add enough French dressing to moisten, and mix well. Fill egg halves, and garnish with parsley. Cover and chill before serving. Makes 16 stuffed egg halves.

Barbara Wicks-Calnan
Andover, MA

Melon Balls

This enticing combination of colors and subtle flavors makes a refreshing first course for summer entertaining.

2 cups small watermelon balls
2 cups small cantaloupe balls
2 cups small honeydew melon balls

½ pound seedless white grapes
  sliced in half
1¼ cups clear melon liqueur

Combine all ingredients and let marinate overnight in glass bowl. Serve as appetizer in small dishes or saucers. Serves 6-8.

Shirley Opitz
Monroeville, PA

Hot or Cold Stuffed Mushrooms

Serve hot with soup for a light supper, or either hot or cold as an appetizer.

1 tablespoon cooking oil
1 teaspoon butter
12 large fresh mushroom caps
  (stems removed and chopped
  for stuffing)
2 tablespoons finely chopped onion
¼ pound sausage meat
½ cup packaged herb-stuffing mix

1 tablespoon chopped parsley

Topping:

2 tablespoons fine bread crumbs
2 tablespoons grated Parmesan
  cheese
1 tablespoon melted butter

Heat oil and butter. Add chopped stems, onion, and sausage meat. Cook and stir until meat is done and liquid from mushrooms has evaporated. Add stuffing prepared according to package instructions. Add chopped parsley. Stuff mushroom caps, and place on ungreased cookie sheet. Mix topping ingredients, and sprinkle over mushrooms. Bake at 400°F. for about 15 minutes. Serves 6 as appetizer, 2 for light supper.

Beatrice Vetrano
New London, PA

Sweet and Fishy Nuggets

This unique and delectable appetizer is a Yankee prizewinner. Serve warm.

2-ounce can anchovy fillets in olive
  oil, drained
2 tablespoons flour
½ cup raisins, chopped

1 package active dry yeast
¾ cup warm water
2 cups flour, sifted
cooking oil for deep frying

Rinse anchovy fillets lightly in tap water, pat dry with paper towels, and chop fine. Combine with 2 tablespoons flour and mix well, taking care that pieces do not stick together. Stir in raisins. Set aside. Sprinkle yeast into ¼ cup of the warm water and stir until dissolved. Add remaining ½ cup warm water. In medium bowl, combine 2 cups flour with anchovy mixture and stir in yeast mixture, mixing until dough becomes sticky and stringy. (To reach this consistency, 2 or 3 tablespoons more warm water may be added if necessary.) Turn dough into lightly greased bowl and cover with plastic wrap or damp towel. Let rise in warm place until doubled in bulk, about 1 hour. Punch down. Repeat. After 2 hours, dough should be bubbly.

Fill deep fryer ⅓ full with oil. Heat oil to 370°F. With wiggling motion of fingers, pinch off golf-ball-size pieces of dough and drop into hot oil. Fry a few at a time, turning with slotted spoon until lightly golden. Remove to paper towels to drain. Makes 3-4 dozen.

Louise M. Keller
Middlebury, CT

Pineapple Chunks

Refreshing as a spiced-fruit hors d'oeuvre, or as a side dish with ham.

No. 2½ can (3½ cups) pineapple
  chunks
¾ cup cider vinegar
1¼ cups sugar

dash salt
1 stick cinnamon
8 whole cloves

Drain pineapple syrup into pan, and add all remaining ingredients except pineapple. Simmer over low heat for 10 minutes. Add pineapple and bring to rolling boil. Remove from heat and cool. May be stored in refrigerator in covered container for 2 months or more. Serve with toothpicks as hors d'oeuvre. Makes 20-25 pieces. As a side dish, serves 6-8.

Linda Long
Reading, MA

Cheesy Spinach Puffs

The corn muffin mix lends a faint sweetness to these little puffs which is surprisingly tasty.

10-ounce package frozen chopped
  spinach
½ cup finely chopped onion
2 eggs, lightly beaten
½ cup grated Parmesan cheese

½ cup blue cheese salad dressing
¼ cup melted butter
⅛ teaspoon garlic powder
8½-ounce package corn muffin mix

Cook spinach and onion in water according to spinach package instructions. Drain well, pressing out all liquid. Combine eggs, cheese, salad dressing, butter, and garlic powder. Add spinach mixture and muffin mix. Mix well. Cover and chill about 3 hours. Shape into 1-inch balls, and bake on greased cookie sheet at 350°F. for 10-12 minutes. Makes about 50 puffs.

Marge Moran
Garden City, NY

Spinach-Cheese Balls

Rich little bombs with a subtle garlic-butter flavor. Good reheated, too.

10-ounce package frozen chopped
    spinach
1 cup coarse bread crumbs
½ cup grated mild Cheddar cheese

2 eggs, beaten
½ cup butter, softened
dash garlic powder

Cook spinach, cool, and drain well. Mix with other ingredients, and roll into balls about 1 inch in diameter. Freeze on cookie sheet for ½ hour, then store in covered bowl until ready to use. Bake on cookie sheet for 15 minutes in 350°F. oven. Let cool slightly before serving. Makes about 20 balls.

Mary Lee Williams
Rochester, NY

CREAM SOUPS

Cream of almost every good thing you can think of — from almonds all the way to tomatoes — except for seafood. You'll find seafood soups and chowders in the section immediately following this one.

Cream of Almond Soup

Rich and subtle to start off a special dinner — add flaked crab meat or small shrimp for a main luncheon dish. Serve hot or cold.

2 cups blanched almonds
3 tablespoons butter
1 small onion, sliced
1 stalk celery, sliced
3 tablespoons flour
2½ quarts hot chicken broth

¼ teaspoon pepper
1 tablespoon salt
2 cups light cream, heated
1 teaspoon almond extract
(flaked crab meat or small shrimp)

Take 30 almonds, cut into slivers, and brown in oven at 200°F. — watch closely, as they can scorch. Crush remainder of almonds very fine (use food processor, meat grinder, or blender). Melt butter in soup pot, and sauté onion and celery until soft. Stir in flour, and cook over medium heat for a moment or two. Add crushed almonds, hot chicken broth, pepper and salt. Mix well and leave to simmer over low heat for 1 hour. Strain. Add in warmed cream and almond extract. Add optional crab or shrimp. Sprinkle toasted almonds over top. Serves 8.

Henry Flory
Southern Pines, NC

Fresh Basil Soup

Light, creamy, and very basil-ly.

2 medium onions, chopped
2 tablespoons butter
6 cups chicken stock

1 bunch fresh basil, chopped
13-ounce can evaporated milk
salt to taste

Sauté onions in butter until soft. Add chicken stock, and bring to boil. Add chopped basil, reduce heat, and simmer for 15 minutes. Add evaporated milk (undiluted), and heat through. Do not boil. Salt to taste. Serves 6.

Michele Verville
Peterborough, NH

Bell Pepper Soup

Hot or cold — sweet green peppers in chicken stock and sour cream with an elusive hint of dill (or thyme if you prefer).

1 cup chopped green pepper
¾ cup chopped onion
¼ cup butter, melted
4 cups chicken stock
½ teaspoon dill or thyme
¼ cup butter

¼ cup flour
½ cup milk
½ cup sour cream
1 sweet red pepper, minced
salt to taste

Sauté green pepper and onion in ¼ cup melted butter until tender. Stir in chicken stock and dill (or thyme), and simmer for 8 minutes. Cool slightly, then puree briefly in blender, and set aside. Melt ¼ cup butter in saucepan, stir in flour, and cook until mixture is smooth and beginning to bubble. Slowly add milk and cook, stirring constantly, until mixture thickens. Add pureed green peppers and sour cream. Stir to blend. Salt to taste. Garnish with sweet red pepper. Serve either hot or cold. Serves 6.

Thérèse Butcher
Santa Fe, NM

Cream of Broccoli Soup

Fresh broccoli, potato, and cream, flavored with nutmeg and wine.

1 large bunch broccoli
1 large potato
4 cups chicken broth
½ cup white wine

1 cup half and half
pinch nutmeg
(salt)

Cut up broccoli and remove tougher stems (they are bitter). Peel and quarter potato. Steam broccoli and potato on rack in chicken broth and wine. Remove from broth and puree in blender immediately to preserve good green color. Return to pan, add half and half and nutmeg, and heat through. Add salt if needed. Serves 6.

Mrs. Anne Seile
Sisters, OR

Cream of Butternut Soup

An Australian squash soup that freezes well and is delicious either hot or cold. You can use pumpkin instead if you wish.

2 pounds butternut squash
water to cover
8 shallots, chopped, white part
    only, or 1 small leek, finely
    sliced
1 tablespoon butter

2 cups milk
3 chicken bouillon cubes
salt and pepper to taste
sour cream or yogurt
parsley

Wash butternut squash, remove seeds, and cut into pieces (leave skin on to retain vitamins). Put into saucepan with water to cover, and cook until tender. Drain off and reserve water. In another saucepan cook shallots or leek in butter over very low heat until soft but not brown. Place cooked squash (skin will be tender enough to eat) in blender with milk. Blend on high speed until smooth, about 1-2 minutes. Pour into saucepan. Dissolve bouillon cubes in reserved squash water and add water enough to make 2 cups liquid. Add to shallots. Pour into blender, and blend until smooth. Add to squash mixture, and heat gently, taking care *not to boil*. Season to taste with salt and pepper. Garnish with dollop of sour cream or yogurt and parsley. Serves 4-6.

Polly Curran
Hancock, NH

Cream of Carrot Soup

A "souper" soup — very pretty way to add color to a meal. Hot or cold, a great introduction to Thanksgiving dinner.

½ cup butter
3 medium onions, chopped
8 large carrots, peeled and sliced
6 cups chicken stock
½ teaspoon thyme

½ cup light cream
2 cups yogurt
salt and pepper
parsley or watercress for garnish

In soup kettle, melt butter, and sauté onions and carrots until onions are tender. Add stock and thyme, cover, and simmer for 30 minutes. Puree in blender, return mixture to soup kettle, and bring to a boil. Remove from heat, stir in cream, yogurt, salt, and pepper. Garnish with snipped parsley or watercress. Serves 10-12.

Carlene Pearre
Manchester, NH

Cheese Chowder

Hot, cheesy, and full of vegetables.

4 medium potatoes, peeled and
    diced
6 carrots, scraped and sliced thin
2 stalks celery, chopped
1 medium onion, chopped
2 cups water
15-ounce can cream-style corn

salt and pepper
¼ cup butter
¼ cup flour
2 cups milk
10 ounces Cheddar cheese
parsley for garnish

Cook vegetables in water about 10 minutes until just done. Add creamed corn, season to taste, and set aside. Melt butter in separate pan, and mix with flour. Gradually add milk, stirring over medium heat until thickened. Add the cheese, cut in small chunks. Heat until cheese is melted; do not allow to boil. When ready to serve, combine cheese sauce with vegetables, heat through, and ladle into soup tureen. Garnish with small sprigs of parsley for color. Serves 6-8.

Mrs. Marion Lovejoy
Worcester, MA

Curry Soup

The pungent, golden taste of India.

2 tablespoons butter
1 small onion, sliced
1 clove garlic, crushed
1 medium apple, peeled and grated
pinch thyme

1 teaspoon curry powder, or to taste
2 tablespoons flour
8 cups hot fish, clam, or chicken
   stock
1 cup heavy cream

Melt butter in soup pot, and lightly sauté onion, garlic, apple, and thyme. Stir in curry powder and flour. Cook over medium heat for 3 minutes. Slowly add stock and cook for another 3 minutes. Add cream and serve. Serves 8-10.

Jeannette Perron
Dublin, NH

Fresh Green Pea Soup

An old French recipe — delicate in color and taste.

4 cups fresh or frozen green peas
2 cups chicken stock
2 cups light cream
1 tablespoon flour

1 teaspoon salt
¼ teaspoon pepper
1 tablespoon butter
mint leaves for garnish

Cook peas in stock until tender. Put peas and stock into blender and puree. Set aside. Scald cream, remove from heat, add flour, and blend with whisk. Cook, stirring over low heat until mixture thickens. Add salt and pepper, stir in pea puree, and add butter. Serve hot, garnished with fresh mint leaves. Serves 6.

Jane Mowry
Tulsa, OK

Potato and Watercress Soup

A light, fresh-tasting soup hearty enough to make a lunch with bread and cheese.

1 bunch watercress
3 large potatoes
5 cups chicken stock

1 cup heavy cream
salt and pepper
1 tablespoon butter

Trim most of stems from watercress, peel potatoes and cube, and cook together in stock until potatoes are tender. Cool and puree in blender until smooth. Pour into soup kettle, stir in cream, add salt and pepper to taste, and cook until heated through. Do not boil. Add butter, stir until melted, and serve. Serves 6.

Bertha Senior
Newburyport, MA

Green Velvet Leek Soup

So rich and smooth, hard to believe it is low-calorie — no butter, no flour, and no cream!

3 leeks — white part and 2 inches
   of green
4 medium onions
4 cups chicken stock

13-ounce can evaporated milk
1 tablespoon vinegar
salt and pepper to taste
chopped chives for garnish

Clean and chop leeks and onions. Put in soup kettle with 1 cup of the chicken stock, and bring to boil. Reduce heat, cover, and steam vegetables over low heat for 15 minutes. Uncover and stir several times to prevent sticking; do not allow to brown. Add rest of stock, and remove from heat to cool a little. Puree in blender, and return to kettle. Add evaporated milk, vinegar, salt, and pepper and heat through but do not boil. Garnish with chopped chives. Serves 8.

Jeannette Perron
Dublin, NH

Versatile Vegetable Soup

Outstanding served cold, but good hot also. Make and serve the same day.

¾ cup chopped onion
½ cup chopped green pepper
2 cloves garlic, chopped
¼ cup olive oil
4 cups chopped peeled fresh
   tomatoes, or two 1-pound cans
4 cups peeled, chopped cucumbers

salt and pepper
4 cups chicken stock
1 teaspoon dill
pulp of 1 large ripe avocado,
   coarsely chopped
1 cup cream

In soup kettle, sauté onion, green pepper, and garlic in olive oil until tender. Add tomatoes, cucumbers, and salt and pepper to taste, and mix well. Add stock and dill, and simmer 25 minutes. Cool slightly and puree in blender, 1 to 2 cupfuls at a time. This can be served hot or cold; so either chill mixture thoroughly or heat until steaming. Just before serving, stir in avocado and cream. Serves 10.

Marina MacMillan
Nashville, TN

Fresh Mushroom Soup

Easy to do and so much better than canned.

¼ cup plus 2 tablespoons butter
2 cups sliced onions
½ teaspoon sugar
1 clove garlic, minced
1 pound fresh mushrooms, sliced
¼ cup plus 1 tablespoon flour

1 cup water
½ teaspoon salt
¼ cup evaporated milk
2 cups chicken broth
1 cup white wine
dash pepper

Melt butter, add onions and sugar, and sauté until onion is tender. Add garlic and mushrooms, and cook 5 minutes, stirring often. Stir in flour, and cook 2 minutes, stirring constantly. Add water. Put contents in blender, and blend to liquefy. Return to saucepan and add salt, milk, broth, wine, and pepper. Heat and serve. Serves 6-8.

Alma Wall
Ridge, MD

Spinach Tarragon Soup

A very attractive, light and tangy soup, good hot or cold.

10 ounces fresh spinach (or 10-
    ounce package frozen)
2 tablespoons butter
3 sprigs parsley
¼ small head lettuce, sliced

⅛ teaspoon pepper
salt to taste
1 teaspoon tarragon
5 cups hot chicken stock
½ cup light cream

Cook spinach and drain well. Add butter, and stir to melt butter. Combine with all other ingredients *except* cream, and puree in blender. Stir in cream and heat over medium heat until heated through. Do not boil. Serves 6.

Jean Brownlee
Victorville, CA

Fresh Tomato Soup

Something nice to do with those garden tomatoes that come all at once!

1 quart fresh ripe tomatoes,
    quartered
1 large onion, cut up
1 quart water
3 tablespoons flour

2 tablespoons sugar
2 teaspoons salt
1 cup milk
1½ tablespoons butter

Boil tomatoes, onion, and water together for 30 minutes. Mix flour, sugar, and salt, and stir into milk. Add to tomatoes, and cook until thickened. Strain to remove skins and seeds. Bring back to boil, and add butter. Serves 6.

Mrs. Lester Anthony
Albany, NY

Cream of Rice Soup

Something old from Mrs. Parloa's New Cook Book, *published in 1880. Wonderful made with brown rice.*

1 cup raw rice	salt and pepper
2 quarts chicken broth	1 quart light cream
1 small onion, chopped	herbs for garnish
1 stalk celery, chopped	

Wash rice and add to broth along with onion and celery. Simmer for 2 hours. Put through sieve or blender; add seasoning and cream. Heat through, but do not boil. Garnish with something green for color — parsley, dill, or basil. Serves 6.

Rhonda Blakely
Scranton, PA

SEAFOOD SOUPS

Just a few. Unless you live in the proper place — by the sea — seafood is hard to get and wickedly expensive these days. Yet there are times when *nothing else will do!*

Crab Bouillabaisse

For really special occasions.

6½-ounce can king crab meat	1 bay leaf
¼ cup cooking oil	1 cup clam juice
3 onions, sliced thin	3 cups boiling water
2 green peppers, cored and sliced	¼ cup tomato paste
1 teaspoon salt	½ teaspoon basil
2 potatoes, peeled and cubed	1 pound white fish fillets, cut up
1 rib celery, diced	½ pound shelled, deveined shrimp
1 garlic clove, minced	

Remove membrane from crab. Heat oil in soup kettle, add onions, and sauté until golden. Add peppers, salt, potatoes, celery, garlic, and bay leaf. Cook together until potatoes are almost tender. Pour in clam juice and water, cover pot, and bring back to boil. Reduce heat and simmer 20 minutes. Remove bay leaf. Stir in tomato paste, basil, and fish. Cover again and simmer 10 minutes. Add shrimp and crab, re-cover, and simmer another 15 minutes before serving. Serves 6.

Doris Chabot
Wilmington, DE

Oysters in Cream Soup

Not for weight watchers, but definitely a treat!

1 pint oysters	1 tablespoon butter
water	salt and pepper
1 quart rich milk	½ cup whipped cream
1 tablespoon flour	1 tablespoon minced parsley

Chop oysters, strain off the liquid and add to it an equal amount of water. Heat liquid slowly, skim often, then add the chopped oysters and cook over medium heat 3 minutes. Remove from heat. Scald milk. Cream together flour and butter, add to milk, and stir over heat until thickened. Add oysters, and heat through. Season to taste. Top each serving with a generous dab of whipped cream, and sprinkle with parsley. Serves 4.

Tena Mohaupt
Woodbury, CT

Salmon Chowder

Quickly made, flavorful, and attractive in color. The corn adds interest and texture. Flavor is best if allowed to stand a bit.

15-ounce can red salmon	3 soup cans milk
1 onion, chopped	15-ounce can cream-style corn
2 stalks celery, chopped	1½ tablespoons butter
2 tablespoons butter	
two 10½-ounce cans cream of celery soup	

Pick over and clean salmon, saving liquid. Sauté onion and celery in butter in bottom of 4-quart soup kettle until tender. Add soup and milk. Stir in corn, flaked salmon, and reserved salmon liquid. Heat through and top with 1½ tablespoons butter. Serves 6.

Linda Long
Reading, MA

Salmon Bisque

Pink and white with a fleck of green. Good for lunch or to start off a special dinner.

15-ounce can red salmon	¼ cup flour
¼ cup butter	1 teaspoon salt
½ cup finely chopped green pepper	¼ teaspoon pepper
½ cup finely chopped onion	4-5 cups milk

(continued)

Clean and flake salmon, reserving liquid. In 3-quart saucepan melt butter, add green pepper and onion, and sauté 7-8 minutes, taking care not to brown vegetables. Blend in flour, salt, and pepper. Gradually add milk and reserved salmon liquid, stirring constantly. Heat to boiling; reduce heat, add salmon, and cook 3 minutes. Serves 4-6.

Audrey Ogden
Albany, OR

Seaside Chowder

Make this chowder a day ahead to get full wonderful flavor. Serve at lunchtime with soda crackers and salad, and you won't be looking for supper for a while.

2 slices bacon
½ cup chopped onion
1 cup sliced celery
1 large potato, peeled and diced
1 pound frozen or fresh haddock, cubed
2 cups water
1½ teaspoons salt

¼ teaspoon pepper
¼ teaspoon thyme
16-ounce can tomatoes with juice
3 tablespoons butter
¼ cup flour
1½ cups light cream (or 1 cup milk and ½ cup cream)

Cook bacon until crisp in large saucepan, crumble, and add onion to sauté briefly. Add celery, potato, haddock, water, salt, pepper, thyme, and tomatoes, including juice. Simmer until potato and fish are tender. In another pot, melt butter, stir in flour, and cook until smooth and bubbly; stir in cream and cook, stirring, for 1 minute. Slowly stir in fish mixture. Heat until hot, but do not allow to boil. Serves 8.

Barbara Barbieri
West Hartford, CT

Egg Balls for Soup

To add some protein to meatless soups, float these tasty little garnishes on top.

4 hardboiled eggs
1 teaspoon salt
dash pepper

1 egg white (raw)
flour
butter or chicken fat

Make a paste of hardboiled eggs in blender, food processor, or mortar. Beat with salt and pepper. Mix with egg white and form into walnut-sizes balls. Roll in flour and fry until brown in butter or chicken fat, being careful not to burn. Float on top of hot soup. Makes ten ½-inch balls.

ASSORTED SOUPS

Soup hot and cold, thick or thin, made from meat, vegetables, fruit, and anything else you can make soup from (which is almost everything!).

Baked Bean Soup

Saturday-night-baked-bean lovers will find happiness in Sunday night bean soup! The electric blender has done away with Grandmother's laborious task of sieving the beans.

2 cups leftover home-baked pea
   beans
¼ cup water

¼ cup tomato catsup
pinch celery salt
water

Puree baked beans with water in electric blender until smooth. Transfer to saucepan. Add catsup, celery salt, and water to bring to the consistency of pea soup. If you prefer a thinner soup, add more water. Heat and serve with toasted garlic croutons, or French bread. Serves 4.

Mrs. Clement F. Richardson
Falmouth, ME

Kidney Bean Chowder

A full-bodied, main-dish soup, quickly made.

6 slices bacon
2 medium onions, sliced
3 medium potatoes, diced
No. 2 can (2½ cups) kidney beans

10½-ounce can tomato soup
1 soup can water
salt and pepper to taste

Fry bacon, remove from pan, and cut into 1-inch pieces. Set aside. Sauté sliced onions in bacon fat until almost soft. Pour off all but 2 tablespoons of the fat. Transfer onions to large soup pot and add potatoes, beans, and tomato soup mixed with water. Cook about 25-30 minutes until potatoes are done, stirring often or soup will stick and burn. Add bacon, season to taste, and cook another minute. Serves 6.

Mrs. H. J. Kent
Hartford, CT

Whi Kroni See Lea
(Pennacook Indian Corn Stew)

The Indians did not have salt, paprika, or pork. They used bear's fat instead of pork or bacon and did not add milk or cream to thin the mixture, as is done today. Still — their stew tasted quite like this.

3 quarts corn, cut from the cob	2 teaspoons salt
1 quart shell beans	¼ cup salt-pork fat
2 quarts sweet red peppers, minced	1 teaspoon paprika
1 quart sliced onions	1 quart boiling water

Combine all ingredients. Stir the mixture well, bring to boil, reduce heat, and simmer for 2 hours. Thin as desired with milk. Serves 8-10.

J. Almus Russell
Bloomsburg, PA

Krupnik

From Poland, a real "stick-to-your-ribs" soup for a cold winter's night.

⅔ cup fine or medium pearl barley	2 potatoes, peeled and diced
3 cups beef broth	1 pound mushrooms
1 large onion, minced	2 tablespoons butter
3 tablespoons butter	4-6 cups beef broth, boiling
2 carrots, chopped	¼ teaspoon thyme
2 stalks celery, chopped	3 tablespoons sour cream

In a 6-quart soup kettle combine barley and beef broth. Bring to boil, reduce heat, and simmer, adding water as necessary to keep barley covered, for 1 hour. Drain, rinse barley, and return to kettle. Sauté onion in 3 tablespoons butter with other vegetables until tender. Add cooked vegetables to kettle. Sauté mushrooms in 2 tablespoons butter until browned and add to kettle. Add enough boiling beef broth to obtain the preferred consistency (thick or thin). Stir in thyme. Simmer soup for 10 minutes. Just before serving, combine the sour cream with ½ cup liquid from the soup, mix well, and stir back into soup. Serve immediately. Serves 6.

Paula Rechnitz
Pepperell, MA

Linsensuppe

Lentil soup with German sausages makes a fine repast, with French bread and green salad.

4 cups dried lentils
water
2 teaspoons salt
⅛ teaspoon pepper
10 strips bacon
1 medium onion, chopped
1 cup chopped celery
2 carrots, thinly sliced

1 cup sliced potatoes
1 bay leaf
pinch each of rosemary, summer
    savory, and basil
1¼ tablespoons vinegar
1 pound German sausage
    (bratwurst, knockwurst,
    bockwurst, garlic, *et al.*)

Soak lentils overnight, drain, and rinse. Place in 6-quart soup pot, cover with water, and bring to a boil. Add salt and pepper, reduce heat, cover, and simmer gently for 1 hour, adding water as necessary to keep lentils covered. Cut bacon in 1-inch lengths and fry crisp. Remove bacon, and sauté onion in fat. To lentils, add bacon, onion, 2 tablespoons bacon fat, vegetables, herbs, and vinegar. Continue simmering for 1 hour, or until vegetables are tender. Twenty minutes before serving, add sausage cut into 1-inch pieces, and simmer until heated through. Remove bay leaf. Serves 10-12.

Mrs. Warren Ralston
Nevada City, CA

Potato Soup with Noodle Bits

The Pennsylvania Dutch noodles give this potato soup an interesting texture.

3 medium potatoes, peeled and
    diced
6 cups chicken broth
1 medium onion, chopped
3 stalks celery, chopped
2 tablespoons chopped green
    pepper

salt and pepper
6 slices bacon

Noodles:

1 egg
1+ cup flour
2 teaspoons minced fresh parsley
½ teaspoon salt

Combine potatoes, broth, onion, celery, and green pepper in kettle and bring to boil. Simmer 30 minutes and add salt and pepper to taste. Meanwhile, fry bacon until very crisp. Drain and dice. In bowl, combine egg, flour, parsley, and salt, stirring to blend. Add enough extra flour to make a crumbly mixture. Stir bacon bits into soup, then stir in crumbly noodle mixture. Bring to boil and cook 15 minutes, stirring occasionally. Serves 4-6.

Ruth Anderson
Pittsburgh, PA

Onion Soup

A simple way to make an old favorite — easier to eat than most.

¼ pound butter
12 onions, chopped or diced thin
1 teaspoon sugar
3 tablespoons flour
end (crust slice) of stale bread,
    crumbled in blender

1½ quarts beef stock, heated
salt and pepper
1 cup freshly grated cheese

Melt butter in soup pot, add onions, cover, and cook for 15 minutes over low heat. Sprinkle sugar over onions, cover, and cook for 15 more minutes. Stir in flour, add crumbs, and gradually stir in heated stock, stirring and cooking until smooth. Season, and simmer over low heat for 15 minutes. Sprinkle grated cheese on top of each serving. Serves 8.

Heidi Beckmann
Sarasota, FL

Piquant Pea Soup

2 cups split green or yellow peas
2 quarts water
ham bone, hock, or few chunks of
    leftover ham
½ cup chopped onions
½ cup diced celery (include some
    leaves)

1 cup sliced carrots
1 bay leaf
½ teaspoon ground cloves
½ teaspoon black pepper
2 tablespoons lemon juice

Wash and pick over peas. Add water and ham, and simmer for 2 hours, stirring occasionally. Add vegetables and spices, and cook for 1 hour. Take out ham bones and bay leaf. Cut meat from bones and return meat to soup. Add lemon juice. Serves 6-8.

Jeannette Perron
Dublin, NH

Brown Rice Chowder

A soup you can sink your teeth into — the brown rice has a chewy texture.

1 pound ground beef
1 tablespoon butter
4 cups water or stock
No. 2 can (2½ cups) tomatoes
1 cup grated carrot, firmly packed
⅓ cup chopped onion

¾ cup uncooked brown rice
2 teaspoons salt
⅛ teaspoon pepper
1 bay leaf
1 cup grated cabbage

Brown meat in butter, add all other ingredients except cabbage, and bring to rapid boil. Turn heat to low, cover, and simmer for 45 minutes, or until rice is tender. Then add cabbage and cook 5 minutes longer. Serves 8.

Mrs. Thomas L. Neill
Magnolia, AR

Tomato Basil Soup

A hearty tomato-rice soup flavored with basil.

2 medium onions, chopped
3 tablespoons butter
2 garlic cloves, crushed
6 cups chicken stock
½ cup raw rice (not Minute Rice)

3 medium tomatoes
1 cup tomato juice
1 bunch fresh basil, finely chopped
salt to taste

Sauté onions in butter in 4-quart soup pot until transparent. Add garlic and cook 1 minute. Add stock, bring to boil, and add rice. Cover and simmer for 30 minutes. Peel and dice tomatoes, and add to pot along with tomato juice and chopped basil. Cook over low heat another 15 minutes. Add salt to taste. Serves 6.

Michele Verville
Peterborough, NH

Jellied Madrilène

Pretty and cool on a hot summer's day.

2 envelopes plain gelatin
1 soup can water
10½-ounce can consommé

1 soup can tomato juice
1 teaspoon lemon juice
lemon slices for garnish

(continued)

Soften gelatin in ¼ cup of the water, bring remaining water to a boil and dissolve gelatin in it. Remove from heat, and add consommé, tomato juice, and lemon juice. Pour into serving cups, chill until set, and garnish each cup with thin slice of lemon. Or pour into a loaf pan, and chill until firm. Cut into cubes, pile into serving cups, and top with lemon slices. Serves 4-6.

Barbara Wicks-Calnan
Andover, MA

Frosted Sherry Soup

A royal purple fruit soup. Serve cold.

3 tablespoons quick-cooking
    tapioca
1½ cups boiling water
2 cups grape juice
2 cups pineapple juice

½ cup sugar
grated rind of 1 lemon
2-inch stick cinnamon
½ cup sherry
1 cup fresh raspberries

Stir tapioca into rapidly boiling water and cook until clear, stirring often. Add fruit juices, and bring to boil. Add sugar, lemon rind, and cinnamon, reduce heat, and simmer 10 minutes. Remove from stove, add sherry and raspberries, and chill thoroughly. Serves 6.

Helen Haaland
Woodbury, CT

Sheep Camp Soup

Our test cook misread the recipe and added 3-4 teaspoons chili instead of ¾ teaspoon — and loved it! Still, even if you like things hot, 1½ teaspoons chili is plenty hot.

2 pounds beef, elk, or venison, cut
    into 1-inch cubes
6 cups water
28-ounce can tomatoes
2 medium onions, chopped
1 cup sliced celery

1 cup carrot slices
1 cup cubed potatoes
2 cloves garlic, crushed
1 tablespoon salt
¾ teaspoon chili powder
¼ teaspoon black pepper

Combine all ingredients in 4-quart dutch oven, and simmer 2 hours until meat is tender. Serves 8.

Mary Thompson
Cora, WY

Grandmother's Saturday Soup

A nourishing meal that can be served any day of the week.

1 fresh beef knuckle bone
water to cover
2 cups pearl barley
½ teaspoon salt
water to cover
1 cup diced potatoes

1 cup diced turnips
1 cup chopped celery
1 cup sliced carrots
1 cup sliced parsnips
1 cup sliced onions
salt and pepper

Place knuckle bone in large soup kettle, cover with water, and simmer for about 2 hours until meat leaves the bone, adding water as needed to keep covered. Place barley in another pot, with ½ teaspoon salt and enough water to cover well, bring to boil, and cook for 50 minutes, adding water as needed. You should end up with soft barley and about 1 quart of thick creamy liquid. When bone is done, remove from kettle to cool. Add vegetables to stock in kettle and boil until all are tender. Add barley and barley liquid. Remove meat from bone and chop into small pieces; combine in kettle with vegetables and barley. Season with salt and pepper to taste. Heat through. Serves 8.

Letitia Bushell
East Aurora, NY

Taco Beef Soup

A hearty Mexican stew with all the fixings made in a jiffy.

½ pound ground beef
¼ cup chopped onion
1 tablespoon butter
1½ cups water
1-pound can stewed tomatoes with
   juice
1-pound can kidney beans
8-ounce can tomato sauce

½ envelope (2 tablespoons) taco
   seasoning mix
1 small avocado, peeled and
   chopped
shredded Cheddar cheese
corn chips
sour cream

In soup pot, brown meat and onion in butter, then drain off fat. Add water, cut-up tomatoes and juice, undrained kidney beans, tomato sauce, and taco seasoning mix. Bring to boil, reduce heat, cover, and simmer 15 minutes. Add avocado. Serve in individual bowls and pass cheese, corn chips, and sour cream. Serves 6.

Jerrianne Plummer
Paradise, CA

CHAPTER TWO

Breakfast, Brunch, Lunch, Supper, and Side Dishes

Magnificent fare can be concocted from the basic ingredients eggs, cheese, milk, cream, rice, barley, and pasta. These few foods offer infinite possibilities of variation, given the host of other ingredients and methods of preparation that can lift these basics to glorious heights through informed invention. Our Good Neighbors have provided Yankee with marvelous examples of just that sort of invention. Granted you can boil, beat, scramble, poach, or fry an egg, here you will find a treasure trove of kitchen-tested recipes, most of which can be used in all of the categories mentioned in the chapter heading, and all of which are guaranteed to enrich your repertoire.

The chapter starts out with pancakes, French toast, and waffles, even a "giant popover for two," continues on to egg and cheese dishes, and ends up with barley, pasta, and rice casseroles. We hope you will enjoy making and eating these recipes as much as we did.

PANCAKES, POPOVERS, FRENCH TOAST, AND WAFFLES

Apple-Yogurt Pancakes

A new kind of apple-spicy, light pancake to serve with maple syrup, apple syrup (melt apple jelly over medium-low heat), or apple syrup and sour cream. Can be frozen; reheat in oven.

1½ cups flour
1¾ teaspoons baking powder
(1 teaspoon salt)
1½ teaspoons cinnamon
½ teaspoon nutmeg
¼ teaspoon ginger

⅛ teaspoon allspice
1 egg
1 cup plain yogurt
¾ cup apple cider
2 large apples, peeled and sliced

Sift together flour, baking powder, optional salt, and spices. Combine egg with yogurt and beat well. Add dry ingredients gradually, alternately with the cider to form a stiff dough. Fold in apples. Cook on oiled, heated griddle over medium-low heat, making one 4-inch pancake (pat flat in pan to 4-inch diameter) at a time. Makes twelve 4-inch pancakes.

Heather Wibben
Dublin, NH

Butter-Thin Hot Cakes

No need to pass melted butter with these tender, puffy pancakes — it's there, in the pancakes.

4 eggs
3 cups half and half
2½ cups flour
3 tablespoons sugar

3 teaspoons baking powder
1 teaspoon salt
½ pound butter, melted

Beat eggs and stir in half and half. Sift together dry ingredients, and gradually beat into egg mixture. Beat well. Stir in melted butter. Cook as for any pancake. Makes sixteen 6-inch pancakes.

Jean Brownlee
Victorville, CA

French Pancakes

Add blueberries, fresh, canned (drained), or frozen, or canned corn (drained), to the batter of this fine standard pancake for variety.

2 eggs	1 teaspoon baking powder
1 cup milk	½ teaspoon salt
1½ cups flour	1½ tablespoons sugar

Beat eggs and milk. Combine dry ingredients, and sift into egg mixture. Cook by ladlefuls on hot, well greased (use cooking oil) griddle until puffed and full of bubbles. Turn and brown on other side. Makes six 6-inch pancakes.

Elaine Kanaby
Croswell, MI

Giant Popover for Two

A luxurious breakfast dish. Sprinkle with confectioner's sugar and lemon juice, and serve with crisp bacon slices, or with Sautéed Apples and Bacon (below).

3 tablespoons butter	½ cup milk
2 eggs, beaten	(dash nutmeg)
½ cup flour	

Preheat oven to 425°F. While oven is heating up, place butter in 9-inch skillet or heavy casserole dish and melt in oven until bubbling. Beat eggs with flour, milk, and optional nutmeg, and pour into skillet or casserole dish. Bake for 15-20 minutes, or until puffed and golden. Serves 2.

Mrs. Philip Ratcliff
Sherman Cooks!

SAUTÉED APPLES AND BACON

A wonderfully tasty side dish to serve with omelet or scrambled eggs, croissants or popovers, or with a pork roast for dinner.

4-5 tart cooking apples	2 tablespoons cooking oil
8 slices bacon	2 tablespoons sugar

Pare, core, and dice apples. Fry bacon until crisp in heavy skillet. Drain bacon on paper. Remove all but about 2½ tablespoons bacon fat from skillet. Add cooking oil to skillet. Over high heat, sauté apples quickly until tender. Sprinkle on sugar. Place apples on warm platter, and surround with bacon. Serves 4.

Dianne Stillings
New York, NY

Raised Pancakes

Made with yeast, these pancakes must be mixed up the night before they are to be used. Serve with butter and maple syrup.

1 package active dry yeast
¼ cup warm water
1¾ cups lukewarm milk
2 tablespoons sugar

1 teaspoon salt
3 eggs, beaten
¼ cup soft butter
2 cups flour

Dissolve yeast in ¼ cup warm water. Add lukewarm milk, sugar, and salt. Cover and let rise in warm place (85°F.) for about 1½ hours. Stir down and refrigerate overnight. Next morning, stir down and cook on greased griddle, ¼ cup at a time. Turn when cakes are puffed and bubbly. Bake until golden brown. Makes about 24 pancakes.

Sylvia E. Walker
Worcester, VT

Sour Cream Pancakes

Very tender and light. Dust with confectioner's sugar, or serve with melted butter and syrup for a substantial, but never heavy pancake breakfast.

2 eggs
1 cup sour cream
5 tablespoons flour

1 teaspoon baking powder
pinch baking soda
¼ teaspoon salt

Beat eggs, add sour cream, and beat together to mix well. Add remaining ingredients, and stir lightly. Cook on hot griddle greased with cooking oil (butter may cause cakes to scorch). Makes 8 medium pancakes.

Jean Brownlee
Victorville, CA

Sour Milk Griddle Cakes

Another light and fluffy cake that stays light inside you! To sour fresh milk, add 2 teaspoons of vinegar to each cup of milk called for.

2 eggs, separated
3 cups sour milk
3 cups flour
1½ teaspoons baking soda

1 teaspoon salt
3 tablespoons sugar
(⅛ teaspoon cinnamon)

Beat egg yolks until light and lemon-colored. Stir in soured milk. Sift together dry ingredients, and gradually add to egg mixture, stirring well after each addition. Beat egg whites until stiff and fold into batter. Bake on well-oiled griddle. Makes 48 pancakes about 3½ inches in diameter. Serves 8.

Dorothy Kennedy
Concord, NH

Swedish Bacon Pancake

Like its close cousins, Yorkshire pudding and popovers, this baked egg cake rises beautifully in the pan as it bakes. Like them, it should be served immediately, as it will fall when taken from the oven. Good alone for breakfast, for brunch, served with toast or a green salad, and also a fine foil for a nippy dish of chili con carne.

½ pound sliced bacon
1 cup flour
1 tablespoon sugar
½ teaspoon salt

2 eggs lightly beaten
2 cups milk
(1 tablespoon chopped chives)

Grease an 8-inch square baking dish, preferably with rounded corners, such as Pyrex or Corningware. Fry bacon until almost crisp in skillet. Drain on paper. Transfer 2 tablespoons of bacon fat to greased baking dish. Cover bottom of dish with overlapping bacon slices. Sift flour, sugar, and salt together into mixing bowl. In another bowl, beat eggs lightly, then beat in milk and optional chives. Add egg mixture to dry ingredients, and blend well. Let stand 1 hour to allow batter to thicken. Pour batter into baking dish over bacon layer, and bake at 400°F. for 40-45 minutes, until puffed and golden brown. Silver knife inserted in center should come out clean. Serves 4.

Ragnhild J. Johnson
Shavertown, PA

Thin Pancakes

A richly eggy, crepe-type pancake, this can be spread with jelly of your choice, with cottage cheese, or with both, then rolled up and dusted with confectioner's sugar. Serve hot. Also good filled with chicken or creamed spinach mixture. These pancakes freeze well.

1 cup flour
½ teaspoon salt

1½ cups milk
3 eggs, well beaten

Sift together flour and salt. Stir in milk and eggs, and beat all together very well. Batter should be like heavy cream. Heat small skillet, and grease lightly. Pour in a little batter, and tilt pan back and forth until batter covers bottom evenly. When pancake is bubbly, turn and brown on other side. Serves 4.

Barb Schneider
Des Plaines, IL

Whole-Wheat Banana Pancakes

Hearty, wholesome pancakes that taste very much like banana bread. Honey can be substituted for the brown sugar in this recipe.

¾ cup whole-wheat flour
¼ cup wheat germ
1 teaspoon baking powder
2 tablespoons brown sugar
1 teaspoon cinnamon

(¼ cup chopped walnuts)
2 eggs, lightly beaten
¼ cup cooking oil
¾ cup milk
½ banana, skinned and diced

Combine dry ingredients (including optional nuts). Mix eggs with cooking oil and milk, and pour into dry ingredients. Stir until just blended. Add bananas. Cook on greased griddle. Enough batter to serve 2.

Cheryl Sanborn
East Thetford, VT

Crispy Waffles

At their crispest when eaten immediately, hot off the iron, with butter and maple syrup. Coarse-ground whole-wheat flour is sold at natural food stores.

1 cup whole-wheat pastry flour
1 cup coarse-ground whole-wheat
    flour
1 tablespoon baking powder
1 teaspoon salt

2 tablespoons sugar
3 eggs, separated
1½ cups milk
½ cup cooking oil

Combine dry ingredients. Beat egg yolks, and stir in milk and cooking oil. Beat egg whites until stiff. Heat waffle iron until ready for baking. When iron is ready, stir dry ingredients into egg mixture and mix well. Fold in egg whites, and begin baking immediately. Bake until steam ceases, and waffles are crisp and a rich brown color. Serve one by one, or keep warm in oven until ready to serve. Make fourteen 4x4-inch waffles.

R. Rossi III
Peterborough, NH

Potato Waffles

Light, moist, and really fine. Potatoes do unbelievable things for waffles. Serve topped with butter and maple syrup, or with cinnamon-sugar. Sautéed Apples and Bacon (page 41) would be good with these.

3 eggs, beaten
2 cups mashed potatoes
1 teaspoon salt
1 cup flour

2 teaspoons baking powder
2 tablespoons melted shortening
1 cup milk

Beat eggs until light and stir in cooled mashed potatoes. Sift together dry ingredients. Stir shortening and milk into potato mixture, then beat in flour mixture. Bake in hot waffle iron until steaming stops. Makes 6 four-section waffles, or enough to serve 3-4.

Mary Cornog
Farmington, CT

French Toast Fondue with Maple Butter

Turn a leisurely weekend breakfast into a delightful occasion for family and friends with this fun-to-make-and-eat fondue. Make the maple butter ahead so it will have time to chill. For a large loaf of bread, double the eggs/milk/salt mixture.

Maple Butter:
1½ cups sifted confectioner's sugar
½ cup soft butter

1 cup real maple syrup
1 egg, separated

Thoroughly cream together sugar, butter, syrup, and egg yolk. Beat egg white until stiff. Fold into creamed mixture. Chill. Makes 2 cups.

French Toast Fondue:
1 loaf French bread
2 eggs, well beaten
½ cup milk

⅛ teaspoon salt
cooking oil
1 teaspoon salt

Cut bread into bite-sized cubes, making sure each cube has some crust on it (this helps keep the cube on the fondue fork). In mixing bowl, combine eggs, milk, and ⅛ teaspoon salt and beat well. Pour cooking oil into fondue pot (or electric frying pan) to half-capacity or to depth of at least 2 inches. Heat to 375°F. Add 1 teaspoon salt to hot oil.

To Cook and Eat:
Spear each bread cube through its crust with fondue fork. Dip bread in egg mixture, and let excess drip off. Cook cube in hot oil until golden brown (1-2 minutes). Transfer to dinner fork, dip in maple butter, and eat. Serves 4-6.

Ruth M. Andrews
Dallas, TX

EGGS AND CHEESE DISHES

Oriental Eggs with Chutney Mayonnaise

The curry butter endows these hardboiled eggs with a lovely gold color and lends them taste. Serve as below, or without the mayonnaise, quartered on lettuce with cold sliced ham.

6 eggs
3 tablespoons butter

1 tablespoon cooking oil
2 tablespoons curry powder

Hardboil eggs, and shell. Heat butter and oil in medium skillet until butter has melted. Stir in curry. Place eggs in skillet, over low heat, rolling them over and over in the curry butter for about 8 minutes, or until each egg is well coated. Take eggs from skillet and chill. To serve, slice and serve with chutney mayonnaise (mix 3 tablespoons chopped chutney with 1 cup mayonnaise). Serves 4-6.

Hazel D. Little
Vienna, VA

Toad in the Hole

An interesting variation on a classic English breakfast-brunch dish. For a brunch, our test cook suggested serving with a compote of fresh fruit.

1 cup flour
¼ teaspoon salt
1 cup milk
2 eggs, well beaten

pinch nutmeg
1 pound pork sausage, either meat
or links
1 tablespoon cooking oil

Mix flour and salt and gradually add milk, stirring to blend well. Add eggs and nutmeg. Cover bowl and let stand for 30 minutes. Shape sausage meat into 1-inch balls, or cut links into 1-inch segments, and prick each segment with fork. Heat oil in skillet, and brown sausages. Place sausage and drippings in 9-inch square baking dish, and bake in preheated 400°F. oven for 2 minutes, or until hot. Remove dish from oven, and pour batter over sausage. Return immediately to oven, and bake 20 minutes at 400°F., then reduce oven temperature to 350°F., and bake 10-15 minutes more, or until puffed and golden. Serves 4.

Jean Brownlee
Victorville, CA

Sunny Meadow Breakfast for Two

Easy to multiply or divide. A satisfying and colorful breakfast dish that gives you a fine start for a busy day.

10-ounce package frozen chopped
   spinach
3-ounce package cream cheese
⅛ teaspoon nutmeg
salt and pepper

2 teaspoons butter
2 eggs, hardboiled and shelled
2 slices whole-wheat toast, buttered
4 slices bacon, cooked crisp and
   drained

Cook spinach according to package directions, and drain well. Place in double-boiler top over boiling water, and add cream cheese, nutmeg, salt and pepper to taste, and butter. Bring water in double-boiler bottom to boil, turn down to medium heat, and cook until cheese mixes easily with spinach. Stir well to blend. Divide the spinach between two warm plates. Quarter eggs and nestle in bed of spinach — four egg quarters per plate. Quarter each slice of toast and place around spinach nest. Garnish each plate with 2 slices of crisp bacon. Serves 2.

O. P. Valhalla
Bedford, NY

Poached Eggs à la Reine

Another great brunch or breakfast dish with a decidedly French accent. Serve not only on toast, but also on toasted English muffins or, for a really fancy touch, on or in puff-pastry rounds (you can buy them frozen). Or add ½ cup of diced ham to the sauce — forget the eggs — and serve over toast, with petits pois jardinières, if you please.

1 cup finely chopped mushrooms
4 tablespoons butter
1 tablespoon chopped shallots
3 tablespoons flour
1¼ cups medium cream
1 cup chopped cooked chicken
¼ cup sherry

salt and pepper
4 eggs
4 toast rounds
pimiento strips, or sprinkling of
   paprika
16 cooked asparagus spears
parsley for garnish

Sauté mushrooms in butter, add shallots, and cook a few minutes longer. Blend in flour, add cream, and cook slowly, stirring, until smooth and thickened. Add chicken and sherry. Season to taste with salt and pepper. Remove from heat, and keep warm in covered oven dish or in double boiler over hot water. Poach eggs and toast bread or English muffins. Place on warm platter, top with eggs, and spoon sauce over all. Garnish each egg with a strip of pimiento or sprinkle with paprika, and arrange asparagus — four spears per egg — around each toast, muffin, or pastry round. Garnish with parsley. Serves 4.

Mrs. Elwyn Dirats
Cooking at Court

Poached Eggs on Toast with Wine Sauce

A truly deluxe egg dish, with a wonderful sauce. If you don't happen to have enough people to consume eight poached eggs, make the sauce full measure anyway, as it is terrific served over broiled or boiled chicken pieces. You can substitute toasted English-muffin halves for the French bread.

1 cup diced ham
¾ cup sliced mushrooms
4½ tablespoons butter
1 cup chopped white onions
1 peeled garlic clove, on toothpick
2 tablespoons flour
10½ ounces beef stock (use half a 10½-ounce can beef bouillon mixed with half a soup can of water)

10½ ounces red wine
pinch thyme
¼ teaspoon pepper
1 sprig fresh parsley
eight ½-inch slices French bread
butter
2 tablespoons vinegar
8 eggs
watercress or parsley for garnish

Sauté ham and mushrooms in 1½ tablespoons of the butter for 3 minutes. Remove from skillet with slotted spoon and reserve. Add 3 tablespoons butter to skillet, and onions. Sauté onions until tender. Add garlic clove. Remove from heat and stir in flour. Return to heat. Add beef stock, wine, thyme, pepper, and parsley sprig. Simmer 20 minutes, stirring now and then. Add ham and mushrooms to sauce, turn up heat, and let boil for several minutes or until slightly thickened. Remove garlic clove and parsley sprig. Keep sauce warm while you fry the bread on both sides in butter in separate skillet, and poach the eggs.

Bring water in two skillets (you'll need two for 8 eggs) to boil. Add 1 tablespoon vinegar to water in each skillet. (The vinegar helps set the whites.) Place 4 muffin rings, egg poachers, or tuna-fish cans with both ends removed in each skillet, and break 1 egg into each mold. Immediately turn down heat to medium or medium-low, and cook until whites are set, spooning water over yolks so that they are just filmed over white. While eggs are cooking, keep fried bread slices just warm in 150-200°F. oven. When eggs are done, place fried bread slices on warmed platter, top each slice with a poached egg, and spoon sauce over all. Garnish with watercress or parsley and serve at once. Serves 6-8.

Marguerite Burchell
Acushnet, MA
Je Me Souviens la Cuisine de la Grandmère

Spinach Omelet

Spinach, eggs, mushrooms, onions, and cheese — a truly delectable combination. Serve this in style with grilled tomatoes and fresh-baked corn bread.

¾ cup sliced mushrooms
3 tablespoons minced onion
2 tablespoons butter
8 eggs
2 tablespoons heavy cream

⅛ teaspoon nutmeg
salt and pepper
10-ounce package frozen chopped
    spinach, cooked and drained
½ cup shredded Mozzarella cheese

Sauté mushrooms and onion in butter until just tender. Beat eggs with cream and seasonings. Add spinach and stir well. Pour egg mixture over mushrooms and onion in skillet; stir, pushing mixture out to sides of pan to form flat cake. Cook over medium heat until bottom is firm. Remove from heat and sprinkle cheese evenly over top. Place under broiler just long enough to melt cheese. Serves 4-6.

Fanny Davenport
Bath, NY

Tomato and Cheese Omelet

Attractive and tasty breakfast for two or three persons. Serve with toast.

6 eggs
2 tablespoons water
½ teaspoon salt
¼ teaspoon pepper
2 tablespoons cooking oil
1 tablespoon butter

2 medium-size tomatoes, sliced
    thinly
½-1 teaspoon oregano
¼ pound Cheddar or Mozzarella
    cheese, shredded

Beat eggs with water, salt, and pepper. Heat oil and butter in heavy skillet, and pour in egg mixture. Preheat broiler. Arrange tomato slices on top of omelet and sprinkle with oregano. Cook over medium heat until eggs are almost set, then remove from heat, and sprinkle cheese evenly over top. Put under broiler just long enough to melt cheese. Remove from skillet, fold in half, and serve. Serves 2-3.

Janice Ryzewski
Shrewsbury, MA

Onion, Potato, and Pepper Frittata

Or omelet, if you prefer. By any name, this makes a hefty and colorful dish for breakfast, brunch, or supper. Serve with a green salad to round out the meal.

¼ cup olive oil
1 large red pepper, cored and diced
2 large potatoes, parboiled and
   cubed

1 large onion, chopped
8 large or 10 medium eggs, beaten
salt and pepper
dash milk

Heat olive oil in large skillet (Teflon-lined, if possible). Place cut-up vegetables in skillet, and cook until potatoes are browned and onions tender. Pour eggs, mixed with salt and pepper and milk, into skillet. Stir mixture, pushing it out to sides of skillet to form a flat cake. When eggs are cooked on the bottom, place a flat dish or plate over skillet and invert skillet so that omelet slides out on plate. Then slide omelet back into skillet to cook other side. Serves 6.

Elsie Stupinsky
Bernardsville, NJ

Cottage Cheese Omelet

A light-textured fluffy omelet — good made with dried parsley (use only 1½ tablespoons), but even better if afforded the slightly peppery taste of fresh parsley. Mrs. Butler's advice to serve "with spinach salad and onion rolls" is right on.

6 eggs, separated
1 cup cottage cheese
¾ cup light cream
salt and pepper

3 tablespoons chopped fresh
   parsley
1½ tablespoons butter

Beat together egg yolks, cottage cheese, cream, salt, pepper, and parsley. Beat egg whites until stiff, and fold into batter. Melt butter in 10-inch skillet. Add egg mixture and cook over low heat until bottom of omelet is cooked to golden brown. Place skillet in 350°F. oven and bake for 15-20 minutes, or until omelet is golden on top and *almost* cooked through. Serves 4.

Mrs. Roger Butler
Cooking at Court

Scrambled Eggs with Spinach

For spinach addicts, this is the perfect *scrambled-egg recipe. Fresh corn kernels are best, but in a pinch you can heat canned corn niblets, drain, and use. Serve with sautéed cherry tomatoes and a good whole-wheat bread for the ultimate in taste and eye appeal.*

4 pounds fresh spinach or four 10-
   ounce packages frozen
4 tablespoons butter
salt and pepper
½ cup cooked fresh corn kernels
2 tablespoons butter

4 tablespoons cream
8 eggs, lightly beaten
3 tablespoons grated Gruyère
   cheese
salt and pepper

Cook washed fresh spinach leaves for 10 minutes in boiling salted water, or cook frozen spinach according to package directions. Drain well. Place spinach in bowl with 4 tablespoons butter and season with salt and pepper. Keep warm. Five minutes before serving, stir in corn kernels. In large skillet, put 2 tablespoons butter, cream, eggs, and cheese. Add salt and pepper as desired, and cook over medium-high heat, turning and mixing constantly for about 3 minutes, or until done. Place eggs in center of serving platter and surround with spinach-corn mixture. Serves 4.

Je Me Souviens la Cuisine de la Grandmère

Gnocchi

Serve these tender little Italian potato dumplings with tomato sauce and grated Parmesan cheese, or combine with ham in a cheese sauce and serve as a main course.

2 medium potatoes, peeled and
   boiled
½ teaspoon salt

3 cups flour
1 egg, lightly beaten
boiling water

Mash potatoes. Add salt, 1 cup of the flour, and egg. With wooden spoon or hands, mix together until potatoes absorb flour. Work in rest of flour gradually until dough is smooth and can be rolled (add more flour if needed). Roll out dough on floured board until 1-inch thick. Cut into strips 1 inch wide. Roll out these strips to ½-inch thickness. Cut into ½-inch lengths. Roll these lengths around your fingers to form shell shapes. (Add flour as needed). Cook a few at a time in boiling water. Boil until gnocchi rise, then cook 5-10 minutes, or until done. Drain in colander. Place in buttered baking dish, add tomato or cheese sauce, and heat at 325°F. until hot. As side dish serves 8.

Adelia Naccarella
Knights of St. John Auxiliary
East Rochester, NY

Broccoli-Cheese Soufflé

A beautiful, high-rise soufflé; for broccoli enthusiasts, use two cups of broccoli.

1 tablespoon butter
1 tablespoon grated Parmesan
   cheese
2 tablespoons butter
3 tablespoons flour
1 cup milk
6 eggs, separated
¾ cup grated Swiss cheese
1 teaspoon Poupon mustard

¼ teaspoon nutmeg
salt and pepper
1 small onion, minced
2 teaspoons butter
1 cup finely chopped cooked fresh
   broccoli, or 10-ounce package
   frozen chopped broccoli,
   cooked and drained

Preheat oven to 400°F. Butter 1½-quart soufflé dish with the 1 tablespoon butter. Sprinkle dish with grated Parmesan, and refrigerate until ready to use. Melt 2 tablespoons butter in saucepan. Add flour, blend, and cook a few seconds, stirring with fork or whisk. Slowly add milk, stirring constantly. Bring to boil and boil for about a minute, stirring. Take from heat and beat in egg yolks. Stir over low heat for a few seconds. Remove from heat and add Swiss cheese, mustard, nutmeg, and seasonings. Let cool for 10 minutes. Sauté onion in 2 teaspoons butter, then add to mixture with broccoli. Beat egg whites until stiff. Whisk ⅓ of beaten egg whites into broccoli-cheese sauce, then fold in the remaining egg whites. Turn into prepared soufflé dish, place dish in preheated oven, and immediately turn oven down to 375°F. Bake 25-35 minutes. Serves 8.

Mary Jane Baylies
An Artist's Cookbook

Mozzarella Croquettes

These little cheese croquettes are delicate, tasty, inexpensive, and versatile. Serve for breakfast with broiled tomatoes and pan-fried slices of ham or bacon, or with spaghetti and tomato or pesto sauce. Or serve with a salad for a nourishing vegetarian meal.

½ pound fresh Mozzarella cheese,
   or ½ pound block Mozzarella
1 tablespoon flour
1 egg, lightly beaten

¼ teaspoon salt
½ cup (or more) flour
1 cup olive oil, or cooking oil

Work fresh Mozzarella in bowl, squeezing until soft and malleable. Or shred block Mozzarella. Work in flour, egg, and salt until well blended. Shape into 1½ inch (walnut-size) balls and roll in flour. Fry in hot oil until browned on all sides. Serve hot. Serves 12.

Dianna Dlugolencky
Sherman Cooks!

Ham, Cheese, and Mushroom Soufflé

In a search for a very different sort of material that required thumbing through past issues of the magazine, we happened on this recipe, published in the September, 1956 issue of Yankee *magazine, the brainchild of Food Editor Nancy Dixon. Serve with a salad of crisped lettuce and tomato slices dressed with oil-and-vinegar and crusty home-made rolls.*

¼ cup butter
3 tablespoons flour
2 cups milk
¾ cup freshly grated cheese
½ cup minced celery
1¾ cups minced pimiento
1½ cups sliced mushrooms, sautéed
    in butter

1 cup chopped cooked ham
4 eggs, separated
¾ teaspoon curry powder
1¾ teaspoons grated onion
salt and pepper

Melt butter in skillet, stir in flour, and cook gently over medium-low heat for 1-2 minutes. Gradually add milk, stirring constantly, until sauce is smooth and thick. Add cheese and stir until cheese has melted. Add celery, pimiento, mushrooms, ham, and well-beaten egg yolks, curry powder, and onion. Season to taste. Cool to lukewarm, then fold in stiffly beaten egg whites. Turn into well-greased 3- to 3½-quart casserole dish, and bake at 350°F. for 35-40 minutes, or until firm and well browned. Serves 6.

Shrimp Strata

This fine "company strata" can be made with diced cooked ham, too. You can make it ahead of time, refrigerate overnight or all day, and have plenty of time to visit with your guests while it is baking. Like so many of the dishes in this chapter, great served simply with greens and rolls.

12 slices white bread, crusts
    removed
12 ounces sharp Cheddar cheese,
    sliced thin
10-ounce package frozen broccoli,
    steamed briefly or parboiled
2 cups cooked shrimp

2 tablespoons instant minced onion,
    or ¼ cup minced fresh onion
6 eggs, lightly beaten
3½ cups milk
½ teaspoon salt
¼ teaspoon dry mustard

Cut up bread into 2-inch squares. Arrange half of the bread squares on bottom of buttered 9x13-inch baking dish or 3-quart casserole dish. Layer cheese slices, broccoli, and shrimp over bread. Arrange remaining bread squares on top and sprinkle with minced onion. Briefly beat together eggs, milk, salt, and mustard. Pour over ingredients in dish. Cover and refrigerate for 6-12 hours. Bake uncovered for about an hour, or until cooked through, at 325°F. Let stand for 10 minutes before serving. Serves 6-8.

Jane Hanson
Boulder, CO

ABOUT QUICHE

You can vary the texture of a quiche according to the type of milk product used. The standard recipe for a 9- or 10-inch quiche calls for 3 eggs, and 1-1½ cups of dairy liquid — milk, half and half, or heavy cream. The difference is in texture. If you use milk, the quiche will be solid and rather bready in texture; a quiche made with half and half will be firm, but less bready, while a quiche made with heavy cream will have a creamier, more custardy consistency — and more calories.

Artichokes and Eggs

The family that tested this recipe for Yankee commented, "If you like artichokes and cheese, you'll love this dish." They did. More quiche than omelet, but with a different texture.

two 6-ounce jars marinated
   artichoke hearts
3-4 green onions, minced
1 clove garlic, minced
4 eggs, well beaten

1 tablespoon chopped parsley
12 soda crackers, crumbled
½ pound sharp Cheddar cheese,
   grated

Drain artichoke hearts, reserving 1 tablespoon oil. Dice. In small skillet, sauté onions and garlic in reserved marinade oil for 2-3 minutes. Remove from heat. In bowl, combine beaten eggs, parsley, crackers, cheese, artichoke hearts, onions, and garlic. Mix well, then turn into well-greased 9x9-inch pan and bake at 325°F. for 40 minutes. Serves 4.

Patricia Foley
Forest Hills Garden Club
Knights of St. John Auxiliary
East Rochester, NY

Breakfast Dish

Somewhere between a crustless quiche, a strata, and a soufflé, yet none of the above, Breakfast Dish is quickly made and reheats happily in a double boiler over hot water. That is if there is any left to reheat.

2 cups onion-garlic or cheese-garlic
   croutons (or 1 cup of either,
   plus 1 cup plain croutons)
1 cup grated Cheddar cheese (4
   ounces)
4 eggs, lightly beaten

2 cups milk
½ teaspoon salt
2 tablespoons chopped chives, or ⅛
   teaspoon onion powder
dash pepper
4 slices bacon, cooked crisp

(continued)

Spread croutons over bottom of buttered baking dish (10x6 inches or 7x11 inches). Sprinkle grated cheese evenly over croutons. Combine eggs, milk, salt, chives or onion powder, and pepper and beat to blend. Pour mixture over croutons and cheese. Crumble bacon over top and bake at 325°F. for 55-60 minutes. (Or, if you prefer your bacon crisp, crumble over dish when you take it from the oven.) Serves 4.

Ann Chambers
Cincinnati, OH

Crab Quiche

Use the very best crab meat to make this fine, firm quiche topped with toasted almonds. Our test cook served it with a green salad and grated carrots vinaigrette for rave reviews.

10-inch unbaked pie shell
1 cup grated Swiss cheese
5¾-ounce package frozen crab meat, thawed (or 7½-ounce can)
2 tablespoons chopped green onion
3 eggs, lightly beaten

1 cup half and half
½ teaspoon salt
½ teaspoon grated lemon peel
¼ teaspoon dry mustard
dash nutmeg
¼ cup sliced almonds, toasted

Chill pie shell 10 minutes in refrigerator. Then sprinkle cheese over bottom of shell. Add crab meat and chopped green onion. Beat together eggs, half and half, salt, lemon peel, mustard, and nutmeg. Pour over crab. Top with almonds. Bake at 375°F. for 45-60 minutes. Serves 8.

Jane Hanson
Boulder, CO

Cheese and Spinach Casserole

Plenty of protein as a main dish for vegetarians; great for brunch, lunch, or supper for anyone. Serve with toasted rye bread or warm French bread and cold sliced beef or ham, if desired. Reheats well.

5 ounces Cheddar cheese, coarsely grated
10-ounce package frozen, chopped spinach, thawed and drained

2 cups cottage cheese
3 eggs, well beaten

Mix all ingredients together and pour into a greased, shallow, 1½-quart casserole dish or 10-inch round cake tin, 2-inches deep. Bake at 300°F. for 1 hour. Serves 4.

Jane Hanson
Boulder, CO

Sausage Quiche

A creamy, spiced-just-right quiche to serve hot or cold. You can use either a baked or an unbaked pie shell, regular or hot sausage.

two 9- to 9½-inch deep dish pie
    shells
1 pound sausage meat
2 cups (8 ounces) shredded Swiss
    cheese
2 cups half and half or light cream
4 eggs, lightly beaten

1 tablespoon cornstarch
½ teaspoon salt
¼ teaspoon nutmeg
dash cayenne pepper
2 tablespoons melted butter
2 tablespoons grated Parmesan
    cheese

Brown sausage meat evenly over medium heat, breaking up all lumps. Remove from heat, and toss with Swiss cheese until well mixed. Pat half this mixture over bottom of each pie shell. In mixing bowl, combine cream, eggs, cornstarch, salt, nutmeg, and cayenne and blend well. Pour over cheese/sausage mixture in pie shells. Drizzle with melted butter, and sprinkle with Parmesan cheese. Bake at 375°F. 20-25 minutes if you used baked pie shells, 35-40 minutes for unbaked pie shells. Let stand 10 minutes before serving hot. Makes two 9- or 9½-inch quiches.

Kathleen H. Beatrice
Lynchburg, VA

Barley, Spinach, and Mushroom Casserole

Barley is a great food that is largely forgotten outside of vegetarian circles in this country. Too bad, as you'll find if you try this casserole. For non-vegetarians, add the optional ham. Either way, an excellent casserole.

6 ounces fresh mushrooms, sliced
    (about 2 cups)
1 medium onion, finely chopped
3 tablespoons butter
10-ounce package frozen chopped
    spinach, cooked and drained
3 cups cooked, drained barley
1½ teaspoons Worcestershire sauce
½ cup sour cream

¼ cup milk
¾ teaspoon salt
¼ teaspoon pepper
¼ teaspoon dry mustard
2 hardboiled eggs, chopped fine
(1 cup cooked diced ham)
bread crumbs
1 tablespoon grated Parmesan-
    Romano cheese

Sauté mushrooms and onion in butter until tender. Stir mushrooms, onion, and spinach into barley and toss well to mix. Stir in all other ingredients except for bread crumbs and grated cheese. Place in buttered 1½-quart casserole or oven-proof bowl and sprinkle lightly with bread crumbs, then with grated cheese. Bake at 350°F. for 25-30 minutes, or until bubbling and heated through. Serves 4.

H. Chapman Little
New York, NY

PASTA AND RICE DISHES

Broccoli Fettucine

Very good and couldn't be simpler to make. Pretty, too, served in a Pyrex bowl as side dish or as vegetarian main course. If you don't have canned bouillon or broth on hand, use 1 bouillon cube dissolved in ½ cup boiling water.

8-ounce package medium noodles
¼ cup cooking oil
1 garlic clove, crushed
10-ounce package frozen chopped broccoli, thawed and drained
½ cup canned condensed beef or chicken broth, undiluted

½ teaspoon dried basil leaves
¼ cup chopped parsley
¼ cup grated Parmesan cheese
1 cup cottage cheese
½ teaspoon salt
dash pepper

Cook noodles according to package directions. Drain. Meanwhile, heat oil in medium skillet, and sauté garlic and broccoli for 5 minutes, stirring. Add broth, basil, parsley, cheeses, salt, and pepper. Stir together over low heat for about 2 minutes. Toss broccoli mixture with noodles. Turn into warmed serving dish. Serves 4.

Janet Hawes
Tigard, OR

Fettucine with Ham

Another fine fettucine dish great for lunch with a lightly dressed salad of tossed fresh greens.

¼ cup chopped onion
1 clove garlic, minced
1-2 cups cubed cooked ham
4 tablespoons butter
8 ounces fettucine, cooked *al dente* and drained

¼ teaspoon thyme
salt and pepper
½ cup heavy cream
¼ cup grated Parmesan cheese

Sauté onion, garlic, and ham in butter until onions are golden and ham is lightly browned. Add to fettucine, along with thyme, and season to taste. Toss to mix well. Add cream and toss again, then Parmesan, and toss once more. Serves 4.

Susan Schneider
Palo Alto, CA

Herbed Garden Pasta Sauce

Here is a pasta sauce for vegetarians or gardeners.

6-ounce can tomato paste
4 large or 6 small tomatoes, chopped, or 1-pound can tomatoes with juice
¾ cup water
1 clove garlic, crushed
1 teaspoon salt
1 teaspoon sugar
1 bouillon cube (chicken, beef, or vegetable)
1 small bunch fresh parsley, chopped fine

3 tablespoons dried basil, or 6 tablespoons chopped fresh basil
¼ cup chopped blanched almonds
⅛ teaspoon dried sage, or ¼ teaspoon chopped fresh sage
¼ teaspoon dried leaf thyme, or ½ teaspoon chopped fresh thyme
1-2 cups mixed or leftover garden vegetables — suggest peas, lima beans, and sliced carrots
grated Parmesan cheese

Combine first seven ingredients, stir until smooth, and bring to boil in 10-inch heavy skillet. Reduce heat to simmer, and add all remaining ingredients except grated cheese. Simmer, covered, for 35-40 minutes (30 minutes if vegetables are already cooked). Spoon over cooked ravioli, spaghetti, or other pasta, and sprinkle with Parmesan cheese. Makes 5-6 cups sauce.

O. P. Valhalla
Bedford, NY

Linguine Pepper Pond

Distinctively flavored with capers and sparked with color — red, green, and black — this is appealing as either a side dish or a main course. Chopped ham or other cold cooked meat can be added if desired.

1 or 2 garlic cloves, minced
2 tablespoons olive oil
3 ripe tomatoes, cut into small pieces
half of 7¾-ounce can pitted ripe black olives, drained and sliced

half of 3½-ounce bottle capers
1 pound package linguine, cooked and drained
1 cup chopped parsley
(Parmesan cheese)

Brown garlic in olive oil. Add tomatoes, olives, and capers. Cook, stirring, until hot, and pour over cooked linguine. Toss, and add parsley. Sprinkle with Parmesan cheese if desired. Serves 6.

Joyce C. Ware
Sherman Cooks!

A Good Neighbor
Remembers the Old Times

"I read with enthusiasm Yankee's plans to publish the *Good Neighbors U.S.A. Cookbook.* In today's world of processed food, we seem to have lost the true taste of natural food. I grew up on a farm, where we went to the chicken coop to gather fresh eggs for breakfast, and garnered wild strawberries, blackberries, and gooseberries right from the place. The grape arbor was heavy with fruit for juice and jam, the likes of which are never to be found in a supermarket. Everything was homemade — cheese, egg noodles, or garden vegetables. Food was an important part of daily family life, and it had to be good.

Early in the morning, my grandfather would bring in wood to start the fire in the cast-iron stove that was the center and focus of the wooden-floored kitchen with its own coffee grinder screwed to the wall. Into the large kettle on the stove went the ingredients for the supper soup or stew, left to simmer all day until time for the evening meal.

Friday was bread-baking day. This also started early in the morning. Eight very large loaves of bread were set to rise in the outdoor oven heated with twigs long before the bread was put to bake. Milk was not homogenized then, and we used fresh cream to make butter. Friday night was a treat of fresh-baked bread and butter.

Basil and other herbs were dried over the stove in the kitchen, as were the strings of peppers and onions. Good meals came out of this simple, farm-raised food. Our neighbors on the hill were of French and German stock. We followed the Italian traditions of our grandparents, who came to America in 1880.

I am enclosing a recipe not from any printed page, but worth so much in memories. However, I too now bow to modern methods, and use a food processor and electric macaroni machine — and I even use frozen rather than fresh spinach!"

Margaret Ree
Elmsford, NY

Egg Noodles with Spinach Sauce

Here is Mrs. Margaret Ree's recipe.

Spinach Sauce:

1 clove garlic, peeled
1 tablespoon olive oil
10-ounce package frozen chopped
   spinach
1 cup heavy cream
½ cup milk
4 tablespoons butter

½ cup grated sharp Cheddar or
   Parmesan cheese
salt and pepper
1 fresh basil leaf, or 1 teaspoon
   dried basil
more grated cheese

Let garlic sit in oil for 1 hour at room temperature. Cook spinach according to package directions. Drain and squeeze dry. Place in blender, add garlic, oil, cream, milk, butter, cheese, salt and pepper, and basil. Blend until smooth. Turn into bowl and set aside to allow flavor to develop. Meanwhile, make noodles.

Noodles:

3 cups flour
2 eggs, lightly beaten
pinch salt
2 tablespoons softened butter

1 cup warm water (approx.)
cornmeal
4 quarts water
1 tablespoon salt

Place flour in large mixing bowl. Add beaten eggs and pinch salt; mix. Work in butter. Slowly add enough water to form firm dough. Turn out on lightly floured board, and knead well until smooth. Cut dough in half, and roll out each half with rolling pin about ¼ inch thick. Cut into strips about ¼ inch wide. As noodle dough is rolled out and cut, spread noodles out on board or table sprinkled with cornmeal and allow to dry about 15 minutes.

    To cook noodles, bring 4 quarts of water to boil with 1 tablespoon salt. Add raw noodles and cook in boiling water for 4-7 minutes, or until tender. Drain and place on platter. Pour spinach sauce over noodles and toss. Sprinkle with more grated cheese if desired. Serves 4-6.

Margaret Ree
Elmsford, NY

Macaroni with Prosciutto-Artichoke Sauce

Quickly prepared, the sauce makes a nice change of pace for any pasta. Prosciutto is best, but it is expensive and sometimes difficult to find. If you cannot obtain prosciutto or its near cousin Virginia ham, use regular ham, but increase the salt to 1 teaspoon.

2 tablespoons butter
¼ pound prosciutto ham, chopped
9-ounce package frozen artichoke
   hearts, chopped
dash salt and pepper
½ cup beef or chicken broth
2 tablespoons butter, melted

¼ pound ricotta cheese
2 eggs
2 tablespoons Parmesan cheese
7-ounce package elbow macaroni,
   cooked and drained
(additional Parmesan cheese)
(bread crumbs and butter dots)

Melt 2 tablespoons butter over low heat in skillet. Add prosciutto, cover, and simmer until ham is browned. Add artichoke hearts, salt, and pepper, and continue cooking over low heat for 15 minutes, sprinkling mixture with broth, a teaspoon at a time, and stirring to keep from sticking to pan. Blend 2 tablespoons melted butter with ricotta. Stir ricotta into sauce. Beat eggs with 2 tablespoons Parmesan cheese. Add to skillet and stir well. Remove from heat. Now, *either* place macaroni on heated platter and spoon sauce over, *or* place mixture in buttered 1½- or 2-quart casserole dish, sprinkle with additional cheese, add optional bread crumbs and butter dots, and bake at 350°F. for 20-25 minutes. Serves 6.

Mrs. Jan Steele-Perkins
Cooking at Court

Noodle Pie

As a side dish, a fine alternative to potatoes. Or add raisins and cottage cheese for a nifty Sunday-night supper. Can also be baked in a buttered casserole dish at 350°F. until browned on top.

8 ounces noodles, cooked and
   drained
2 eggs, lightly beaten
salt and pepper

(⅓ cup seedless raisins)
(⅓ cup boiling water)
(⅔ cup cottage cheese)
cooking oil

To noodles, add eggs, salt, pepper, and optional raisins (first plumped in boiling water for 10-15 minutes and drained) and cottage cheese. Mix well. On high heat, heat 10-inch skillet with enough cooking oil to just coat bottom until a drop of water dances in the oil. Add noodle mixture, smoothing out to make a flat cake. Reduce heat to medium. Cook until golden brown on bottom, checking occasionally to prevent scorching. Then invert noodle cake onto plate, and gently slide back into skillet to brown other side. Serves 6 as side dish, 4 as Sunday-night supper.

Barbara Ackerman
Sherman Cooks!

Spinach-Noodle Casserole

A quick and filling family casserole to serve alone or with browned sausage links.

8-ounce package tiny (thin) noodles
two 10-ounce packages frozen
    chopped spinach
10½-ounce can cream of mushroom
    soup

½ pound mild Cheddar cheese,
    shredded

Cook noodles according to package directions and drain. Cook spinach and squeeze dry. Add canned soup to spinach and mix well. Butter a 2½-quart casserole dish, and put in ½ the noodles, then ⅓ of the cheese, followed by all of the spinach mixture. Then top with another ⅓ of the cheese, the remaining noodles, and lastly the remaining cheese. Cover dish, and bake at 350°F. until heated through and bubbly, about 20-30 minutes. Serves 6.

Katherine Bombara
Simsbury, CT

Brown Rice, Tomato, and Cheese Casserole

One recipe where American cheese comes into its own. Serve with cole slaw or buttered beans.

1 cup thinly sliced onions
4 tablespoons chopped green
    pepper
3 tablespoons cooking oil
No. 2½ can tomatoes, or 3½ cups
    sliced fresh tomatoes

1 cup grated American cheese
3 whole cloves
1 bay leaf
1 tablespoon sugar
1½ teaspoons salt
3¾ cups cooked brown rice

Sauté onions and pepper in oil until tender but not brown. Add tomatoes, cheese, cloves, and bay leaf (we suggest enclosing cloves and bay leaf in a cheesecloth bag so that you can easily remove them). Add sugar and salt, and simmer for 15 minutes. Remove cloves and bay leaf, add rice, and mix. Turn into greased 1½-quart casserole dish. Bake at 375°F. for 30 minutes. Serves 6.

Dora Thorp
Sherman Cooks!

Brown Rice and Sausage Curry

An inexpensive, easily made curry for brunch, lunch, or supper.

8 pork link sausages
1 cup white (Chablis) wine
1 onion, thinly sliced
1 tablespoon butter
14½-ounce can tomatoes, with juice
1 rib celery, diced
1 apple, peeled, cored, and diced
2 teaspoons curry powder

1 tablespoon apricot jam
½ teaspoon thyme
1½ ounces (¼ cup) raisins
3 cups cooked brown rice
shredded coconut
(chopped almonds or peanuts)
chutney

Cook sausages, drain on paper towel, and cut each sausage into four pieces. Pour off fat in pan. Deglaze pan with white wine. In separate pan, sauté onion in butter until golden. Add onion to wine, along with tomatoes, celery, apple, curry, jam, thyme, raisins, and sausages, and simmer gently until celery is tender — about 10 minutes. Combine with rice, and turn into greased 2-quart casserole dish. Bake at 325°F. for 20-30 minutes, or until heated through. Sprinkle with coconut and optional nuts, and serve with chutney. Serves 4-6.

Virginia Klingenstein
Warren, VT

Rice Pilaf I

Serve this wonderful, spicy pilaf as a side dish or all by itself as a vegetarian brunch. For variation, you can add 1-1½ cups diced apple and/or diced ham or chicken. Reheat in double boiler over boiling water.

2 cups raw white long-grain rice
½ cup butter
1 medium onion, chopped
1 garlic clove, chopped
4 cups boiling water
12 cloves
12 cardamom seeds

2 teaspoons salt
1 teaspoon allspice
1-inch piece stick cinnamon
½ teaspoon turmeric
2 tablespoons butter
¼ cup slivered almonds
½ cup raisins

Wash rice under cold water and drain. Melt butter in large skillet, and sauté onion and garlic. Add rice, and cook, stirring, for 5 minutes over medium heat. Add boiling water and all seasonings. Cover, and simmer for 30 minutes, or until rice is tender and all water has been absorbed. Melt 2 tablespoons butter in skillet, add almonds, and sauté until golden. Stir almonds and raisins into cooked rice. Serves 8.

Mrs. Edwin Smith
Cooking at Court

Rice Pilaf II

A colorful pilaf dotted with bits of celery, carrots, green onion, and parsley.

1 cup raw rice	6 tablespoons chopped celery
3 tablespoons butter	6 tablespoons chopped carrots
2 cups boiling consommé	6 tablespoons chopped parsley
½ teaspoon salt (seasoned, if you prefer)	¼ cup chopped green onion
	½ cup slivered almonds

Brown rice in butter. Place in 2-quart casserole dish, and mix with 1½ cup consommé and salt. Cover and bake at 350°F. for 30 minutes. Remove from oven, add remaining ingredients, including the remaining ½ cup consommé, and mix with a fork. Cover dish, return to oven, and bake 30 minutes longer. Serves 6.

Mrs. Celia Orelup
Sherman Cooks!

Spanish Rice

Tangy rice side dish to serve with roast or fried chicken or with pork.

1 onion, chopped fine	1 tablespoon capers
1 green pepper, cored and diced	salt and pepper
1 garlic clove, minced	15-ounce can tomato sauce
2 tablespoons cooking oil	above can full of boiling water
8-10 pimiento-stuffed Spanish olives, chopped	1 cup raw long-grain rice

Sauté onion, pepper, and garlic in oil until onion is tender. Add remaining ingredients. Simmer, covered, until rice is cooked — about 30 minutes. Serves 6.

Teresa Miller
Valatie, NY

Walnut-Cheddar Loaf

A crunchy, nutritious, and filling loaf for those who prefer to obtain their protein from a source other than meat. Should there be any leftovers, slice, dip slices in flour, fry in oil or butter, and serve with tomato or horseradish-sour-cream sauce.

½ cup raw brown rice
1 cup boiling water
¼ teaspoon salt
2 tablespoons cooking oil
2 cups chopped onions

1 cup ground walnut meats
1 cup grated Cheddar cheese
2 eggs, beaten
1 teaspoon caraway seed
salt and pepper

Add rice to boiling water and ¼ teaspoon salt. Bring back to boil, stir, cover, turn down heat, and simmer over medium-low heat for 40-50 minutes, or until rice is fluffy. Sauté onions in cooking oil until tender. Combine rice with onions, walnuts, cheese, eggs, and caraway seed. Season to taste with salt and pepper. Butter 7x4-inch loaf pan, pour in batter, and bake at 350°F. for 30 minutes. Serves 4-6.

Clair Marcus
An Artist's Cookbook

Wild Rice Casserole

From Minnesota, where it grows! Excellent as a main dish, or as a side dish for a duck or chicken dinner.

1 pound pork sausage meat
1 pound fresh mushrooms, thinly
   sliced
1 cup chopped onion
2 cups raw wild rice
8 cups boiling water
1 teaspoon salt
¼ cup flour

½ cup heavy cream
2½ cups chicken broth
pinch each of oregano, thyme, and
   marjoram
salt and pepper
(1 tablespoon Worcestershire
   sauce)

Brown sausage and drain. In sausage fat, sauté mushrooms and onion and mix with sausage meat. Wash wild rice *well* by placing rice in large strainer and running cold water from tap through rice until water runs clear. Place rice in boiling water, add salt, bring back to boil if necessary, then reduce heat and simmer, covered, for about 1 hour, or until rice is tender and fluffy. Drain. Mix flour with cream until smooth. Add chicken broth, and cook, stirring, over medium heat until thickened. Add seasonings including optional Worcestershire sauce. Stir in rice and sausage mixture and mix well. Turn into buttered 3-quart casserole dish, cover, and bake for 30 minutes at 350°F. Serves 8.

Betty McGill
Bloomington, MN

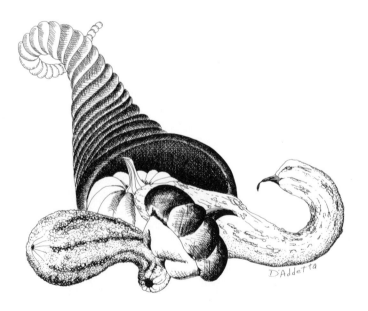

CHAPTER THREE

Chicken and Turkey

High in protein, low in fat and cholesterol content, and certainly the most reasonably priced of all meats, chicken has rightfully taken its place as a major American food staple. Its versatility has taken it out of the proverbial "pot." Now you can find the bird anywhere: blanketed between two pieces of bread, aromatically roasting on a spit, or swimming in a champagne sauce on a silver platter.

Since Good Neighbors come from all over the world and all walks of life and each one has a favorite chicken recipe, you will find included in this chapter chicken dishes for the fanciest dinner party, an after-ski supper, or a backyard cookout. There are recipes with the international flavors of Italy, France, Mexico, India, China, and the Philippines — not to mention fascinating inventions using to delicious effect ingredients all the way from lobster and artichokes to maple syrup and even Coke! And since one of the glories of chicken is that it is just as tasty the second time around, we have included many good ideas for leftovers. (Almost any dish calling for cooked chicken can be made equally well with cooked turkey meat.)

CHICKEN BREASTS

Chicken Breasts with Apples

Smells great while it's cooking, and that's just the half of it.

1 medium onion, finely chopped
4 tablespoons butter, divided
5 tablespoons flour, divided
salt and pepper
1 tablespoon paprika
4 chicken breasts, halved

1 quart apple juice or cider
juice of 1 lemon
6 apples, peeled, cored, and cut
   into eighths
¼ cup sherry
¼ cup slivered almonds, toasted

In large, heavy skillet sauté onion in 1 tablespoon of the butter until soft. Remove onion, and set aside. Place 2 tablespoons of the flour, salt, pepper, and paprika in a paper bag. Shake chicken in bag, one piece at a time, until well coated. Add remaining 3 tablespoons butter to skillet, and brown chicken. Blend in 3 tablespoons flour, onion, and cider. Cover, and simmer 45 minutes. Add lemon juice and apples, and continue cooking for 15 minutes. Add sherry and almonds, and serve over rice or noodles. Serves 6-8.

Mrs. William C. Roux
Madison, CT
Vittles Unlimited

Vermont Apple Chicken

Apples and chicken are always good together — add brandy and cream as here, and you've really got something.

6 tart (Granny Smith) apples,
   cored
1 cup cider
2 chicken breasts, boned, skinned,
   and halved

4 tablespoons minced onion
4 tablespoons butter
¼ cup slightly warmed brandy
salt and pepper
1 cup heavy cream

Slice apples into ½-inch rings and poach in cider. Remove apple rings when almost soft, reserving the cider. Brown chicken and onion in butter in medium skillet. Pour brandy over chicken and ignite. When flames die down, add salt, pepper, and cider to chicken. Place all in greased 9x13-inch baking dish, and bake 50 minutes in 350°F. oven. Add cream, and continue cooking for 10 minutes. Arrange apple rings on top of chicken, spoon some sauce over tops, and run under broiler until lightly browned. Serves 4.

Favorite Foods

Apricot Chicken

A real holiday dish. Elegant tasting and beautiful to look at — golden chicken and apricots set off by green parsley. Good with wild rice and broccoli or asparagus.

4 chicken breasts, split in half
2+ cups dry white wine (not Vermouth)
1 cup dried apricots
water and wine

4-6 tablespoons butter, softened
4-6 tablespoons honey
salt and freshly ground pepper
parsley for garnish

Marinate chicken in 2 cups wine in 9x13-inch baking dish for several hours. Remove chicken; drain thoroughly, leaving marinade in dish. Soften apricots for 15 minutes in simmering liquid, half water and half wine — enough to cover apricots. Combine butter and honey in equal amounts, and spread half over chicken pieces. Place chicken and drained apricots in marinade in baking dish. Season with salt and pepper, cover, and bake in 350°F. oven for 1 hour. Remove cover, brush chicken with remaining butter-honey mixture; return to oven and bake 10-15 minutes longer. Place chicken on warm platter, arrange apricots over and around the chicken, then pour a *little* of the wine marinade over all. Garnish with sprigs of parsley. Serves 4.

Mrs. Roger Butler
Cooking at Court

Chicken and Artichokes

A subtle party dish neither rich nor greasy and easily prepared — in advance, if you wish. Serve a side dish of mushrooms.

9-ounce package frozen artichoke hearts, thawed
2 tablespoons water
1½ teaspoons salt
¼ teaspoon pepper

1 pound chicken breasts, or 2 whole breasts, halved
½ cup dry vermouth
¼ teaspoon oregano
3 strips bacon

Cover bottom of lightly greased 8x12-inch oval, or 7x11-inch oblong baking dish with single layer of artichoke hearts. Add water, salt, and pepper. Cover hearts with chicken pieces, skin side up. Combine vermouth and oregano, and pour over chicken. Lay bacon on top, and bake at 350°F. for 1 hour. Serves 4.

Mrs. Edward Bridgman
Cooking at Court

Chicken Breasts Archduke

If the Archduke can't come, serve this to the King. Elegant looking and tasting!

3 chicken breasts, boned and
    halved
¼ cup brandy
salt and pepper
4 ounces mushrooms, chopped
6 tablespoons butter
1 teaspoon lemon juice
½ cup minced boiled ham
½ cup finely diced Swiss or
    Gruyère cheese
1 teaspoon chopped tarragon

flour for dusting
½ teaspoon meat glaze (Chinese
    brown sauce or Bovril)
½ teaspoon tomato paste, or 1
    tablespoon tomato sauce
3 tablespoons flour
1 cup chicken stock
½ cup heavy cream, whipped
artichoke hearts or bottoms, sliced
Mozzarella cheese, sliced

Cut pocket on inside (not skin side) of each chicken breast, and rinse pocket with brandy. Sprinkle breasts with salt and pepper on pocket side. Sauté mushrooms in 2 tablespoons of the butter. Add lemon juice, and cook briskly 2 minutes. Stir in ham, cheese, and tarragon. Stuff each pocket with a good tablespoon of this filling.

In large skillet, melt remaining 4 tablespoons butter. Fold chicken pieces in two, with stuffed pocket inside. Dust lightly with flour and place in melted butter, skin side down. Cover pan with foil, and place heavy weight on top. (The weight flattens and seals the chicken packages.) Brown slowly on one side. Remove weight and foil, and brown chicken on other side. Pour ¼ cup brandy over chicken, then remove chicken from pan and keep warm.

Off fire, stir in meat glaze, tomato paste, and 3 tablespoons flour. Gradually stir in chicken stock, heating over medium-high heat until boiling. Reduce heat; stir in whipped cream, mixing well. Return chicken to pan, cover, and simmer for 15-20 minutes. (Dish may be made to this point ahead, then reheated several hours later.) To serve, arrange chicken pieces in ovenproof serving dish. Spoon sauce over chicken and top each piece with artichoke slice and thin slice Mozzarella. Place under broiler just long enough to melt cheese. Serve hot. Serves 6.

Mrs. John A. Elliot
Bon Appétit

Breast of Chicken Sauté

Chicken enhanced by grapes and mushrooms in a delicate wine sauce.

½ cup flour
salt and pepper
6 chicken breasts, halved, skinned, and boned
½ cup butter
½ cup finely chopped onion

1 cup dry white wine
2 cups chopped fresh mushrooms
1 cup seedless grapes
1½ cups light cream
chopped parsley

Season flour with salt and pepper. Dredge chicken in seasoned flour, and sauté in butter in large skillet over medium-high heat until lightly browned. Reduce heat to medium. Add onion, and cook until tender but not browned. Add wine and mushrooms. Cover, and simmer gently for 25-30 minutes. Add grapes, and cook 3-5 minutes longer. Remove chicken to heated platter. Stir cream into mushroom mixture. Heat through and pour over chicken. Garnish with parsley. Serves 6-8.

Connecticut Cooks

Chicken Gloria

Sautéed chicken and vegetables in tomato sauce — can be made in a wok.

2 large chicken breasts, boned and skinned
3 green onions
3+ tablespoons butter
3 tablespoons chopped green pepper
10-12 large mushrooms, sliced
2 tablespoons white wine or sherry
1 medium tomato, cut in chunks

¼ teaspoon garlic salt
½ teaspoon onion powder
2 teaspoons grated Parmesan cheese
8-ounce can tomato sauce
salt and black pepper
1 teaspoon dried parsley
⅛ teaspoon paprika

Cut chicken breasts into bite-sized pieces. Chop green onions, including 1 inch of green stalks. In large, heavy skillet or wok, melt butter, and sauté green pepper and mushrooms until soft. Remove and set aside. Place chicken pieces in skillet, adding more butter if necessary. Add wine or sherry, tomato chunks, garlic salt, onion powder, and Parmesan cheese. Cook covered over low heat until chicken is cooked through, 6-8 minutes, stirring once or twice. Add green pepper, mushrooms, and tomato sauce. Mix gently, seasoning to taste with salt and pepper. Heat through. Sprinkle parsley, green onions, and paprika over top, and serve over rice or pasta. Serves 4.

Gloria Williams
Moorestown, NJ

Chicken in Fresh Tomato Sauce

Spectacular variation on chicken cordon bleu. Must be made a day ahead.

Sauce:
8 ripe tomatoes, peeled
½ teaspoon fresh basil
½ teaspoon oregano
½ teaspoon salt
½ teaspoon pepper
1 bay leaf

Chicken:
3 chicken breasts, boned, skinned
    and halved

½ pound ham, sliced
½ pound Mozzarella cheese, sliced
salt and pepper to taste
Tabasco sauce
flour for dredging
oil for deep frying
½ cup white wine
1 tablespoon chopped fresh basil

Cook tomatoes with other sauce ingredients in dutch oven for 3 hours. Remove cover for last half-hour. Pound chicken thin between wax paper. Cut slice of ham and one of cheese to fit each pounded chicken breast-half. Place first ham, then cheese on breast. Sprinkle with salt, pepper, and a few drops Tabasco. Roll up breasts, tucking in edges, and secure with round, wooden toothpicks. Dredge chicken with flour, shaking off excess. Deep fry in oil until golden brown, 5-8 minutes. Drain chicken on paper. Pour off all oil except 3 tablespoons. Add white wine and tomato sauce. Bring to hard boil, uncovered, and boil to reduce sauce for 10 minutes. Place chicken in casserole dish, cover with tomato sauce, and sprinkle with fresh basil. Cover, and refrigerate overnight. When ready to serve, bake uncovered at 350°F. for 1 hour. Serves 4-6.

Favorite Foods

Coq Au Vin

A good, honest recipe — French country cooking at its best. This would make a wonderful after-ski dinner. Serve with barley or rice, salad, and a crusty French bread.

12 slices bacon
flour, seasoned with salt and
    pepper
5 whole chicken breasts, boned and
    cut in chunks

2 cups sliced carrots
2 cups thickly sliced onion rings
1 cup sliced fresh mushrooms
2+ cups chicken bouillon
2+ cups red wine   *(continued)*

In large frying pan, cook bacon until crisp. Drain and crumble over bottom of 4-quart dutch oven. Place seasoned flour in paper bag. Shake chicken pieces in seasoned flour to coat, then brown in bacon grease, drain, and put in dutch oven over bacon. Add carrots, onions, mushrooms, 2 cups bouillon, and 2 cups wine. Bring to boil. Reduce heat, and simmer until carrots are cooked — about 1 hour. As liquid evaporates, add more broth and wine in equal parts. Serves 8-12.

Meredith M. Thayer
The Well Tempered Kitchen

International Dateline Chicken

Succulent chicken in a lightly curried sauce fruited with dates and oranges and accented with green peppers. An eye-appealing luncheon dish. Serve with noodles and perhaps a crisp cucumber salad.

3 large chicken breasts, halved
¼ cup butter
10½-ounce can chicken broth
½ teaspoon curry powder
1 tablespoon minced onion
¼ teaspoon pepper

1 teaspoon salt
1 teaspoon lemon juice
11-ounce can mandarin oranges
2 tablespoons cornstarch
1 cup thin green pepper slices
1 cup chopped dates

In large skillet sauté the chicken breasts in butter until brown. Combine broth, curry powder, onion, pepper, and salt. Pour over chicken, cover, and simmer for 45 minutes. Remove chicken to serving platter and keep warm. Combine lemon juice, syrup drained from the oranges, and cornstarch. Stir into skillet, and mix with broth in pan. Cook, stirring constantly, until thickened and clear. Add green pepper and dates. Simmer 3-4 minutes. Stir in orange sections, and pour sauce over chicken. Serves 6.

Myra Meyer
The Rockport Heritage Cookbook

Chicken Breasts Priscilla

Serve with noodles, barley, or rice, curried or plain. Freeze either before or after cooking, but do not freeze rice in the same container.

4 chicken breasts, skinned and
    halved
1½ cups rosé or red wine
½ cup sunflower oil
2 cloves garlic, minced

½ teaspoon oregano
½ cup soy sauce
¼ cup water
2 teaspoons ground ginger
2 tablespoons brown sugar, packed

Place chicken breasts in large casserole dish. Mix other ingredients together in small mixing bowl, and pour over chicken. Cover, and refrigerate overnight, or up to 2 days. Remove from refrigerator at least 1 hour before cooking. Bake at 375°F. for 1 hour. Baste chicken well with sauce before serving. Serves 6-8.

Kerilyn Fruchter
Ann Arbor, MI

Layered Chicken Casserole

Chicken baked with mushrooms and sour cream for very special everyday fare. Serve over Kaluchi soup noodles, or other noodles, with broccoli or beans.

3 chicken breasts, halved, boned, and skinned
flour for dredging
2 tablespoons dry bread crumbs
seasoned salt
pepper
paprika
2 tablespoons butter
2 tablespoons cooking oil
¾ cup diced onion
2 cloves garlic, crushed
1 cup (½ pound) sliced fresh mushrooms
½ cup slivered almonds
10½-ounce can chicken noodle soup
⅓ cup dry white wine, or chicken stock
1 cup sour cream
parsley flakes

Pound each breast half slightly to flatten a bit. Mix flour, crumbs, and seasonings, and coat chicken pieces well with mixture. Brown a few pieces at a time in butter and oil. Remove chicken to platter. In same skillet sauté onion until limp (add more butter as necessary). Add garlic, mushrooms, and almonds, and cook, stirring, for 3-4 minutes more. Now add soup and wine (or stock), and cook 2-3 minutes, stirring constantly. If sauce is thin, sprinkle in, stirring, 1-2 tablespoons of the seasoned flour used for dredging, and cook until thickened slightly. Slowly, over low heat, stir in sour cream — do not let sauce boil. Correct seasoning.

Layer one third of sauce in bottom of 9x13-inch casserole dish. Add layer of chicken pieces, more sauce, remaining chicken, and rest of sauce. Cover, and bake at 325°F. for 1 hour, removing cover for final 10 minutes. Garnish with parsley and spoon over noodles. Serves 4-6.   *Laurel Gabel*
Wellesley, MA

Broiled Chicken Oriental Style

Very low in calories but high in flavor, this versatile chicken dish is great for family or company — even as an hors d'oeuvre (cut breasts into chunks, and cook en brochette).

1 scallion, minced
1 clove garlic, crushed
¼ cup orange or pineapple juice
2 tablespoons sherry
1 tablespoon Tamari (soy sauce)
1 tablespoon minced fresh ginger root
1 whole chicken breast, boned, skinned, and halved

Combine all ingredients but chicken in small, shallow glass or enamel pan. Add chicken breasts, and marinate for 2 hours, turning occasionally. Grill chicken, or broil 4 inches away from flames for 3-4 minutes on each side, or until chicken is a rich brown. Baste occasionally with marinade. Serves 2.

Alice Freeman
Newfane, VT

Pineapple Chicken and Rice

A satisfying dish, not too sweet, which can be made a day ahead and heated in the oven. Serve with Madeira Spinach (page 171) and sliced ripe tomatoes for an attractive green, red, and yellow meal.

¼ cup currants or raisins
hot water to cover
3 whole chicken breasts, boned and skinned
½ cup flour
1½ teaspoons salt
¼ teaspoon pepper

water or milk
8 tablespoons butter
1 medium onion, coarsely chopped
1½ cups raw rice, brown or white
¼ cup light rum
1 large can crushed pineapple
½ cup brown sugar, packed

Cover currants or raisins with hot water, and set aside. Cut each chicken breast into quarters. Mix flour with salt and pepper. Dip chicken pieces in water or milk and roll in seasoned flour. Melt 6 tablespoons of the butter in large skillet, and cook chicken over medium heat until cooked through, about 10-15 minutes, turning to brown evenly. Meanwhile, melt remaining 2 tablespoons butter in small skillet, and sauté onion until golden. Cook rice. When chicken is done, spread onion over top, and cook 5 minutes more. Drain currants, and combine with rum, pineapple, and brown sugar. Pour mixture over chicken, cover, and simmer 15 minutes, stirring frequently to prevent sticking. Place rice in shallow 10-inch casserole dish and top with chicken and sauce. Serves 4-6.

Patricia D. Partridge
Lovell, WY

Chicken and Wine Casserole

Tender breasts of chicken in a warm brown sauce. Serve with noodles or rice, a crisp vegetable, and a green salad.

3 chicken breasts, boned and halved
3 tablespoons lemon juice
2 cloves garlic, crushed
salt and pepper
4 tablespoons olive oil

½ pound mushrooms, sliced
4 tablespoons flour
2 cups chicken broth
½ cup dry white wine
½ teaspoon rosemary

Place chicken in Pyrex baking pan, and sprinkle with lemon juice, garlic, salt, and pepper. Cover and refrigerate overnight. Next morning, in large skillet brown chicken in olive oil. Remove chicken to deep 2-quart casserole dish. Sauté mushrooms in the olive oil. Add flour and then broth, stirring over low heat until thickened. Add wine and rosemary. Pour sauce over chicken, cover dish, and bake at 350°F. for 45 minutes to 1 hour. Serves 4-6.

Elsie Stupinsky
Bernardsville, NJ

Spinach Chicken Gratin

Crumbed chicken and spinach in a herb-flavored, creamy sauce for an attractive party dish.

3 chicken breasts, boned, skinned,
    and halved
2 eggs, beaten
1½ cups crushed stuffing mix
3 tablespoons butter
½ cup white wine
1 cup chicken broth

1 clove garlic, crushed
dash marjoram
dash basil
⅓ cup heavy cream
two 10-ounce packages frozen leaf
    spinach, cooked and drained
½ cup grated Parmesan cheese

Preheat oven to 350°F. Dip chicken in eggs, then in stuffing mix until well coated. In large skillet, sauté in butter until chicken begins to brown. Turn once, lower heat, and add wine. Simmer until wine has almost evaporated. Remove chicken from pan. Stir broth, garlic, marjoram, basil, and cream into pan juices to make sauce. Place half the spinach in bottom of buttered 2-quart casserole dish. Add chicken, and top with remaining spinach. Pour sauce over all, sprinkle with Parmesan, and bake, uncovered, for 30 minutes. Serves 6.

Alice H. Rogers
Sherman Cooks!

CHICKEN PARTS

Apple-Stuffed Chicken

Very good, and inexpensive, too. Toasty bundles of chicken wrapped around a filling of apple, cheese, and raisins in a gingered-up apple sauce.

4 chicken thighs
salt and pepper
2 small eating apples, cored and
    quartered
¼ cup grated Swiss cheese
4 teaspoons raisins
2 teaspoons flour

¼ cup cooking oil
1 tablespooon cornstarch
1 tablespoon sugar
¼ teaspoon ground ginger
⅛ teaspoon salt
¾ cup water

Remove bone from chicken thighs by placing each thigh, skin-side down, on a cutting board; cut meat along bone. Starting at one end of bone, cut away meat, pulling it back as you cut. Discard bone. Sprinkle meat with salt and pepper. Cut 1 apple-quarter lengthwise into 4 slices. Place an apple slice, some cheese and a few raisins in center of each chicken piece. Fold meat over stuffing and secure with toothpicks, making sure stuffing is covered.

(continued)

Coat chicken with flour. In a 10-inch skillet over medium-high heat, brown chicken in oil, turning frequently. Reduce heat to medium-low, cover, and cook 15 minutes, or until chicken is tender, turning once while chicken is cooking. Meanwhile prepare sauce: cut remaining apple into chunks. In saucepan over medium heat, heat apples, cornstarch, sugar, ginger, 2 teaspoons raisins, salt, and water to boiling, stirring constantly. Boil 1 minute. Serve over chicken. Serves 2.

Sallie Lathrop Klemm
The Well Tempered Kitchen

Curried Chicken and Rice

A quick and easy curry with a very authentic taste. Serve with chutney and dishes of "boys": raisins, chopped peanuts, flaked coconut, chopped hard-cooked eggs, and crushed bacon.

2 whole chicken breasts, boned, skinned, and cubed
2 chicken thighs, boned, skinned, and cubed
3 tablespoons butter
2 small onions, minced
1 cup cooked rice
1½ teaspoons brown sugar, packed

¾ teaspoon poultry seasoning
1½ teaspoons curry powder
1-2 cloves garlic, crushed
salt and pepper
¾ cup sherry
1 teaspoon dry chicken bouillon, or
1 chicken bouillon cube

In a 10-inch skillet sauté cubed chicken in butter. Add onions and sauté until golden. Add rice, sugar, and seasonings, stirring to mix. Add sherry and bouillon. Bring to a boil while stirring. Reduce heat, cover, and simmer 30 minutes. Serves 4.

Kathleen Hanning
West Warwick, RI

Kauilani Chicken

A snap to prepare — the kids will love it.

4 chicken breasts, boned, skinned, and halved
4 chicken thighs, boned and skinned
20-ounce can pineapple chunks
1 small onion, chopped

1 green pepper, chopped
2 tablespoons mustard
2 tablespoons vinegar
2 tablespoons Worcestershire sauce
1 cup catsup
2 tablespoons cornstarch

Place chicken in single layer in buttered 10x16-inch baking dish. In saucepan, combine pineapple, onion, pepper, mustard, vinegar, Worcestershire sauce, and catsup. Simmer 5 minutes, then add cornstarch. Cook until thickened. Pour over chicken. Bake, covered, at 350°F. for 1 hour, or until chicken is tender. Serves 6 (2 pieces each).

Mrs. Ralph Cortis
Cooking at Court

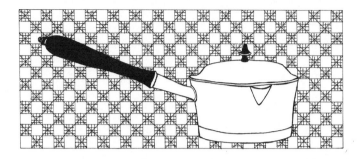

Chicken Tamale Pie

Festive "High Mexican" — a meal in one dish. Serve with Sangría, and pass sour cream and hot sauce.

Broth:
2 pounds chicken breasts
2 pounds chicken thighs
water to cover
½ teaspoon salt
2-3 stalks celery, chopped
1 onion, sliced

Sauce:
¼ cup butter (approx.)
2 large onions, chopped
½ cup flour
7½-ounce can pitted black olives, sliced, drained
28-ounce can solid pack tomatoes, undrained

1 teaspoon salt
1 tablespoon chili powder
dash hot-pepper sauce
¾ cup grated Monterey Jack cheese

Batter:
1 cup flour
1 cup yellow cornmeal
¼ pound butter, melted
2 teaspoons baking powder
1 teaspoon salt
2 cups milk

Cook chicken parts with salt, celery, and onion in water to cover until chicken is tender. Cool in broth, then remove meat from bones. Skim fat from broth, and add enough butter to chicken fat to make ½ cup. Strain broth and reserve. Heat fat in skillet, and sauté onions until tender. Stir in flour. Add olives, tomatoes, salt, chili powder, and hot-pepper sauce; simmer 10 minutes. Add a little reserved broth if needed. Meanwhile, mix batter ingredients in medium bowl. Cut chicken into bite-sized pieces and place in buttered 3-quart casserole dish. Cover with sauce. Pour batter over all, and bake uncovered at 350°F. for 1 hour, or until top is thoroughly cooked and brown. Five minutes before pie is done, top with grated cheese. Serves 6-8.

Mrs. William Davies
San Diego, CA
Vittles Unlimited

Shy Thighs

Marvelous name for a very impressive dish. Great for company, but inexpensive, too. Chicken thighs stuffed with sausage, encased in pastry, and served in a creamy mushroom sauce.

½ cup corn oil
6 brown-and-serve sausage links
6 broiler-fryer chicken thighs, skinned
2 chicken bouillon cubes
¼ cup boiling water
water to make 1 cup liquid
½ cup all-purpose flour
¼ teaspoon salt
¼ teaspoon paprika
⅛ teaspoon freshly ground black pepper

10¾-ounce can cream of mushroom soup
½ pint sour cream
¼ cup dry white wine
6-ounce can sliced mushrooms, drained
11-ounce box pie-crust sticks
water to prepare according to directions on box
2 tablespoons heavy cream
parsley for garnish

Heat corn oil in skillet over medium heat. Add sausages and brown; remove from pan and drain on paper. Add chicken to skillet, and brown on all sides. Dissolve bouillon cubes in boiling water. Add to skillet. Cover, and simmer about 20 minutes or until fork can be inserted in chicken with ease. Remove chicken from broth, cool, and carefully remove bones. Discard bones, and set aside meat.

Pour broth from skillet into measuring cup; add water to make 1 cup liquid. Return liquid to skillet. Mix together 3 tablespoons of the flour, salt, paprika, and pepper. Add to broth. Stir to blend over low heat. Add soup and cook, stirring constantly, until mixture bubbles. Gradually add sour cream and wine; blend well and remove from heat. Add mushrooms and mix well. Place browned sausage in bone cavity of each thigh, roll tightly, and set aside.

Using remaining flour, sprinkle work area. Prepare pie-crust mix according to box directions. Divide mix into 6 equal portions. Roll each portion out into a thin 6-inch circle. Place stuffed thigh in the center of each circle and top with 2 tablespoons of mushroom sauce. Fold pastry over and seal seams. Brush with cream, and place in lightly greased 2-quart Pyrex baking dish. Bake at 400°F. in preheated oven for about 30 minutes, or until golden brown. Remove from oven. Heat remaining mushroom sauce, and serve with chicken. Garnish with parsley. Serves 4-6.

Mrs. Nelda Young
Jacksonville, FL

Chicken and Walnuts

Chicken and walnuts in a delectable sauce. A good main dish any time, and a fine entrée for an all-Chinese meal. Serve with fried rice and stir-fried vegetables.

6 chicken thighs or 4 breasts
1 egg, beaten
1 tablespoon cooking oil
1 teaspoon cornstarch
1 cup walnuts
boiling water
2 tablespoons Hoisin sauce

1 teaspoon grated fresh ginger root
1 teaspoon sugar
1 teaspoon soy sauce
¼ teaspoon sesame oil
½ cup cooking oil
4 green onions, chopped fine, for garnish

Bone and skin chicken, and cut into ½-inch pieces. Combine egg with 1 tablespoon oil and cornstarch. Add chicken pieces and toss gently to coat. Set aside. Chop walnuts into quarters and place in bowl. Pour boiling water over nuts, and let stand for 5 minutes. Remove nuts and pat dry. Set aside. Combine Hoisin sauce, ginger, sugar, soy sauce, and sesame oil in small bowl. Set aside. Heat ½ cup oil in large skillet or wok over medium-high heat. Add walnuts and fry 45 seconds till golden. Remove with slotted spoon, and drain on paper towels. Add chicken to skillet, and cook over medium-high heat till golden, about 3-4 minutes. Remove with slotted spoon, and drain well. Pour off all but film of oil from skillet. Add Hoisin-sauce mixture, and cook over medium heat until sauce is bubbly, about 1 or 2 minutes. Add chicken and walnuts and mix thoroughly with sauce. Transfer to warm serving dish and garnish with finely chopped green onions. Serves 4.

Dottie Dobson
Exeter, NH

Debbie's Chicken Wings

Savory and tender chicken wings. They are spicy and a bit tangy. A great appetizer or meal.

1 star anise
2 tablespoons hot water
⅓ cup soy sauce
1 teaspoon dry mustard
½ teaspoon ground ginger

2 cloves garlic, crushed
¼ cup vegetable oil
(dash M.S.G.)
up to 5 pounds chicken wings

Remove anise seeds from pod and crush. Combine crushed anise seeds and hot water. Let stand 15 minutes. Strain out and discard seeds, and put flavored water in small bowl. Add all other ingredients except chicken, and mix well with wire whisk. Disjoint chicken wings into three sections; discard tips, or save for another use. Place other sections in large bowl, pour marinade over, and mix to coat. Marinate 3 hours, or overnight in refrigerator. When ready to cook, place wings on rack in low-sided cookie sheet (to catch drippings) so that they do not touch each other. Bake in 350°F. oven for 45 minutes. Serves 6.

Dottie Dobson
Exeter, NH

WHOLE OR CUT-UP CHICKEN

Barbecued Chicken on a Spit

The slightly sweet basting sauce produces a lovely, golden-brown chicken. Great summer fare for outdoor rotisserie. A Weber kettle cooker with indirect heat accomplishes the same thing as a rotisserie.

3-4 pound whole fryer	1 teaspoon Worcestershire sauce
¼ cup water	¼ teaspoon Tabasco sauce
½ cup vinegar	¼ teaspoon black pepper
4 tablespoons butter	salt to taste
1 tablespoon sugar	

Wash fryer thoroughly and pat dry. Center bird on spit and secure with tines. With cord, bind wings to bird, then bind legs together and to spit skewer. Two or three small birds may be placed on one skewer. Combine sauce ingredients in a small saucepan. Heat and stir until butter has melted and ingredients are well-combined. Cook over medium-hot fire, basting chicken inside and out with sauce (use a bulb baster) immediately after placing over fire, and approximately every 15-20 minutes until chicken is golden brown. Keep pan containing sauce close to heat to keep warm. Serves 4.

Maybelle M. Scheetz
Topeka, KS

No-Tomato Barbecued Chicken

Be sure to make more than you think they'll eat. You'll be glad you did. When outdoor cooking is impossible, just finish cooking in the oven or under broiler.

1 cup white wine or sherry	2 tablespoons lemon juice
1 cup cooking oil	2 tablespoons mayonnaise
3 tablespoons Worcestershire sauce	1 teaspoon salt
3 teaspoons chopped thyme	3 teaspoons pepper
1 medium onion, grated	3 broilers, cut in pieces
2 cloves garlic, grated	

A day ahead, blend all ingredients but chicken in food processor or electric blender. Marinate chicken in this mixture overnight, turning several times. When ready to cook, remove chicken, and place in single layer in large baking pan, reserving marinade. Bake in preheated 350°F. oven for 20 minutes. Finish cooking over low fire on grill, brushing marinade on chicken every few minutes. Have a bowl of water on hand to keep coals from flaming. Serves 6-8.

Ann Skelly
Hancock, NH

Broiled Chicken with Cayenne

A four-star recipe! Don't let the amount of cayenne scare you. Use it all for a sauce that is spicy but not explosive. (Sauce works beautifully on spare ribs or pork chops, too.)

½ cup lemon juice
2 cloves garlic, crushed
1½ teaspoons cayenne pepper
½ cup cooking oil
2 tablespoons tomato paste

½ teaspoon salt
1 teaspoon paprika
4½ pounds cut-up chicken or 4
    whole chicken breasts

In a bowl large enough to hold chicken, beat well the first seven ingredients. Add chicken, and marinate for 4 hours. Drain chicken, reserving marinade. Broil chicken, turning occasionally and basting with remaining sauce until done. Serves 4-6.

Mary Thompson
Cora, WY

Marinated Broiled Chicken

The most tender broiled chicken ever, subtly flavored.

½ cup cooking oil
2 tablespoons lemon juice
2 teaspoons salt
¼ teaspoon black pepper

¼ teaspoon garlic powder
¼ teaspoon poultry seasoning
1 broiling chicken, cut up into 6
    pieces

Combine oil, lemon juice, and spices and mix well. Place chicken pieces in shallow dish and pour marinade over them. Use a dish large enough to hold chicken in a single layer, so that the marinade comes about halfway up each chicken piece. Let marinate at least 2 hours, turning once. Brush chicken pieces with marinade and broil, 15-20 minutes, turning once and brushing again with marinade. Serves 6.

Caroline Day
The Rockport Heritage Cookbook

Chicken Baked in Beer and Tomatoes

A heartily flavored dish, tastes even better if made the day ahead. Serve over rice.

two 2½-pound fryers, cut up
⅓ cup flour
2 teaspoons salt
¼ teaspoon pepper
½ teaspoon paprika

⅓ cup bacon drippings
1 clove garlic
¾ cup chopped onion
¾ cup chopped green pepper
4 medium tomatoes

(continued)

Shake chicken pieces in paper bag with flour, salt, pepper and paprika. In large skillet, brown chicken pieces in bacon drippings and garlic. Transfer chicken to a 5-quart casserole dish. Discard garlic. In pan drippings, sauté onion and green pepper until tender. Sprinkle over chicken. Peel and quarter tomatoes and arrange over chicken. Add sauce.

Sauce:

2 cups beer	**½ teaspoon thyme**
¼ cup tomato paste	**1 teaspoon salt**

Blend all ingredients and pour over chicken. Can be made a day ahead up to this point. When ready to serve, bake uncovered in a 350°F. oven 1½ hours. Serves 8.

Connecticut Cooks

Spiced Cola Chicken

Chicken in a spectacular deep-red sauce. Divulge the secret ingredient, or keep it secret! Serve with rice, green beans, and fruit salad.

1 cup flour	**2 tablespoons peanut oil**
1 teaspoon ground ginger	**¼ cup catsup, or onion-flavored**
1 teaspoon cinnamon	**barbecue sauce**
½ teaspoon salt	**1 cup bottled cola beverage**
1 broiling chicken, cut up	

Mix flour, ginger, cinnamon, and salt in paper bag. Toss chicken, one piece at a time, in bag to coat. Sauté chicken in peanut oil in frying pan until golden brown. Pour off fat. Add catsup and cola, stirring to blend. Cover, and simmer 20 minutes. Uncover, and cook 30 minutes more. Serves 4.

Shirley Opitz
Monroeville, PA

Easy Maple Chicken

A New England family favorite.

1 frying chicken, cut into 8 pieces	**¼ cup soy sauce**
1 cup chopped onion	**¼ cup lemon juice**
1 cup chopped green pepper	**1 teaspoon salt**
1 cup maple syrup	**½ teaspoon pepper**

Arrange chicken pieces in single layer in baking dish. In a small bowl, mix together onion, green pepper, maple syrup, soy sauce, lemon juice, salt, and pepper. Pour over chicken and marinate overnight. Preheat oven to 350°F. Roll chicken in marinade, remove, and bake skin side down for the first 30 minutes. Turn chicken, and continue baking for 1 hour, basting with marinade every 15 minutes. Serves 4.

Charlotte Stone
Dublin, NH

Chicken with Lemon Sauce

Pretty enough to be the centerpiece at your table, this is tender chicken swimming in a cream-wine-citrus-cheese sauce. Serve with rice.

two 2-pound chickens, cut up
¼ pound butter
3 tablespoons dry sherry
3 tablespoons dry white wine
grated rinds of 1 orange and 1
    lemon
2 tablespoons lemon juice

salt and pepper
1½ cups heavy cream
¾ cup grated Gruyère or Swiss
    cheese
8 wafer-thin lemon slices
parsley

Using two large skillets (or one in shifts), cook chicken pieces in butter until golden brown. Cover pan, and cook over low to medium heat for 40-50 minutes. Remove chicken to heat-proof platter, reserving pan juices. Preheat broiler. Stir sherry, wine, grated rinds, and lemon juice into skillet. Add salt, pepper, and cream. Bring sauce quickly to boil, then pour over chicken. Sprinkle chicken with cheese, arrange lemon slices over top, and brown under broiler about 10 minutes. Garnish with parsley sprigs. Serves 6.

Richard F. French
Sherman Cooks!

Poulet en Cocotte

Savory chicken and vegetables roasted in wine for a delicious Sunday dinner.

½ cup butter, softened
1-2 cloves garlic, minced
3- to 4-pound roasting chicken
¼ teaspoon thyme
6 carrots, scraped and cut into
    1-inch pieces

3 large potatoes, quartered
1-pound can boiled onions, drained
¼ cup dry red wine
2 tablespoons water
parsley

Blend 2 tablespoons of the butter with garlic. Spread inside chicken cavity. Truss chicken, and rub outside with 2 tablespoons of the butter. Place in large casserole dish, and roast for 30 minutes in preheated 375°F. oven. Meanwhile, melt remaining butter in skillet. Add thyme, carrots, and potatoes. Sauté 5 minutes, stirring frequently. Arrange these vegetables with onions around the chicken in casserole dish. Pour in wine and water. Return to oven and roast about 1 hour and 15 minutes, basting several times. To serve, transfer to a warm platter and garnish with parsley. Serves 4.

Mrs. Elwyn Dirats
Cooking at Court

Chicken Tarragon

Delicately flavored chicken pieces. Serve with herbed rice and a crisp vegetable or salad.

2 to 2½-pound broiler, cut into
   pieces
1 cup dry white wine
1 tablespoon crushed tarragon
   leaves

¼ cup butter
½ teaspoon salt
⅛ teaspoon pepper
1 tablespoon flour
¼ cup dry white wine

Wipe chicken with damp paper towels. Arrange in single layer in 9x9-inch shallow baking dish. Combine 1 cup wine with tarragon, and pour over chicken. Cover and refrigerate several hours or overnight, turning chicken several times. Drain, reserving marinade. In large, heavy skillet melt butter and sauté chicken a few pieces at a time, turning until brown. Remove pieces as they brown, and sprinkle with salt and pepper. Pour off all but 2 tablespoons drippings from skillet. Add chicken and ¼ cup reserved marinade. Cook, covered, over low heat until chicken is tender, about 25-30 minutes. Remove to heated platter.

Make sauce. Combine flour with ¼ cup white wine, stirring until smooth. Pour mixture into skillet with remaining marinade, stirring constantly. Heat just to boiling, then reduce heat, and simmer several minutes. Pour over chicken. Serves 4.

Alice Freeman
Newfane, VT

Two-Continent Chicken

Curry, raisins, and hot sauce mixed with marinara sauce — India meets Italy! Serve over rice.

1 frying chicken, cut up
¼ cup flour
1½ teaspoons salt
¼ cup vegetable oil
1 medium onion, chopped
1 clove garlic, minced
1 green pepper, sliced

8-ounce can tomato sauce
1½ cups water
1 teaspoon curry powder
¼ teaspoon Tabasco sauce
¼ cup currants or raisins
2 tablespoons slivered almonds,
   toasted

Shake chicken, one piece at a time, in paper bag containing flour and salt. In large skillet or dutch oven, brown chicken in oil; remove. Add onion, garlic, and green pepper. Cook 3 minutes. Blend in tomato sauce, water, curry, Tabasco, and raisins, mixing well. Return chicken to pot. Cover and simmer 30 minutes. Garnish with toasted almonds. Serves 4.

Mela Baughman
Hanover Center Cooks

COOKED CHICKEN

Bihon Guisado

A recipe from the Philippines with a nice fresh flavor.

5 garlic cloves, minced
½ cup vegetable oil
1 medium onion, sliced
¼ pound cabbage, coarsely
    shredded
1 medium carrot, sliced
1 stalk celery, sliced
1 pound fresh shrimp, shelled and
    deveined

2 cups diced, cooked white chicken
    meat
2 cups chicken broth
4 tablespoons soy sauce
2 teaspoons salt
three 8-ounce packages rice
    noodles, pre-soaked

In 16-inch skillet, sauté garlic in oil until golden. Add vegetables, shrimp, and chicken, and simmer 2 minutes. Add chicken broth, soy sauce, and salt. Boil 5 minutes over medium-high heat. Add noodles, carefully stirring with wooden spoon so as not to break. Continue to boil until noodles are cooked — a few minutes. Serves 6-8.

Connecticut Cooks

Chicken and Crab Valentine

Tender chicken and crabmeat in a pink, velvety-smooth sauce. Serve with a tart salad.

3 cups diced, cooked chicken
2 cups frozen or fresh crab meat
3-4 cups cooked rice (1 cup raw)
8 slices crisp bacon, crumbled
parsley or watercress for garnish

Sauce:

6 tablespoons butter

6 tablespoons flour
1½ cups chicken broth
1½ teaspoons salt
pinch pepper
¾ teaspoon paprika
1 tablespoon sherry
2¼ cups sour cream

In saucepan, melt butter, add flour, and cook over low heat for 2 minutes, stirring constantly. Add chicken broth and cook, stirring, until smooth and thickened. Add salt, pepper, paprika, and sherry. Cover, and cook 10-15 minutes, stirring occasionally. Take off heat, add sour cream, and keep hot in top of a double boiler over boiling water. Fold chicken and crab meat gently into sauce, and heat through. Pour over bed of rice. Sprinkle bacon over all and garnish with parsley or watercress. Serves 6.

Mrs. Edward Lee
Cooking at Court

Chicken Crescent Squares

Delightfully different and easy!

3-ounce package cream cheese,
   softened
3 tablespoons butter, melted
2 cups cubed cooked chicken
¼ teaspoon salt
⅛ teaspoon pepper

2 tablespoons milk
1 tablespoon finely chopped onion
1 tablespoon finely chopped
   pimiento
8-ounce can crescent rolls
¾ cup seasoned bread crumbs

Blend together cream cheese and 2 tablespoons of the melted butter. Add chicken, salt, pepper, milk, onion, and pimiento. Mix thoroughly. Separate crescent rolls into four rectangles, sealing perforations. Place about ½ cup chicken mixture on each rectangle. Pull four corners of dough to center and seal. Brush tops with remaining 1 tablespoon butter. Dip into bread crumbs. Bake on ungreased cookie sheet at 350°F. for 20-25 minutes. Serves 4.

Carol L. Dembeck
A Taste of New Hampshire

Curried Chicken and Lobster

A subtly deluxe curry dish. Serve over hot rice or in patty shells.

1 tablespoon butter
1 tablespoon flour
2 teaspoons curry powder
¼ teaspoon salt
⅛ teaspoon cayenne pepper
1 egg yolk, beaten

1 cup cream
1½ cups diced, cooked chicken
1½ cups diced, cooked lobster
12-ounce can apricots, drained and
   each half cut into four pieces

Melt butter in top of double boiler. Mix flour, curry powder, salt, and pepper, and blend into melted butter. Cook about 1 minute, stirring constantly. Add beaten egg yolk to cream, then add this to roux, stirring until smooth and thick. Add chicken and lobster and mix in apricots. Bake at 350°F. for 15 minutes. Serves 4.

Bon Appétit

Chicken and Green-Chili Enchiladas

A south-of-the border hit.

10-ounce can enchilada sauce
12 corn tortillas
1½ cups shredded Cheddar cheese
1½ cups shredded Monterey Jack
    cheese
1½ pounds chicken pieces, cooked,

boned, and skinned, or meat
    from a 2- to 3- pound chicken
4-ounce can green chilis, diced
sour cream
sliced ripe olives
green onion slices

Heat enchilada sauce in small frying pan. Soften tortillas by briefly dipping each in warm sauce. Mix cheeses together. On each tortilla, place chicken in center, and top with about 2 tablespoons cheese mixture, and 2 tablespoons chilis. Roll tortillas and place seam side down, side by side in a greased 9x13-inch baking dish. When finished, pour remaining sauce over all, and sprinkle with remaining cheese. Bake uncovered in 375°F. oven 15-20 minutes, or until cheese is melted and bubbly. Spoon sour cream down center, and sprinkle with olives and onion slices. Makes 12 enchiladas.

Deb Christenson
Brookline, NH

Gratin Italienne

A supreme layered casserole of noodles, spinach, tomatoes, and cheese with buried gems of sherried chicken chunks. Looks and tastes truly impressive. Serve with garlic bread and red wine.

Chicken:
2 tablespoons butter
1 medium onion, chopped fine
1 pound chicken meat, minced
1 tablespoon flour

3 tablespoons sherry
1 cup chicken stock
salt
pepper

Melt butter. Add onion and cook until soft. Increase heat. Add chicken and stir well until meat begins to brown. Blend in flour, sherry, and stock. Bring to boil. Season with salt and pepper, then simmer gently for 1½ hours.

Tomato Coulis:
1 medium onion, thinly sliced
1 tablespoon butter
16-ounce can Italian tomatoes,
    undrained
8-ounce can tomato puree

1 bay leaf
½ teaspoon chopped basil
salt and pepper
1 teaspoon arrowroot mixed with 1
    tablespoon water

Cook onion slowly in butter until soft. Add tomatoes (breaking up well), tomato puree, herbs, salt, and pepper. Cover and simmer until pulpy and
(continued)

rich, about 1 hour. Take off heat. Remove bay leaf, and add arrowroot mixed with water. Bring back to boil. Remove from heat.

Spinach and Noodles:

2 pounds fresh spinach	**8 ounces noodles**

In large pot blanch spinach for 3 minutes. Drain in sieve, pour cold water through, then press between two plates to remove excess moisture. Boil noodles 4-5 minutes. Drain and tip into large mixing bowl. Cover with lukewarm water (this prevents them from sticking together).

Cheese Sauce:

3 tablespoons butter	**salt and pepper**
3 tablespoons flour	**2 ounces grated cheese (Cheddar or**
1½ cups milk, warmed	**Parmesan)**

Melt butter over low heat. Stir in flour. Remove from heat, and stir in warmed milk. Return to heat, and add salt, pepper, and cheese, stirring until thickened. Cover with buttered wax paper to prevent skin from forming.

Assembly:

3 tablespoons butter	**1 cup grated cheese**
pepper	

Heat 1½ tablespoons of the butter until brown. Add spinach and heat gently until any remaining moisture evaporates, but don't let it dry. Place half the spinach on bottom of deep, buttered 4-quart casserole dish, and cover with half the cheese sauce. Drain noodles. Place in large pan with remaining butter, and toss over heat until well coated with butter and all water has evaporated. Season with pepper and turn into gratin dish. Cover with tomato coulis, then spoon in chicken mixture. Put remaining spinach over meat and cover with rest of cheese sauce. Sprinkle grated cheese over top and bake at 350°F. for 30-40 minutes. Serves 8-10.

Connecticut Cooks

Leftover Chicken

The night after a dinner of roast chicken and baked potatoes, try this. Good also with leftover pork or ham. The amounts of soy sauce and brown sugar may vary according to personal taste.

4 medium onions, thinly sliced	**4 large baked potatoes, thinly**
water to cover	**sliced (skins on)**
4 tablespoons butter	**⅓ cup soy sauce**
3 cups diced cooked chicken	**¼-⅓ cup brown sugar, packed**

Place onions in a large skillet with enough water to cover. Cook over high heat until onions are soft. Drain. Turn heat down to medium, and add butter, then chicken, potatoes, soy sauce, and brown sugar. Stir until chicken and potatoes are hot, and soy sauce and brown sugar have cooked into other ingredients. Serves 4-6.

Ronald Sands
Waitsfield, VT

Chicken Noodle Delight

A nifty way to serve leftover chicken — a whole meal in one dish. It will remind you of Fettucine Alfredo.

8-ounce package wide noodles	½ teaspoon dried parsley flakes
10-ounce package frozen green beans, cooked	¼ teaspoon garlic powder
8-ounce carton yogurt	½ teaspoon salt
½ cup mayonnaise	⅛ teaspoon pepper
½ cup dry white wine	3 cups cubed cooked chicken
	½ cup grated Parmesan cheese

Cook noodles according to package directions. Rinse in cool water and drain well. Drain beans well. In medium bowl, combine yogurt, mayonnaise, wine, parsley, garlic powder, salt, and pepper. In 2½-quart casserole dish, layer half the noodles, followed by half each of beans, chicken, yogurt mixture, and cheese. Repeat the layers. Cover, and bake in a 350°F. oven for 30 minutes. Uncover, and continue baking for 15-20 minutes, or until heated through. Remove from oven, and let stand for 5 minutes. Serves 6-8.

Mrs. Randall Carr
Lancaster, NH

Broiled Chicken Salad

Chicken-salad flavor all year long. Serve with a tossed green salad.

2 cups diced cooked chicken	⅓ cup sour cream
1½ cups diced celery	¼ cup slivered almonds, toasted
¼ cup French dressing	1½ cups fresh bread crumbs
salt and pepper	1 cup grated Cheddar cheese
½ cup mayonnaise	

Marinate chicken and celery in French dressing for 1 hour. Season with salt and pepper. Combine mayonnaise, sour cream, and almonds, and add to chicken mixture. Spoon into 8-inch square baking dish. Toss bread crumbs and cheese together, and place on top of chicken. Run under broiler just until cheese melts, then serve. Serves 4.

Elizabeth Fox
Guilford, CT

Hot Chicken Salad

As this bakes only 10-15 minutes, even in a heat wave it doesn't heat up the kitchen too much. Equally good made with turkey or tuna fish. Serve with fruit salad and rolls for a luncheon or light supper dish.

2 cups cooked and chopped
    chicken, turkey, or tuna
1-2 cups finely chopped celery, to
    taste
½ cup slivered almonds, toasted
½ teaspoon salt
2 teaspoons lemon juice
1 cup mayonnaise
½ cup grated Cheddar cheese
1 cup crushed potato chips

In large bowl, combine all ingredients except cheese and potato chips. Pile lightly into 9-inch square casserole dish, or individual baking dishes. Sprinkle with grated cheese and chips. Bake at 450°F. about 10 minutes, or until mixture bubbles. Serves 6.

Frances Miller
Community Baptist Church
Whitefield, NH

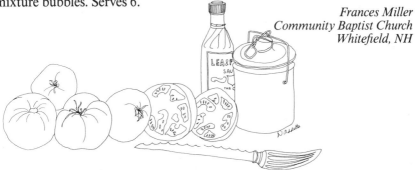

Chicken Soufflé on Tomatoes

Unusual and attractive brunch dish. Garnish with whole mushrooms, parsley sprigs, and cherry tomatoes for color.

1 egg, beaten
¼ cup bread crumbs
½ teaspoon poultry seasoning
½ teaspoon grated onion
½ teaspoon salt
½ cup mayonnaise
1 cup chopped cooked chicken
3 medium tomatoes, sliced ½ inch
    thick
2 tablespoons cooking oil
¼ teaspoon salt
dash thyme
6-ounce can mushroom crowns,
    drained and sliced

Combine the first seven ingredients. Arrange tomato slices on bottom of buttered 10-inch square baking dish. Spoon chicken mixture over tomatoes. Combine oil, salt, thyme, and sliced mushrooms, and sprinkle over top. Bake at 350°F. until firm. To brown on top, place under broiler for a second. Serves 2-3.

Mrs. Robert Polk
Madison, CT
Vittles Unlimited

Chicken and Turkey / **91**

CHICKEN LIVERS

Chicken Livers in Madeira

A treat for liver lovers. Serve over rice cooked in chicken broth, with garden peas.

1 medium onion, finely chopped
¼ pound mushrooms, sliced
4 tablespoons butter
1½ pounds chicken livers
1 tablespoon flour, plus flour for
    dusting

1 cup chicken broth
½ cup Madeira wine
1 teaspoon fresh chopped parsley

In large skillet, sauté onion and mushrooms in butter until onion is soft and golden. Dust livers with flour, and add them to pan. Sauté for 3-4 minutes until brown on all sides. Remove to plate and keep warm. Stir 1 tablespoon flour into pan drippings. Gradually add chicken broth, Madeira, and parsley. Cook, stirring, until smooth and thickened. Return livers to pan and cook over low heat about 10 minutes. Serves 4.

Ann Skelly
Hancock, NH

Chicken Livers Stroganoff

A rich, but relatively low-cost stroganoff. Serve immediately.

1 cup thinly sliced onions
½ cup butter
1 cup halved chicken livers
½ teaspoon salt
dash pepper

1 tablespoon paprika
1 cup sour cream
¼ cup sherry
hot cooked rice
parsley

Sauté onions in butter until tender. Add chicken livers, salt, pepper, and paprika. Cook livers gently for 10 minutes until browned. Stir in sour cream and sherry, heat through (do not boil), and ladle over rice. Garnish with parsley. Serves 4.

Mrs. Donald Richards
Cooking at Court

TURKEY

Roast Turkey with Wine

Try this turkey on a non-holiday for a new twist to an old standby. Neatest trick of the week to stuff a bird: place stuffing in center of large cheesecloth square and gather up cheesecloth like a sack; push sack into neck or body cavity and roast turkey. When turkey is done, simply extract sack, and empty dressing into a serving bowl. No mess!

(continued)

Stuffing:

2 cups chopped celery
1½ cups butter
16 cups bread cubes
2 cups seedless raisins, plumped in
    boiling water and drained
2 medium tart apples, peeled,
    cored, and diced

½ cup chopped fresh parsley
½ teaspoon rosemary
1 tablespoon salt
2 teaspoons poultry seasoning
1 cup rosé wine

In a large pan sauté celery in melted butter until soft. Add bread cubes, raisins, apples, parsley and seasonings. Toss gently before adding enough wine to moisten. Toss again.

Turkey:

15-pound turkey
3-4 teaspoons salt

butter, softened

Rub inside of bird with salt. Wrap enough dressing in double layer of cheesecloth to lightly fill neck cavity. Fasten skin over cavity with skewer. Place remaining dressing in square of double-thick cheesecloth to fill large cavity. Rub turkey with soft butter, and place in roasting pan with breast up.

Basting Liquid:

1 cup rosé wine

1 cup chicken bouillon or broth

Mix ½ cup wine with ½ cup broth. Pour over turkey. Cover bird with heavy foil tent. Roast at 325-350°F. until done according to weight of turkey. Baste several times with liquid prepared from the remaining ½ cup wine and ½ cup broth. Remove foil 20 minutes before total cooking time to allow turkey to brown.

Shirley Opitz
Monroeville, PA

Red Flannel Turkey Hash

Use this recipe for the bits and pieces still in the fridge when everyone says "Please no more leftover turkey!" No one will know he's eating turkey, and every bit will disappear.

⅔ cup diced salt pork
2 cups finely chopped or ground
    cooked turkey
2 cups finely chopped cooked beets

2 cups mashed potatoes
4 tablespoons chopped onion
salt and pepper

In large skillet, fry salt pork until crisp. Remove with slotted spoon and set aside. In medium bowl, combine turkey, beets, potatoes, and onion. Salt and pepper to taste, being conservative with salt because of salt pork. Fry this mixture in hot salt-pork fat until a crust forms on bottom. Flip and continue cooking until heated through and onion is cooked, about 20 minutes in all. To serve, break into portions and sprinkle with crisp salt pork. Serves 4.

Jeannette Perron
Dublin, NH

Turkey-Spinach Crepes

An impressive and attractive dish not difficult to make. Crepes not used can be frozen. You can prepare the filling a day ahead.

Crepes:

1 cup cold water
1 cup cold milk
4 eggs

½ teaspoon salt
2 cups sifted flour
4 tablespoons melted butter

Place all ingredients in blender or food processor, and mix for 1 minute. Refrigerate at least 2 hours. Place 6-inch crepe pan over medium-high heat, and brush with a little oil. Heat. When oil is almost smoking, add some batter, tilting to cover bottom of pan. When crepe is lightly browned, turn with spatula. Cool on wire rack. Stack until ready to fill. Make filling.

Filling:

4 tablespoons butter
1½ cups chopped onions
1 pound mushrooms, sliced
3 cups chopped cooked turkey
¾ cup chopped cooked spinach

6 tablespoons sour cream
3 tablespoons sherry
½ teaspoon salt
dash of cayenne

Melt butter in large skillet. Add onions and sauté until golden. Add mushrooms and cook 4 minutes, stirring occasionally. Stir in turkey, spinach, and other ingredients. Remove from heat and cool. When ready to fill, place ⅓-½ cup of filling along center of each crepe. Fold 1 side over, then the other, covering filling. Place filled crepes, seam-side down, side by side in a single layer in greased baking dish.

Sauce:

4 tablespoons butter
4 tablespoons flour
2 cups chicken broth
1 cup milk
½ cup grated Parmesan cheese
½ cup grated Swiss or Cheddar
  cheese

salt
dash cayenne
⅛ teaspoon saffron
½ cup sherry

Melt butter in saucepan, blend in flour, and cook for 2-3 minutes. Add broth and milk, stirring constantly, until thickened a bit. Add cheeses, salt, cayenne, and saffron, and continue cooking until cheeses have melted. Remove from heat; add sherry. Pour 1-2 tablespoons sauce over each crepe, and bake at 350°F. for 15 minutes. Pour remaining sauce over crepes, and bake 15 minutes more. Serve immediately. Serves 8 (2 crepes per person).

Flossie H. Ukena
Sherman Cooks

CHAPTER FOUR

Meat and Meat Casseroles

Beef, veal, lamb, and pork share the honors with poultry and seafood as mainstays of the dinner menu. In this chapter you'll find some eye-opening and mouth-watering inventions. Some take a little longer to prepare than others, but while the outcome of such effort may appear elaborate, the cook will need no special ingredients or expertise. We have included veal recipes despite the currently sky-high price of that meat — *if* you can find it at all — because there are times when you feel like splurging, and should you happen on the real thing (*not* "baby beef"), it would be a shame not to seize the opportunity!

BEEF FILLETS, STEAKS, AND POT ROASTS

> You can use meat from the first three cuts of top round beef (approximately 1 inch thick) to simulate filet mignon medallions. Sprinkle top round with meat tenderizer as the package directs, and marinate in a little wine (any kind) for 1-2 hours or overnight, as convenient. Then trim all fat from the meat, and cut meat into medallions 3-4 inches in diameter. Cook as directed for filet mignon.

Beef Fillets Wellington with Golden Tarragon Sauce

Use tenderloin fillets or first-cut top round for this impressive entrée.

eight 5-ounce fillets of beef	½ teaspoon salt
olive oil	pepper
1 pound ground sirloin of beef	8 frozen patty shells, thawed
1 clove garlic, crushed	1 egg white, slightly beaten
1 tablespoon chopped parsley	

Place fillets in freezer for 20 minutes. Remove and brush with oil. Brown in hot skillet for 5 minutes on each side. Refrigerate. Combine ground sirloin, garlic, parsley, salt, and pepper. Divide mixture into eight meat patties, and place one of these on top of each fillet. Refrigerate. Roll out each patty shell into a 9x5-inch rectangle ⅛ inch thick. Place one fillet, sirloin side down, on each rectangle. Fold one side of pastry over meat, then end, then other side, and finally other end. Seal, place seam side down in shallow baking pan. Refrigerate until ready to bake. Before baking, brush with beaten egg white. Bake in 450°F. oven 10 minutes for rare, 12 minutes for medium rare, and 15 minutes for medium. Serve with sauce. Serves 8.

Sauce:

3 egg yolks	¼ teaspoon salt
½ cup butter, melted	1 teaspoon chopped parsley
2 tablespoons lemon juice	⅛ teaspoon dried crushed tarragon
2 tablespoons hot water	

Beat egg yolks in top of double boiler with wire whisk until smooth and fluffy. Add butter, lemon juice, water, and salt. Place over hot, not boiling, water. Over medium heat, beat until sauce starts to thicken, about 5 minutes. Stir in parsley and tarragon. If mixture begins to separate, add a small amount of cold water, and beat. Makes about ¾ cup.

Mrs. J. Albert Hessian
West Islip, NY
Vittles Unlimited

Beef Tenderloin in Claret

For a festive touch, pour 2 tablespoons warm brandy over meat on serving platter at table, and ignite.

3-pound beef tenderloin, trimmed
salt and pepper
4 shallots, minced
4 tablespoons butter
½ cup claret
½ cup beef consommé

1 teaspoon cornstarch
½ teaspoon sugar
½ teaspoon lemon juice
2 tablespoons parsley
(2 tablespoons brandy)

Rub tenderloin with salt and pepper. Roast in 300°F. oven for 1 hour. Sauté shallots in butter. Add claret and cook until the liquid is reduced by half. Add consommé mixed with cornstarch and sugar, and simmer until thickened. Add lemon juice and parsley. Pour over meat. Run under broiler until hot and bubbly. Flame with brandy if desired. Serves 6.

Favorite Foods

Beef Stroganoff

The mustard lends zip to this stroganoff. Serve over rice or noodles.

1½ pounds beef tenderloin, cut into
    strips approximately 2 inches
    long by ½ inch wide (or
    thinner)
salt and pepper
4 tablespoons flour

1 cup beef consommé or bouillon
1 teaspoon prepared hot mustard
½ cup sour cream
1 onion, thinly sliced
3 tablespoons butter

Place meat in a bowl, sprinkle with salt and pepper, cover bowl, and let stand for 1 hour at room temperature. Dissolve 2 tablespoons flour in a little of the beef broth, then stir in the remaining broth. Place in saucepan or double-boiler top. Stir in mustard, and bring to a boil. Remove from heat, and add sour cream. Dust meat with remaining 2 tablespoons flour. Sauté onion in butter, then remove onion and discard. Sauté meat on both sides in this butter. Add meat to mustard sauce. Place in top of double boiler over hot water. Cover, and cook over boiling water for 20-30 minutes, stirring from time to time. Serves 4-6.

Tivvy Carr
Bonds Corner, NH

Minute Steaks in Sauce Marsala

If there is any of this wonderful sauce left over, use it and some Mozzarella cheese to top an omelet. When the omelet is done and the cheese melted, roll up and serve.

½ cup butter
2 onions, chopped fine
six ½-inch steaks cut from eye of
    round and pounded to ¼-inch
    thickness

¼ cup chopped mushrooms
3 tablespoons chopped parsley
2 tablespoons Worcestershire sauce
2 tablespoons Marsala wine
salt and pepper

Melt ¼ cup of the butter and sauté onions in it. Remove onions and reserve. Add steaks to skillet, and sauté for 1 minute on each side. Keep steaks warm on heated platter while you make the sauce. Melt remaining ¼ cup butter, and sauté mushrooms and parsley in it until mushrooms are tender. Add onions, Worcestershire sauce, and Marsala. Bring to boil. Add salt and pepper if desired, and drizzle sauce over steaks on platter. Serve at once. Serves 4.

H. Chapman Little
New York, NY

COOKING WITH WINES

For best results, do not use the so-called "cooking wines." An average table wine will be much less thin and sour, and *without salt* (supermarket "cooking wines" are heavily salted). Table wines, however, must be well cooked, so if the recipe does not call for long cooking, it is best to reduce the wine by half before adding to the recipe. This is not the case, however, with the heavier, fortified wines such as port, Marsala, Madeira, or sherry.

Other things to keep in mind are: a good dry white wine can be substituted for champagne; gin will provide the same flavor as hard-to-find juniper berries; warm brandy for about a minute — just enough to bring the fumes to the top before igniting. Cold brandy will not flame, and brandy heated too long will have all the alcohol fumes driven off, so will not flame either.

Braggiolotini Hélène

For summer enjoyment add vegetables to the skewers and serve as tender kabobs. Freezing the meat makes it easier to slice thin.

5 pounds eye of round
2 cups Italian-flavored bread crumbs
3 tablespoons grated Parmesan cheese
1 teaspoon oregano

⅛ teaspoon garlic powder
2 tablespoons olive oil
¼ pound butter
¼ pound sharp cheese, cut into small cubes

Put meat in freezer for 1 hour. Remove and slice as thinly as possible with a very sharp knife. Mix bread crumbs, Parmesan cheese, and seasonings. Moisten with oil. Set slices out on counter. Place small piece of butter, 1 teaspoon crumb mixture, and small square of sharp cheese in center of each slice. Fold sides in and roll up. Place four or five meat rolls on each of several skewers. Broil close to flame over a broiling pan for 2 minutes on each side. Serve hot. Makes 6 skewers.

Mrs. Edwin Smith
Cooking at Court

Stuffed Marinated Flank Steak

The marinade flavors and tenderizes the steak. The succulent stuffing makes for attractive slices. Surround meat on platter with broccoli or other green vegetable.

1½ pounds flank steak
½ cup Italian salad dressing
¼ cup finely chopped onion
¼ cup finely chopped fresh mushrooms

½ cup finely chopped celery
4 tablespoons butter
1 egg, beaten
½ cup seasoned bread crumbs
water for pan

Several hours before baking time score steak on both sides. Place meat in shallow pan, and marinate in salad dressing, turning several times. Sauté onion, mushrooms, and celery in butter for 10 minutes. Remove from heat. Combine egg with crumbs. Stir in celery, onion, and mushrooms. Remove steak from marinade and spread surface of meat with crumb mixture. Roll steak, small end first, in jelly-roll fashion, and tie in center and at both ends. Place meat on rack in shallow pan. Cover bottom of pan with water. Bake in 350°F. oven for 1 hour. Slice meat, and arrange slices down center of heated platter. Serves 6.

Mrs. Elizabeth J. Fox
Guilford, CT

Sukiyaki

A dramatic Japanese stir-fry dish that can be cooked before guests in 10 minutes. Serve with tea as the beverage and vanilla ice cream with candied ginger for dessert.

2 pounds round steak
1 teaspoon meat tenderizer
¼ cup vegetable oil
1 large onion, sliced thin
2 cups sliced celery
12 scallions, cut in 3-inch pieces
¼ pound mushrooms, sliced

¼ pound fresh spinach leaves, torn
5-ounce can water chestnuts, drained
½ cup soy sauce
1 cup bouillon
1 tablespoon sugar
3 cups hot cooked rice

Cut beef in thin, diagonal slices, across the grain, and sprinkle lightly with tenderizer. Dip in oil and let stand 30 minutes. On large serving platter, arrange vegetables and water chestnuts attractively. This dish is meant to be admired before cooking as well as after. Heat oil in large skillet or chafing dish. (An electric skillet that can be brought to the table is perfect.) When oil is hot, add meat and brown lightly, then push to the sides of the pan. Add onion, celery, scallions, and mushrooms, and toss for 1-2 minutes in the hot oil. Combine soy sauce, bouillon, and sugar. Add to pan and mix well. Add spinach and water chestnuts. Cover and steam for 5 minutes. Spoon over hot rice. Serves 6.

Mary Lou Kelly
West Concord Woman's Club
GFWC-NHFWC Complete Menu Cookbook

Potted Beef

An easy supper dish with an excellent flavor. Yankee's test cook suggests serving it with noodles and a dish of sliced carrots, turnips, and parsnips, sautéed together until tender.

¼ cup olive oil
3- to 5-pound rump roast
1 carrot, chopped
1 stalk celery, chopped
1 onion, chopped
1 garlic clove, chopped

2 bay leaves, crumbled
salt and pepper
½ pound mushrooms
1 cup red wine
6-ounce can tomato paste
2 cups warm beef broth

In heavy casserole dish, heat oil, and brown meat well. Add carrot, celery, and onion. Sauté until onion is browned. Add garlic, bay leaves, salt, and pepper. Stir, and cook 3 minutes over low heat. Add mushrooms and cook another 3 minutes. Add wine, tomato paste, and warm broth. Spoon sauce and vegetables over meat, cover pan, and bake in 325°F. oven for 2½ hours, turning at least once. Skim fat from surface, and discard. Puree vegetables and gravy in blender or food mill, return to casserole dish, and reheat briefly before serving. Serves 6-8.

Mrs. Roger Butler
Cooking at Court

Beer Pot Roast

Subtly imbued with flavor from the beer and gin, but not with the alcohol, which evaporates during cooking.

5 pounds beef rump or flank steak
salt and pepper
6 slices bacon
2 onions, sliced thin
2 carrots, sliced
2 turnips, sliced thin
2 bay leaves

2 good pieces lemon rind
¼ cup gin
30-36 ounces beer
2 tablespoons butter
2 tablespoons flour
salt and pepper

Trim fat from meat and pound meat with mallet. Rub with salt and pepper. Place bacon in bottom of 4-quart dutch oven, and place beef on top. Arrange vegetables, bay leaves, and lemon rind around meat. Sprinkle with gin. Pour in beer just to cover, and bring pot to boil. Turn down heat, cover pot, and leave to simmer 2½ hours. Drain, reserving broth. Remove bay leaves. Place meat on heated platter and keep warm while you make the sauce. Melt butter, stir in flour, and cook over low heat a few minutes until smooth and *lightly* browned. Gradually add 2 cups of the reserved broth, and stir over medium heat until thickened and smooth. Season sauce to taste and pour over meat. Serves 10.

Adele Merrill
Bedford, NY

Slivered Beef à l'Italienne

A stir-fried variation on an Italian theme. Serve with pasta.

6 slices bacon
1 pound lean beef, slivered
1 large onion, thinly sliced
1 cup water
½ cup red wine

1 beef bouillon cube
sprinkling of dried red pepper
    flakes
salt and pepper

Fry bacon until crisp. Remove from frying pan and drain on paper. Stir-fry beef in bacon fat until lightly browned. Add onion and continue to stir-fry until onion is tender. Add bacon broken into bits. Add water, wine, and bouillon cube. Cover and simmer over low heat until beef is fork-tender. Add seasonings. Simmer a few more minutes. Serves 4.

Mrs. Helen G. Smith
Lancaster, PA

Sweet and Sour Brisket

A good do-ahead dish for a casual supper.

4- to 6-pound fresh brisket of beef,
    trimmed
1 envelope dry onion soup mix
½ cup cider vinegar
1 cup catsup
½ cup light brown sugar, packed
beef broth, as necessary

Place brisket in dutch oven. Combine soup mix, vinegar, catsup, and sugar, and pour over meat. Cook over medium heat until sauce boils. Reduce heat, and simmer for 1 hour. Turn meat, and simmer 1 hour more, or until brisket is fork-tender. If sauce thickens during cooking time, thin with beef broth to avoid scorching. When meat is tender, take from pot, slice, and return to sauce. Refrigerate overnight. Next day, skim off fat from sauce, reheat gently, and serve. Serves 6-8.

Favorite Foods

Beef and Beans

Delicious, different, easy to prepare, hearty, and healthy. What more can one ask?

2 tablespoons butter
2 tablespoons corn oil
2 cups sliced onions
1 tablespoon flour
1 tablespoon paprika
1 teaspoon minced garlic
freshly ground pepper
8 cups water
1 cup dried navy beans
1½ cups dried small lima beans
½ cup medium pearl barley
1½ teaspoons salt (or to taste)
4-pound fresh brisket of beef,
    chuck, or bottom round

In heavy 7-quart pot, heat butter and oil. Add onions, and sauté over medium heat about 5 minutes until limp and pale gold. Stir in flour, paprika, garlic, and pepper. Add water. Add washed and drained beans. Sprinkle in barley and salt. Bring to boil. Push meat down into liquid. It should be ¾ covered by liquid. Bring to simmering point. Cook, covered, as slowly as possible for 5 hours. Serves 8-10.

Ferne Matthews
Cridersville, OH

Glazed Corned Beef

Tastes as good as it looks.

4-5 pounds corned beef
3 thick slices onion
1 bay leaf
1 clove garlic
1 teaspoon rosemary
1 stalk celery, chopped
10 whole cloves

(continued)

Place meat in large pot. Cover with water. Add remaining ingredients except cloves. Simmer, covered, for 4 hours until tender. Remove bay leaf, and transfer beef to baking dish, stick cloves into it, and bake in 350°F. oven for 30-45 minutes, basting every 10 minutes with sauce (see below). Slice and serve with sauce. Serves 8-10.

Sauce:

2 tablespoons butter	3 tablespoons vinegar
5 tablespoons catsup	½ cup brown sugar, packed
1 tablespoon prepared mustard	

Stir ingredients together in 1-quart saucepan and bring to a boil. Use as above. Makes about 1 cup.

Mrs. Frederick W. Watriss
The Flavor of Concord

STEWS, GROUND-BEEF, AND ORGAN-MEAT DISHES

Beef Bravado

Some unusual ingredients that make up into a marvelous bright red stew. Good made with venison, too. A Yankee prizewinner.

2 pounds stewing beef	8-ounce can tomato sauce
1½ teaspoons salt	1 cup carbonated lemon-lime soda
⅛ teaspoon pepper	½ beef bouillon cube
2 tablespoons cooking oil	1 tablespoon parsley
1 tablespoon butter	1½ teaspoons brown sugar, packed
1½ cloves garlic, crushed	½ teaspoon each of marjoram and
½ cup chopped onion	thyme
½ cup thinly sliced celery	1 tablespoon butter
2 tablespoons flour	½ pound fresh mushrooms, sliced

Sprinkle meat on all sides with salt and pepper. Heat oil and butter in skillet or stew pot. Brown meat. Add garlic, onion, and celery. Cook, stirring, about 3 minutes. Blend in flour, add remaining ingredients except 1 tablespoon butter and mushrooms, cover, and bring to boil. Reduce heat and simmer for 2½ hours. About 15 minutes before serving, melt 1 tablespoon butter in skillet and sauté mushrooms until just tender. Add to stew and serve. Serves 4-6.

Florence Ogden
Livingston, NY

Country Beef Curry

Serve with rice into which ¼ cup parsley has been mixed just before serving.

1½ pounds bottom round,
  tenderized with unflavored
  tenderizer according to
  package directions
flour
salt and pepper
¼ cup olive oil

1 medium onion, chopped
1 green pepper, chopped
1 clove garlic, minced
½ teaspoon curry powder
1-pound can tomatoes, undrained
½ cup water
(⅓ cup raisins)

Cut beef into large cubes. Shake in a bag with flour, salt, and pepper. Brown in oil in skillet. Remove meat to casserole dish. Add onion, pepper, and garlic to skillet, and cook for 3-4 minutes. Add the curry, tomatoes, and water, and mix gently but well. Pour the sauce over the meat in the casserole dish. Cover and bake in 350°F. oven about 1 hour until meat is tender. For an Eastern touch, add optional raisins and bake 15 minutes longer. Serves 4-6.

Favorite Foods

Curried Beef

Pungent and spicy, yet not hot. Refrigerate overnight and reheat for maximum commingling of flavors. Serve with white rice and crisp french-cut green or wax beans.

1 pound beef chuck, cut into small
  pieces
3 tablespoons cooking oil
2 cups water
1 teaspoon salt
1 large onion, chopped
1 tablespoon curry powder

1 tablespoon chili powder
1 teaspoon ground cumin
½ teaspoon dry mustard
¼ teaspoon ground cloves
2 tablespoons catsup
1 apple, cored and chopped

Brown chuck in 2 tablespoons of the oil in 10-inch skillet. Add water and salt. Simmer 1 hour. Drain, reserving broth. Sauté onion in remaining 1 tablespoon oil until tender. Add reserved broth, spices, and catsup. Simmer 5 minutes. Add meat. Simmer 10 minutes. Add apple and simmer 15 minutes more. Sauce should be fairly thick. Serves 4.

Mrs. Joseph Harbey
Cooking at Court

Phyl's Matrosen Beef

Yes, that's right, anchovy paste! We bet your guests will never guess the ingredients that produce the tantalizing flavor of this richly brown stew. Serve on a bed of hot, buttered noodles.

2½ pounds bottom round, cut in
   1½-inch cubes
4 tablespoons cooking oil
1 medium onion, sliced
2 tablespoons vinegar
1 cup red Bordeaux wine
1 teaspoon anchovy paste
1 bay leaf, crumbled
¼ teaspoon thyme

1 clove garlic, crushed
2 carrots, coarsely grated
1 apple, grated
2 stalks celery, diced
1 tablespoon cooking oil
1 cup beef consommé
salt and pepper
(1 tablespoon butter)
(1 tablespoon flour)

Sear beef in 4 tablespoons hot oil in heavy 4-quart dutch oven. Remove meat, and lightly brown onion in same pan. Add vinegar, wine, anchovy paste, bay leaf, thyme, and garlic. Bring to a boil. Return meat to pan. Cover and simmer 30 minutes. Sauté carrots, apple, and celery in 1 tablespoon oil, stirring constantly, for 5 minutes. Add to meat, along with consommé, salt, and pepper. Cover, and bake in 350°F. oven for 1½ hours, or until meat is tender. Let cool, skim off fat, and reheat when needed. To thicken sauce, just before serving mix together with your fingers the optional 1 tablespoon butter and 1 tablespoon flour and add to hot sauce, stirring until well blended. Serves 6.

Mrs. Roger Butler
Cooking at Court

Stuffed Cabbage

Serve this Old World version with good red wine, rye bread with plenty of real butter, and a tossed salad. Can be prepared ahead and baked before serving.

1 large head cabbage
1 cup uncooked rice
1 medium onion, chopped
1 egg, beaten
salt and pepper

1½ pounds ground beef
¼ pound butter, cut into dots
8-ounce can tomato sauce
1 cup water

Parboil cabbage and set aside in colander to cool. When cool, separate leaves. Cook rice. While rice is cooking, stir together onion, egg, salt, and pepper in large bowl. Add meat, and mix well. Place butter on top of ground beef mixture. Add hot cooked rice and mix well. The hot rice will melt butter and soften ground beef so that all mix nicely. Line buttered 9x13-inch baking dish with the outer leaves of the cabbage. Take separated cabbage leaves, place 2-3 tablespoons of meat mixture on each leaf, fold in edges, roll and place seam side down in baking dish. Pour tomato sauce and water over all. Place any leftover cabbage leaves over top to seal in juices. Cover and bake in 350°F. oven for 2½ hours. Serves 4-6.

Susan Butterfield
Southampton, MA

Baked Macaroni, Venetian-Style

Meat, vegetables, and pasta, all in one simple low-budget, and good-to-eat dish.

1 pound pasta or macaroni, any shape
3-ounce can mushroom stems and pieces
3 tablespoons olive oil
2 onions, thinly sliced
½ cup diced celery

½ cup chopped green pepper
1 clove garlic
1 carrot, grated
1 pound ground beef
17-ounce can peeled Italian tomatoes, with juice
½ cup grated Parmesan cheese

Boil pasta or macaroni in salted water until *al dente*. Drain and place in 2- to 2½-quart buttered baking dish. Drain mushrooms, reserving liquid, and sauté in olive oil for 5 minutes. Remove mushrooms with slotted spoon and spread over macaroni. In oil in pan, sauté onions, celery, pepper, garlic, and carrot for 10 minutes. Add beef. Cook until beef is well browned. Add tomatoes, and liquid from mushrooms, and cook 15 minutes more. Pour sauce over macaroni. Sprinkle cheese over top. Bake in 350°F. oven until casserole is bubbling and cheese is lightly browned. Serves 8-10.

Janice Ryzewski
Shrewsbury, MA

Bohemian Meatballs with Dill Sauce

An adaptation of an old German recipe. Serve with noodles, rice, or spaetzle and a green salad.

1 pound ground beef
⅓ cup minced onion
¼ cup fine bread crumbs
1 large egg, beaten
1 teaspoon salt
dash pepper
¼ teaspoon poultry seasoning
1 tablespoon snipped parsley

2 tablespoons butter
10-ounce can beef broth or bouillon
3½-ounce can chopped mushrooms, drained
1 tablespoon flour mixed with 2 tablespoons water until smooth
1 cup sour cream
1 teaspoon dill weed

Mix together beef, onion, bread crumbs, egg, salt, pepper, poultry seasoning, and parsley. Form into roughly twenty-four 1½-inch balls. Brown slowly on all sides in butter in large frying pan. Remove from frying pan. Add broth and mushrooms to pan, and heat to boiling. Return meatballs to pan, cover tightly, and simmer 30 minutes. Mix together flour-water mixture, sour cream, and dill. Pour over meatballs and stir until thickened. Serves 5-6.

Eleanor Austin
Portsmouth, NH

Summer Squash and Meatballs

A lightly spiced summer dish to serve with green noodles and cold sliced tomatoes sprinkled with basil and just a little sugar.

1½ pounds lean ground beef
½ teaspoon salt
¼ teaspoon pepper
2 tablespoons cooking oil
1 clove garlic, minced
1 large young yellow summer
    squash, seeded and cut into
    1½-inch cubes

1 tablespoon cornstarch mixed with
    2 teaspoons cold water
½ teaspoon soy sauce
1 cup chicken broth
1 cup sliced cooked mushrooms

Mix beef with salt and pepper. Roll into small balls. Brown in hot oil in 10-inch skillet. Remove from pan and set aside. Add garlic and squash to oil in pan. Turn heat on high and keep stirring for a few minutes until almost done. Add cornstarch/water mixture and soy sauce. Blend well. Add hot chicken broth. Stir well. Cook until thickened. Add meatballs and mushrooms, and cook until thoroughly heated. Serve hot. Serves 4.

Thomas Roberts
North Easton, MA

Surprise Meatballs

These rich little meatballs make a wonderful appetizer, too. For a main dish, serve over hot noodles, barley, or rice.

2 eggs, lightly beaten
1 cup bread crumbs
1 small onion, finely chopped
1 teaspoon salt
¼ teaspoon pepper
⅔ cup sauterne wine

2½-ounce can deviled ham
1 pound lean ground beef
blue cheese (about ½ pound)
2-3 tablespoons cooking oil
10¼-ounce can beef gravy
½ cup sauterne wine

Mix eggs with bread crumbs, onion, salt, pepper and ⅔ cup sauterne. Add ham and beef, and mix well. Break up cheese into crumbs about the size of large peas. Mold meat mixture into balls, putting a piece of cheese in center of each ball. Brown balls in hot oil a few at a time. Remove browned meatballs to warm plate. When all are browned, pour off fat from pan, and return meatballs to pan. Combine gravy with ½ cup sauterne wine and pour over meatballs. Bake at 325°F. for about 1 hour. Serves 4-6.

Frances M. Higgins
Lancaster, PA

Sweet and Sour Meatballs

Rice makes a good bed for the tangy sauce. Halve recipe for a smaller amount, or make meatballs and freeze unused portion. Good as appetizer, too — serve with toothpicks and sauce for dipping.

2 pounds ground beef
1½ cups unseasoned bread crumbs
1 cup milk
2 eggs, beaten
½ cup minced onion
2 tablespoons pineapple juice (from can of chunks)
1 teaspoon salt
½ teaspoon pepper
⅔ cup minced onion

6 tablespoons olive oil
2 cups catsup
⅔ cup lemon juice
¼ teaspoon salt
7 tablespoons brown sugar, packed
1 cup water
4 teaspoons prepared mustard
4 tablespoons Worcestershire sauce
No. 2 can (2½ cups) pineapple chunks

Combine beef, bread crumbs, milk, eggs, ½ cup minced onion, pineapple juice, 1 teaspoon salt, and pepper in large bowl. Mix well with hands. Roll into 1½-inch balls. Sauté ⅔ cup onion in oil in large frying pan until tender. Add catsup, lemon juice, ¼ teaspoon salt, brown sugar, water, mustard, and Worcestershire sauce. Simmer until blended. Add half the meatballs and simmer 30 minutes. Remove meatballs from pan and keep warm. Add remaining meatballs to pan and simmer for 30 minutes. When done, put all meatballs in serving dish, add pineapple chunks to sauce, and pour over meatballs. Makes about 50 meatballs. Serves 10.

Audrey Lindsay
Roslindale, MA

Persian Meat Loaf

A spicy, round meat loaf with spinach, green onions, and nuts baked right in. Serve with mashed potatoes or noodles, and sliced cucumbers or a green salad.

1½ pounds ground beef
3 tablespoons melted butter
1 large onion, chopped
3 whole pimientos, sliced
10-ounce package frozen chopped spinach, cooked and drained
½ cup chopped green onions

⅓ cup chopped parsley
1 teaspoon curry powder
½ teaspoon cinnamon
½ cup chopped walnuts
salt and pepper to taste
4 eggs, slightly beaten
plain yogurt

Combine all ingredients except yogurt. Mix well, and press into greased 9-inch casserole dish. Bake at 350°F. for 1 hour, or until firm. Pour off grease and tip onto platter. Pass yogurt. Serves 8.

Jane Hanson
Boulder, CO

Meat Loaf Wellington

Serve hot with spinach and broiled tomatoes. Also good served cold with mustard, or fried in butter and served with brown gravy or mushroom sauce.

1 loaf frozen white bread dough,
thawed
1 pound ground beef
¼ pound ground pork
¼ pound ground veal
2 eggs, beaten
¾ cup bread crumbs

½ cup tomato sauce
½ cup minced onion
¼ cup chopped parsley
¼ cup finely chopped chives
1 teaspoon salt
¼ teaspoon pepper
1 egg, beaten

Thaw and soften bread dough. Combine ground meats with 2 beaten eggs, bread crumbs, tomato sauce, onion, parsley, chives, salt, and pepper. Mix well. Mold meat mixture into loaf a little smaller than the 5x9-inch loaf pan you place it in. (You will rebake meat loaf in dough wrapping, so leave room for dough.) Bake in 375°F. oven for 1 hour. Roll thawed bread dough out into a rectangle about 8x16 inches. Brush surface with beaten egg. Center hot meat loaf on rectangle of dough and carefully wrap dough around meat, moistening edges of dough and pinching together to seal. Let sit 30 minutes. Prick sides and top of dough with fork, brush with beaten egg, and replace loaf in washed, greased loaf pan. Bake in 375°F. oven for 30 minutes, or until golden. Serves 8-10.

T. Raffle
Boston, MA

Puffle Pot

Substitute a different canned soup — cream of celery or golden mushroom, for example — for a very different but equally tasty dish. Prepare, place in oven, and cook 1½ hours before dinner.

4 medium potatoes, peeled and
sliced ¼ inch thick
1 pound ground beef (chuck or
round)
1 large onion, chopped
2 tablespoons butter

⅛ teaspoon garlic powder
salt and pepper
3 large carrots, scraped and sliced
⅛ inch thick
10½-ounce can tomato soup

Butter a 2½-quart casserole dish. Line it with half the potatoes. Brown beef and onion in butter in skillet. Season with garlic, and sprinkle with salt and pepper. Layer beef evenly over potatoes. Add layer of carrots. Cover with remaining potatoes. Sprinkle lightly with salt and pepper. Stir soup and pour over the top and spread evenly. Cover and bake in 350°F. oven for 1½ hours. Do not uncover. Serves 4-6.

Mary Lee Williams
Rochester, NY

Steak and Kidney Pie

This can also be made using 1 pound veal kidneys and 1 pound beef. Veal kidneys do not need pre-soaking.

½ pound lamb kidneys soaked
    overnight in milk to cover
1½ pounds tenderized beef
2 tablespoons butter
2 tablespoons flour
1 cup beef broth
2 medium onions, diced

½ teaspoon salt
⅛ teaspoon pepper
2 teaspoons Worcestershire sauce
¼ cup sherry
2 hardboiled eggs, finely chopped
rich pastry to cover 3-quart dish

Drain off milk from kidneys, and remove membranes and cores. Cut in ½-inch dice. Trim fat from beef (reserve), and cut beef in ½-inch dice. Melt beef fat over medium heat. Add butter. Remove unmelted fat pieces. Add flour and cook for 2 minutes. Add broth and simmer, stirring, for about 4 minutes until thickened. Combine with meat and all remaining ingredients (except pastry) in deep 2½- to 3-quart casserole dish. Cover with rich pastry. Cut slit in pastry to allow steam to escape. Bake in 350°F. oven for 1 hour. Serves 6.

Diana Mac Veagh
Marlborough, NH

Calves' Liver Provençale

A truly great dish. To clarify butter, melt 3-4 tablespoons in skillet, then skim off solids.

2 pounds fresh calves' liver
2 tablespoons clarified butter
1 onion, finely chopped
2 cloves garlic, crushed

juice of ½ lemon
salt and pepper
½ cup white wine

Cut calves' liver into small pieces. Add to clarified butter over high heat with onion, garlic, lemon juice, salt, and pepper. Cook for 5 minutes, shaking pan. Before serving, add white wine, and cook 3 minutes longer. Serves 6.

Mrs. Frances Mellen
The Flavor of Concord

VEAL

Veal Roast

Moist and flavorful. Also good cold, served with stewed tomatoes, French bread and cheese, cucumbers in sour cream, and fruit. The same recipe can be used for a pork roast, served hot with roast potatoes and cucumber salad.

olive oil
2 tablespoons chopped parsley
2 tablespoons chopped chilies
1 tablespoon tarragon
1 tablespoon chervil
1 teaspoon onion salt
2 shallots or scallions, chopped

1 bay leaf, crumbled
dash nutmeg
salt and pepper
3- to 5-pound veal roast
2 teaspoons red wine vinegar
2 tablespoons butter

Add enough olive oil to herbs and seasonings to make a paste. Rub paste all over meat, wrap meat in aluminum foil, and refrigerate for 3 hours. Roast, still wrapped, in 350°F. oven about 30 minutes to the pound. Twenty minutes before roasting time is up, unwrap meat carefully and slide into open roasting pan to catch the juices. Return to oven to brown. At end of roasting time, remove meat to heated platter and set aside. Put roasting pan on top of stove, add wine vinegar and butter to pan juices, mix well, and serve as sauce with roast. Serves 8-14, depending on size of roast.

Eileen Toumanoff
Washington, DC

Veal Chops Louise

Glamorous enough for dinner guests, yet quick and easy to prepare. Serve with noodles or rice.

4 thick veal chops
2 tablespoons butter
2 tablespoons sherry or white wine
2 egg yolks, beaten

1 cup heavy cream
salt and pepper
1 cup sliced mushrooms sautéed in
  2 tablespoons butter

Brown chops in butter in 10-inch frying pan over medium-high heat. Reduce heat, cover pan, and simmer about 20 minutes more, turning chops once during cooking. Remove chops to heated platter and keep warm. Add wine to frying pan and scrape up the brown bits. Beat egg yolks and cream together and add to frying pan. Heat slowly until thick, stirring constantly. Do not boil. Season with salt and pepper. Add sautéed mushrooms to sauce and pour over chops. Serves 4.

E. C. Mac Veagh
Santa Barbara, CA

Veal Scallopine

Serve with rice, green salad, and cold lemon soufflé for a company dinner.

2 pounds veal scallops
salt and pepper
½ cup flour
3 tablespoons olive oil
2-4 tablespoons butter
3 cups fresh mushrooms, sliced

juice of 1 lemon
½ cup plus 2 tablespoons Marsala
  wine or dry sherry
¼ cup light cream
chopped parsley

Trim fat from meat, then pound veal slices paper thin. Season both sides of scallops with salt and pepper. Dip each slice in flour. In large skillet, heat olive oil and 2 tablespoons butter to sizzling. Cook veal scallops 3-4 minutes on each side. Do not allow slices to overlap. Remove to shallow casserole dish. To fat in skillet, add mushrooms and lemon juice, and cook for a few minutes, adding more butter if necessary. Sprinkle mushrooms over veal. Add wine or sherry to skillet, and cook over high heat until boiling. Scrape sides and bottom of skillet into sauce. Cook for about 1 minute, then reduce heat to simmer. Return veal and mushrooms to pan, cover pan, and simmer for 10-15 minutes. Before serving, fold in light cream, and heat through but do not boil. Serve immediately, garnished with chopped parsley. Serves 6.

Favorite Foods

Veal Scallops in Cream

Very good and even easier than the preceding recipe.

⅛ cup flour
½ teaspoon salt
pepper
4 veal scallops
4 tablespoons butter

½ cup heavy cream
1 tablespoon lemon juice
parsley
twist of lemon peel

Mix flour, salt, and pepper. Dip veal scallops in mixture. Sauté in butter over medium heat about 7 minutes on each side, until brown and tender. Place scallops on heated platter, and keep warm. Mix cream and lemon juice together. Add to pan and scrape up the brown bits. Heat thoroughly for about 2 minutes. Do not boil. Pour over veal and serve. Garnish with parsley and a twist of lemon. Serves 4.

Louis Thoron
New York, NY

Veal Stew

Serve this over rice or noodles, accompanied by a colorful garden salad.

3 slices bacon
1 large onion, sliced
3 green peppers, chopped
3 tablespoons butter
2 pounds boneless veal, cut in 1½-inch cubes
2 tablespoons flour
1½ teaspoons salt
¼ teaspoon pepper

⅛ teaspoon oregano
½ cup water
1 cup sour cream
½ pound fresh mushrooms, sliced and sautéed in 2 tablespoons butter
chopped parsley or chives for garnish

Cut bacon into 1-inch pieces. Stir and cook over medium heat in a large, heavy frying pan until lightly cooked but not brown. Add onion, peppers, and butter. Stir and cook until partially cooked, but not brown. Roll veal in flour seasoned with salt, pepper, and oregano. Add to skillet and brown. Add water. Cover and simmer for 1 hour. When veal is fork-tender, push to one side of pan. Stir sour cream into drippings. Add sautéed mushrooms and stir all together. Cover, and cook over low heat for 15 minutes more to blend the flavors. Serve over noodles. Garnish with parsley or chives. Serves 4-6.

Martha Logan
Chicago, IL

LAMB

Leg of Lamb

An elegant roast flavored with garlic and mustard, basted with coffee and brandy, and served with currant-cream sauce.

5- to 6-pound leg of lamb
1 clove garlic
1 tablespoon salt
1 teaspoon dry mustard
1 cup strong coffee
2 teaspoons sugar
2 teaspoons cream

2 tablespoons brandy
¼ cup water

Sauce:
5 tablespoons flour
¾ cup cream
2 tablespoons currant jelly

Trim fat from lamb. Rub lamb with garlic, salt, and mustard. Roast uncovered in preheated 350°F. oven for about 2½ hours. When half-done, turn roast, and baste all over with mixture of coffee, sugar, cream, brandy, and water. Baste at least once more before roasting time is up. When done, keep lamb warm while making sauce. Scrape up drippings from roasting pan, combine with flour, add cream and currant jelly, and stir with wire whisk over low heat until sauce is thick and smooth. Pass sauce in gravy boat with warm lamb. Serves 8.

Edith Huey
Santa Barbara, CA

Roast Lamb with Sour Cream Sauce

An impressive holiday entrée. Serve with mashed potatoes, peas, and a fresh mushroom salad.

6- to 7-pound leg of lamb
1½ teaspoons salt
¼ cup butter, softened
4 cloves garlic, crushed
½ teaspoon thyme
2 cups sliced onions
⅓ cup butter, melted
2 cups chicken broth

Rub lamb with salt. Combine ¼ cup soft butter, garlic, and thyme to make a paste. Cut a number of deep slits in lamb with sharp knife, and push butter paste into slits. Arrange onions on bottom of roasting pan, and place leg of lamb on top. Cover roasting pan and place in preheated 350°F. oven. Roast 20 minutes per pound. Baste lamb from time to time with mixture of melted butter and chicken broth. Uncover lamb for last ½-hour of cooking, and continue to baste. When lamb is done, remove to warmed platter. Skim off fat from juices in pan. Make sauce (see below). Serves 6-8.

Sauce:
pan juices
½ cup dry bread crumbs
2 tablespoons vinegar
grated rind of 1 lemon
⅛ teaspoon nutmeg
1 bay leaf
hot water
1 cup sour cream

Add to pan juices all sauce ingredients *except* sour cream, and heat, stirring, to mix well, adding enough hot water to get a gravy consistency. Strain, return to pan, and add sour cream. Over medium-low heat, heat through. Put sauce in gravy boat, and pass with lamb.

O. P. Valhalla
Bedford Hills, NY

Lamb Stew with Ginger

A rich full flavor. Lamb neck meat has a gelatinous quality which gives body to the sauce. Serve with rice and carrots.

3 pounds lamb neck slices
4 tablespoons flour
2 tablespoons butter
2 cups chicken broth
8-ounce can tomato sauce
2 medium onions, sliced
1 bay leaf
1 tablespoon salt
¼ teaspoon pepper
¼ cup vinegar
⅓ cup gingersnap crumbs
¼ cup warm water
⅛ teaspoon ground ginger

(continued)

Trim excess fat off lamb. Coat meat with flour, and brown in butter in dutch oven over medium heat. Add broth, tomato sauce, onions, seasonings, and vinegar. Bring to a boil, cover, and simmer 1½ hours. Stir occasionally. Add more water if necessary. (If you are making this a day ahead, cool and refrigerate. Before serving, skim off fat and reheat.) Add gingersnap crumbs, softened in water, and ginger. Simmer until gravy is thickened. Serves 6.

Mrs. Edward Lee
Cooking at Court

Lamb Shanks Dinner

Inexpensive and delicious family fare.

4 tablespoons cooking oil	**1½ cups chicken broth (or more)**
8 lamb shanks	**¼ teaspoon thyme**
1 carrot, chopped	**½ teaspoon salt**
1 rib celery, chopped	**¾ cup rice**
1 small onion, chopped	**½ pound green beans**
½ yellow turnip, cubed	**2 ripe tomatoes, quartered**

Heat oil in heavy casserole dish. Brown lamb, then remove from dish. Add carrot, celery, onion, and turnip. Cook in oil until glazed. Return lamb to casserole dish; add broth and seasonings. Cover, and cook about 1 hour, or until lamb is tender. Add rice, stirring lamb to top, so that rice is submerged in liquid. Add more broth if necessary to cover rice by 1 inch. Add beans and tomatoes. Cover casserole dish tightly. Return to boil, then reduce heat, and simmer about 20 minutes, until rice is done and lamb very tender. Serves 4.

Isabelle R. Alter
Haverhill, MA

Orange Lamb Shanks

Serve with hot rolls, or rice, and enjoy every drop of the spicy sauce.

2 tablespoons cooking oil	**2 tablespoons soy sauce**
3 lamb shanks	**1 clove garlic, minced**
2 teaspoons grated orange rind	**1 teaspoon curry powder**
¾ cup orange juice	

Heal oil in 10-inch skillet. Brown lamb shanks in oil; drain off fat. In bowl, combine orange rind and juice, soy sauce, garlic, and curry powder. Pour over meat in skillet, cover, and simmer 2-2½ hours, or until meat is tender, turning occasionally. Skim fat from pan juices. Serve meat and pan juices over rice. Serves 3.

Mrs. Margaret Skinner
Carlstadt, NJ

Moussaka

Authentic moussaka is always made with lamb, but ground beef can be substituted.

2 large eggplants, sliced ½ inch thick	½ cup chopped parsley
salt	1 cup tomato paste
3 potatoes, pared and thinly sliced	¼ cup dried bread crumbs
4-6 tablespoons olive oil	⅓ cup flour
2 large onions, chopped	2 cups milk
1 pound ground lamb	2 eggs, separated
6 tablespoons butter	¼ cup grated Romano cheese
	dash nutmeg

Sprinkle eggplant with salt. Set aside for 15 minutes. Drain eggplant slices well, and pat dry. Brown eggplant and potato slices in olive oil. Drain on paper towels, and set aside. Sauté onions and meat in 2 tablespoons of the butter until brown. Add parsley and tomato paste, and simmer for 10 minutes. Dust greased 9x13-inch baking dish with bread crumbs. Layer dish with potatoes, next eggplant, then meat mixture. Repeat layers, ending with eggplant. Melt remaining 4 tablespoons butter. Combine with flour, and cook over low heat for 2-3 minutes, stirring, then increase heat to medium-high, and add milk ½ cup at a time, stirring constantly, until thickened. Cool slightly. Beat egg yolks until light, combine with cheese and nutmeg, and add gradually to sauce, stirring constantly. Beat egg whites until stiff, and fold into sauce. Pour sauce over eggplant and meat layers. Bake at 350°F. for 45-55 minutes, or until golden brown. Serves 10-12.

Roberta Anne Brush
GFWC-NHFWC Complete Menu Cookbook

PORK, HAM, AND SAUSAGE

Fruit-Stuffed Pork Loin with Apricot Glaze

A real pièce de résistance! *Serve with mashed potatoes and peas or carrots. Cold slices make a festive summer dish.*

12 dried apricots	1 teaspoon salt
⅔ cup brandy	½ teaspoon ground ginger
4-pound pork loin, boned and rolled	½ cup apricot preserves
12 canned prunes, pitted	1 teaspoon soy sauce

(continued)

Cook apricots in brandy for 3 minutes. Remove from heat, cover pan, and let stand 1 hour or more. Drain, reserving liquid. With a knife, cut a slit in the center of the roast, from top to bottom. Insert a long, thin, round tool — a skewer or steel knife-sharpener — in slit, pushing tool all the way down through the loin, turning tool to enlarge hole. Remove, and push apricots and prunes alternately down into tunnel with handle of a wooden spoon. Rub meat with salt and ginger. Place in small roasting pan on rack. Roast at 325°F. for 35 minutes to the pound, or until meat thermometer registers 170°F. Mix reserved apricot/brandy liquid, preserves, and soy sauce. During roasting, brush pork often with this mixture. Place roast on warm serving platter; remove strings. Baste again with apricot mixture on platter. Pass remaining sauce. Serves 8-10.

Diana Boullet
East Burnham, NH

Savory Skillet Pork Chops

The beer combines with the other ingredients to make a rich brown sauce with a succulent flavor. A good cold-weather meal. Serve with a green vegetable.

4 pork chops
1-2 tablespoons cooking oil
1 large onion, sliced
1 clove garlic, chopped
4 medium potatoes, peeled and
  sliced ¼ inch thick

1 teaspoon salt
¼ teaspoon pepper
1½ teaspoons brown sugar, packed
½ teaspoon thyme
12-ounce can beer

In heavy 10-inch skillet, brown chops on both sides in oil. Remove chops from pan. Add onion and garlic. Cook 5 minutes until softened. Return chops to pan and add potatoes. Sprinkle with salt, pepper, sugar, and thyme. Add beer. Cover, and cook over medium heat about 40 minutes, or until done. Serves 4.

Mrs. Rudolph C. Reers
Narrowsburg, NY

Pork Pepper Boats

Green pepper halves hollowed out and filled with a tasty stuffing of pork, vegetables, bread crumbs, and cheese.

3 large green peppers
1 pound ground pork
½ cup chopped onion
½ cup chopped carrot
½ cup chopped celery
1½ cups herb-seasoned stuffing
   mix
½ cup hot water

½ chicken bouillon cube, or ½
   teaspoon chicken bouillon
   granules
1½ cups shredded Monterey Jack
   cheese
1 tablespoon butter, melted
1 tablespoon grated Parmesan
   cheese

Cut peppers in half lengthwise. Remove stems, seeds, and membranes. Drop in boiling salted water, and cook for 5 minutes. Drain on paper towels. Combine pork, onion, carrot, and celery in a heavy skillet. Cook slowly until pork is done and vegetables are tender. Drain off fat. Blend 1 cup stuffing mix into pork mixture. Combine hot water and chicken bouillon. Stir to dissolve. Add to meat mixture, and mix well. Stir in Monterey Jack cheese, and heap mixture into pepper shells. Place in greased 7x11-inch baking dish. Combine remaining ½ cup stuffing mix with butter and Parmesan cheese. Sprinkle over peppers. Bake at 350°F. for 30-35 minutes, or until peppers are tender and stuffing is browned. Serves 6.

Dorothy Butler
Arlington, MA

Barbecued Spareribs

Tender ribs in a spicy sauce with a bit of zing.

3 pounds country-style spareribs,
   cut in pieces
1 lemon sliced paper-thin, or ¼ cup
   lemon juice
1-2 teaspoons liquid smoke
1 cup catsup

¼ cup Worcestershire sauce
1 teaspoon salt
1 teaspoon chili powder
1 cup water
1 teaspoon celery seeds

Place ribs in shallow baking pan, meaty side up. Roast at 450°F. for 30 minutes. If using lemon slices, arrange slices over ribs. If using juice, sprinkle over ribs. Combine remaining ingredients. Bring just to boiling point, and pour over ribs. Continue baking at 350°F. for about 40 minutes until tender, basting every 15 minutes. Serves 4.

Juanita Coleman
Big Bear City, CA

Tourtière

An authentic French-Canadian pork pie, hearty and rich. Lard makes the flakier crust here.

Crust:

1 cup lard or vegetable shortening	½ teaspoon salt
4 cups sifted flour	1 cup water

Cut lard or shortening into flour and salt until consistency of small peas; add water, and mix with fork. Refrigerate at least 2 hours. Roll out half the dough to medium pie-crust thickness, and line a deep 9-inch pie plate. Fill (see below), and cover with top crust.

Filling:

1½ pounds ground lean pork	¼ teaspoon pepper
1 small onion, minced	¼ teaspoon sage
½ cup boiling water	pinch ground cloves
1 garlic clove, chopped	3 medium potatoes, boiled and
1½ teaspoons salt	mashed
¼ teaspoon celery salt	

Combine all filling ingredients except potatoes, in a 3-quart saucepan. Cook over low heat, stirring constantly, until meat loses its red color, and about half the liquid has evaporated. Cover, and cook about 45 minutes longer. Add mashed potatoes. Cool. Fill deep 9-inch pie plate, lined with pastry. Cover filling with top crust. Flute and seal edges; slash top crust. Bake in preheated 450°F. oven for 10 minutes. Reduce heat to 350°F. and bake 30-40 minutes longer. Serves 6.

Mrs. Robert Descoteaux
Je Me Souviens la Cuisine de la Grandmère

Ham with Champagne Sauce

Champagne refers to the lovely golden color of the sauce.

2-pound ham steak	½ teaspoon prepared mustard
¼ cup brown sugar, packed	1½ tablespoons cornstarch
4 tablespoons vinegar	¾ cup seedless grapes
4 tablespoons water	

Sprinkle ham with sugar. Mix vinegar, water, mustard and cornstarch. Pour over ham. Bake in 325°F. oven for 45 minutes. Two minutes before end of cooking time, top with grapes, to heat them through. Serves 4.

Vittles Unlimited

Gingerale Ham Steak

A very tender, well-seasoned ham steak with its own sweet golden sauce.

1 ham steak, cut 1 inch thick   **3-5 tablespoons brown sugar**
1 teaspoon dry mustard   **gingerale**

Place ham in large iron skillet, and sprinkle evenly with mustard. Pat mustard into meat. Sprinkle brown sugar over steak. Pour gingerale into skillet until liquid comes halfway up sides of steak. Bake at 350°F. for 40 minutes, or until sugar has melted on top of ham. Remove from oven, and place skillet on stove burner. Bring sauce to boil, and let boil until reduced to golden syrup. Place ham on platter, and pour syrup over. Serves 4.

Phyllis Burt
Dublin, NH

Spinach and Ham Roll-ups

Perfect for the busy hostess, this can be prepared ahead and baked 30 minutes before serving.

10½-ounce can cream of mushroom   **2 eggs, beaten**
    soup   **½ cup finely chopped onion**
1 cup sour cream   **¼ cup flour**
2 tablespoons prepared mustard   **18 slices boiled ham (about 1½**
2 cups cooked rice   **pounds)**
10-ounce package frozen chopped   **salt and pepper**
    spinach, thawed and pressed   **buttered bread crumbs**
    dry on paper towels   **paprika**
1 cup small-curd cottage cheese   **parsley**

In small bowl mix soup, sour cream, and mustard. In larger bowl combine ½ cup of this soup mixture with rice, spinach, cottage cheese, eggs, onion, and flour. Mix well. Place about 1½ tablespoons mix on each ham slice. Roll up from small end. Place close together, seam-side down in 13x9-inch baking dish. Spoon remaining soup mixture over middle of ham rolls and top with crumbs. Sprinkle with paprika. Bake in 350°F. oven for 30 minutes. Garnish with parsley. Serves 6.

Jean Brownlee
Victorville, CA

Savory Soufflé Roll

Puffy and light, nice for a special lunch. The filling may be prepared the day before and reheated.

Filling:

2 tablespoons butter
4 tablespoons chopped onion
4 mushrooms, chopped
1 cup cooked chopped spinach,
    drained

1 cup cooked chopped ham
6 ounces cream cheese
1 tablespoon Dijon mustard
¼ teaspoon nutmeg
salt and pepper

Melt butter, and sauté onion until tender. Add mushrooms and cook for 5 minutes. Add drained spinach, ham, cream cheese, and seasonings. Cook, stirring, until heated through. Keep warm while you make the Roll (see below).

Roll:

4 tablespoons butter
½ cup flour
½ teaspoon salt

⅛ teaspoon pepper
2 cups milk
5 eggs, separated

Grease, line with wax paper, and grease again a 10x15-inch jelly-roll pan. Dust lightly with flour. Melt butter, and add flour, salt, and pepper. Cook, stirring, for 1 minute. Add milk and bring to a boil. Cook 1 minute, then remove from heat. Beat egg yolks and slowly add hot sauce to yolks, beating constantly. Return to pan and cook 1 minute longer, over low heat. Do not boil. Cool to room temperature. Beat egg whites until stiff, but not dry. Fold into cooled sauce, and spread in prepared pan. Bake in preheated 400°F. oven for 25-30 minutes, until well puffed. Turn onto a clean towel, spread with warm filling, and roll up. Slide onto warm serving platter seam side down. Serves 4-5.

Mrs. Charles McPherson
Cooking at Court

Ham Puff

So much like a soufflé that you must serve it right away.

¼ cup butter
5 tablespoons flour
1½ cups milk

4 egg yolks, lightly beaten
2 cups ground ham
4 egg whites, beaten stiff

Melt butter, add flour, and blend. Gradually add milk, and cook over low heat until thick, stirring constantly. Gradually beat this mixture into beaten egg yolks. Stir in ham. Fold in egg whites. Pour into greased 2-quart casserole dish. Bake at 350°F. for 50 minutes. Serves 4.

Je Me Souviens la Cuisine de la Grandmère

Ham Loaf

The fine texture slices easily. Delicious cold in sandwiches with cheese and Dijon mustard. Good sliced and browned in butter for breakfast with eggs or pancakes.

1 cup soft bread crumbs
1 egg, beaten
½ cup milk
3 tablespoons condensed tomato
    soup

1½ pounds ham, ground
1 pound ground pork
1 teaspoon paprika

Combine bread crumbs and liquids. Add remaining ingredients, and mix well. Place in lightly greased 9x5-inch loaf pan. Bake in 350°F. oven for 1½ hours. Serve with mustard sauce (see below). Serves 6-8.

Mrs. Robert Lane
Cooking at Court

Mustard Sauce:

½ cup condensed tomato soup
½ cup prepared mustard
½ cup apple cider vinegar

½ cup light brown sugar, packed
2 large egg yolks

Beat together all ingredients in 1-quart saucepan. Cook over medium-high heat, stirring constantly, until hot and thickened. Makes about 2 cups.

Linda Bensinger
Dublin, NH

Hot Italian Sausage Chili

A marvelous cross-cultural version of the chili pot that you'll make from now on. Serve with warm corn bread.

1 pound hot Italian sausages, cut
    up
2 cloves garlic, chopped fine
1 onion, chopped
1 green pepper, chopped
½ pound fresh mushrooms,
    chopped
12-ounce can tomato paste
3 cups water

2 tablespoons brown sugar, packed
dash lemon juice
dash Tabasco sauce
salt and pepper
1½-2 tablespoons chili powder
two 1-pound cans kidney beans or
    1 cup dried kidney beans
    soaked overnight, simmered
    until tender, and drained

Fry sausage pieces in skillet over low heat until pink is gone. Lift out sausages and drain on paper towel. Sauté garlic, onion, and pepper in sausage fat for 5 minutes. Add mushrooms, and continue cooking until mushrooms wilt. Meanwhile, in medium saucepan, combine tomato paste, water, sugar, juice, and seasonings. Stir in sausages, vegetables, and drained kidney beans. Simmer about 1 hour. Serves 4-5.

Cheryl Sanborn
East Thetford, VT

Italian Sausage Casserole

Flavorful and easy to prepare after a hard day.

water
1 pound Italian sausages, parboiled
for 8 minutes and sliced
5 potatoes, boiled until almost
done, and cut up

1 onion, sliced thin
10-ounce package frozen peas or
string beans, thawed
¼ cup Parmesan cheese
3 tablespoons butter

Cover bottom of 1¾-quart casserole dish with water. Add sausages, potatoes, onion, and peas or beans. Sprinkle with cheese. Dot with slivers of butter. Cover and bake at 350°F. for 1 hour. Serves 4.

Audrey Lindsay
Roslindale, MA

Sausages and Lentils

Economic and inviting, this protein-rich dish is easily reheated, or recycled into a soup served with sour cream on the side. For a meatier dish, use 1½ pounds sausage links. Serve with sour cream.

1 pound dried lentils
1 teaspoon salt
1 pound sausage links
2 tablespoons butter
2 onions, finely chopped
1 cup chopped celery stalks and
leaves
1 clove garlic, minced

1 tablespoon chili sauce, or 1
teaspoon chili powder plus ½
teaspoon sugar
¼ teaspoon salt
¼ teaspoon marjoram
½ teaspoon dry mustard
½ teaspoon pepper
½ cup tomato sauce (or more)

Soak lentils overnight in water to cover. Drain, cover with boiling water, add salt, and simmer 1½ hours. While lentils are simmering, cook sausages. Drain off fat and discard. Set sausages aside, and in same skillet, melt butter and sauté onions, celery, and garlic until tender. When lentils are done, drain, and place in 3-quart casserole dish. Stir in sautéed vegetables, seasonings, and tomato sauce. Top with sausage links, or cut up the sausages and stir the pieces into lentils. Bake at 325°F. for 1 hour. Check after 30-40 minutes, and add a little more tomato sauce or water, if needed. Serves 6-8.

Lucy Grey
Northfield, VT

Sausage Loaf

A convenient, versatile loaf to serve on a busy Christmas Eve with oyster stew, for Sunday brunch with an omelet, or any day with potatoes, green beans, and baked apples (or Sautéed Apples and Bacon, page 41).

1 pound bulk sausage	**½ teaspoon poultry seasoning**
1 medium onion, minced	**1 teaspoon mustard**
1 cup fine dry bread crumbs	**1 egg, beaten**
1 cup corn-flake crumbs	**5-ounce can evaporated milk**

In a large bowl, combine all ingredients, and mix together thoroughly, as for any meat loaf. Form into loaf, and place in 5x9-inch loaf pan. Bake at 375°F. for 1 hour. Let sit 5 minutes, then transfer to serving platter. Serves 6.

Lynn Sullivan-Walsh
Peterborough, NH

CHAPTER FIVE

Fish and Seafood

A heavenly galaxy of ways to serve up the fruits of the sea, all easily mastered. Included are recipes using frozen and canned seafood as well as fresh, so that even if you are not lucky enough to live within calling distance of salt water, you can still indulge that yearning for seafood that seizes us all on occasion, and that those raised by the seaside never quite can escape.

Landlubbers should remember that seafood is toughened by overcooking. Poultry and meats of all kinds will far more readily forgive the absent-minded cook than will any kind of seafood. Heed the directions and cooking times, or end up with an expensive hunk of nothing!

FISH

Baked Bluefish with Mustard Sauce

If you think of bluefish as oily, let this recipe change your mind. Use fresh chopped dill when in season to add that little extra spark of flavor.

2 tablespoons butter
3 pounds bluefish fillets
2 tablespoons mayonnaise
2 tablespoons sour cream
2 tablespoons Dijon mustard

2 tablespoons lemon juice
½ teaspoon salt
¼ teaspoon black pepper
chopped dill or parsley

Butter a 9x13-inch baking dish. Lay fish fillets in dish, skin side down. Combine mayonnaise, sour cream, mustard, lemon juice, salt, and pepper, and spread evenly over fish. Sprinkle with chopped dill or parsley. Bake at 350°F. for 30-40 minutes (adjust baking time according to thickness of fillets). For added color, place under broiler for last 5 minutes. Serves 6-8.

Mrs. Juris Udris
An Olde Concord Christmas

Salt Codfish with Egg-Caper Sauce

The capers make this an extra special dish. It can be served as is, on toast points, or, more elegantly, in pastry patty shells.

1 pound salt codfish
2 tablespoons butter
2 tablespoons flour
2 cups milk
¼ cup grated Cheddar cheese
4 hardboiled eggs, chopped

1 tablespoon capers
2 strips bacon, cooked crisp and
   crumbled
salt
freshly ground black pepper

Soak codfish in water for 24 hours, changing the water several times. Drain. When ready to prepare, put in saucepan with cold water, bring to boil, and cook 20 minutes. Drain codfish, return to pot, cover with water, and boil again for 5 minutes. Drain. Let cool, then remove skin and bones, and cut fish into 2-inch squares. Keep warm. Melt butter in skillet over low heat. Stir in flour, and mix well. Add milk gradually, stirring constantly until sauce is smooth and thickened. Do not let sauce boil. Add cheese, and stir until smooth. Add chopped eggs, capers, and bacon. Pour sauce over warm fish pieces, season to taste, and serve. Serves 4.

Joan Pesce
Stockton, CA

Mediterranean Salt Codfish

After all the soaking, the codfish tastes very nearly fresh. The generous amount of black pepper flavors this just right. Or, try experimenting with additional Italian seasonings.

1 pound salt codfish
flour
½ cup olive oil
3 onions, chopped
3 cloves garlic, minced
16-ounce can Italian plum
    tomatoes, drained and cut up

16-ounce can chick peas
    (garbanzos)
½ teaspoon salt
¾ teaspoon black pepper
(chopped parsley)

Soak codfish in water for 24 hours, changing water several times. Drain well. Bone, and cut fish into 2-inch pieces. Dust fish pieces with flour. In large skillet, heat olive oil, and fry codfish pieces until brown on both sides. Take fish from pan, and set aside. In same skillet, sauté onions and garlic in the remaining oil. Add tomatoes and chick peas to onions and garlic, and simmer mixture for 20 minutes. Season with salt and pepper. Lay fish in 2-quart casserole dish or 9x13-inch baking dish. Cover with sauce. Bake at 350°F. for 15 minutes. Garnish with parsley. Serves 4.

Theresa Giordano
Fresno, CA

Filets Piquants

No particular fish is specified here, as this combination of ingredients lends itself well to almost any fish. Regard cooking time carefully.

2 pounds fresh or frozen fish fillets
¾ cup dry bread crumbs
½ cup melted butter
1 tablespoon vinegar
1 tablespoon lemon juice

1 tablespoon Worcestershire sauce
1 teaspoon prepared mustard
1 teaspoon salt
⅛ teaspoon pepper
paprika

If using frozen fillets, thaw them partially. Sprinkle half the crumbs over bottom of greased baking dish. Lay fillets on top. Sprinkle remaining crumbs over fillets. Mix together melted butter, vinegar, lemon juice, Worcestershire sauce, mustard, salt, and pepper. Pour sauce over fish. Bake at 450°F., allowing 10 minutes cooking time per inch-thickness of fresh fish, and 20 minutes per inch-thickness of frozen fish. When done, fish will flake easily. Sprinkle with paprika before serving. Serves 4.

Je Me Souviens la Cuisine de la Grandmère

Fish Cakes in Spicy Tomato Sauce

You can use fresh or leftover mashed potatoes for this and almost any kind of fresh or frozen fish. In favorable months, try adding finely chopped fresh herbs to the fish cakes — 1 tablespoon chopped parsley, or 2 teaspoons chopped chives, for example.

Cakes:

2 cups flaked cooked fish	½ teaspoon salt
2 cups mashed potatoes	⅛ teaspoon pepper
1 tablespoon butter	½ cup flour
1 egg, beaten	6 tablespoons butter

Combine fish, potatoes, butter, egg, salt and pepper. Shape into round, flat cakes, then dredge in flour. Melt butter in skillet, and fry cakes until golden brown on both sides. Keep warm in oven while preparing tomato sauce. Serves 6.

Tomato Sauce:

3 tablespoons butter	¼ teaspoon cloves
2 tablespoons flour	½ teaspoon allspice
1 cup canned tomatoes (reserve juice)	½ teaspoon salt
	⅛ teaspoon pepper
1 tablespoon sugar	(tomato juice)

Melt butter in saucepan. Add flour and stir until well blended. Add tomatoes, sugar, and seasonings. Continue stirring and bring mixture to a boil. Remove from heat and beat well until creamy. If mixture appears too thick, thin with tomato juice. Pour sauce over fish cakes. *Hazel D. Little*
Vienna, VA

Baked White Fish Fillets with Herb Topping

Here again, you can use any white fish. Serve with wild rice and broccoli, and garnish fish with lemon slices and parsley sprigs.

¼ cup raisins	⅛ teaspoon basil
2 tablespoons dry white wine	½ teaspoon oregano
2 tablespoons boiling water	1 large tomato, chopped fine
2 tablespoons cooking oil	1½ teaspoons salt
1 onion, finely diced	pepper
1 clove garlic, chopped	3 pounds white fish fillets
1⅔ cups dry bread crumbs	(salt and pepper)
3 tablespoons cooking oil	dry white wine (about 1¼ cups)
⅓ cup chopped walnuts	½ teaspoon salt
¼ cup dry white wine	
4 tablespoons chopped fresh parsley, or 2 tablespoons dried	

(continued)

Place raisins in measuring cup and add wine and boiling water. Let sit for 15 minutes. Drain off liquid, and chop raisins fine. Heat 2 tablespoons cooking oil in small skillet over medium heat, add onion and garlic, and cook until tender. Transfer to mixing bowl, add bread crumbs, 3 tablespoons oil, walnuts, ¼ cup wine, raisins, parsley, basil, oregano, tomato, salt, and pepper. Mix well. Butter 9x13-inch baking dish and lay fillets in it. Sprinkle with additional salt and pepper if desired. Spoon topping over fish in even layer. Pour in wine until wine comes ½ inch up sides of dish. Bake at 350°F. until fish flakes — about 30 minutes. Serves 6.

Priscilla Speare
Maplewood, MO

Fish Baked in White Wine

Elegant and flavorful! Vary by substituting chopped dill (weed), or oregano, or rosemary for the parsley.

2 pounds white fish fillets	pinch nutmeg
1 onion, chopped	pinch ground cloves
8 mushrooms, sliced	1 tablespoon brandy
1¾ cups white wine	1 tablespoon butter
1 teaspoon lemon juice	1 tablespoon flour
2 tablespoons chopped parsley	pinch ground cayenne or red
½ teaspoon salt	pepper
¼ teaspoon pepper	

Lay fillets in buttered 8x10-inch baking dish. Spread onion and mushrooms on top, then pour wine over all. Sprinkle with lemon juice, parsley, salt, pepper, nutmeg, and cloves. Bake at 350°F. for 30 minutes, or until fish flakes easily. Remove fish and place on warm serving platter. Keep warm. Prepare sauce. Scrape juices from baking dish into small saucepan. Reduce over high heat to about 1 cup. Strain sauce into bowl and add brandy. Melt butter over medium heat, then add flour to make a smooth paste. Stirring constantly, add strained sauce in slow, steady stream. Cook and stir until sauce thickens slightly. Add cayenne and pour over fish. Serves 6.   *Fanny D. Rogers*
Bath, NY

Fish Fillets in Herb Sauce

Another delectably flavored sauce. . . . Gauge the poaching time according to the thickness of the fish you use, being careful not to overcook it. Serve over rice.

1¼ cups sliced onions
4 tablespoons butter, melted
1¼ cups white wine vinegar
1 teaspoon salt
½ teaspoon mace

⅔ cup chopped parsley
1 teaspoon thyme
1 teaspoon rosemary
2 pounds fish fillets

Sauté onions in melted butter until tender. Stir in vinegar, salt, mace, parsley, thyme, and rosemary. Cover and simmer gently for 15 minutes. Arrange fillets in skillet on top of broth. Cover and simmer 12-15 minutes, turning fish once during cooking time. Fish is poached when it flakes easily. Transfer fillets to heated serving dish, pour sauce over, and serve. Serves 4.

Margaret Tuve
Boise, ID

Fish Matelote with Red Wine

The sauce in this recipe is like something you'd expect with beef, but does marvelous things for fish. If you don't feel up to flaming the brandy, simply add, unflamed, to fish along with wine, carrot, etc.

2 pounds pike, perch, or haddock
 fillets
2 cups red wine
1 carrot, sliced
1 onion, minced
2 cloves garlic, halved
1 teaspoon salt

¼ teaspoon pepper
2 teaspoons *Herb de Provence**
 mixture
3 tablespoons brandy
3 tablespoons melted butter
2 tablespoons flour
2 tablespoons chopped parsley

In large, heavy skillet place haddock fillets in a single layer. Add wine, carrot, onion, garlic, salt, pepper, herbs, and brandy if you do not intend to flame brandy. Slowly bring to boil over medium heat. If you do flame brandy, warm brandy in small saucepan. Ignite, and pour immediately over fish. When flame has burned out, cover pan, and cook 15-20 minutes, or until fish flakes. Remove fillets, and keep warm while you finish the sauce. Strain and reserve cooking liquid. In same skillet, blend melted butter with flour, and stir until smooth. Cook over low heat until mixture bubbles. Gradually stir in cooking liquid. Stirring constantly, cook rapidly until sauce thickens, about 2-3 minutes. Pour over fish and garnish with parsley. Serves 4.

Je Me Souviens la Cuisine de la Grandmère

*A special herb mixture available in specialty food stores.

Russian Fish Pie

Serve with a sweet-sour vegetable such as pickled or Harvard beets or red cabbage and a green vegetable.

Pastry:

1 package active dry yeast
¼ cup warm water
½ cup milk
¼ cup melted butter
½ teaspoon salt
2-3 cups flour
milk

Filling:

¼ cup melted butter

1 cup cooked rice
2 pounds cooked haddock or other
    white fish fillets, flaked
3 hardboiled eggs, chopped
½ cup chopped parsley
2 teaspoons dill weed
1 teaspoon salt
½ teaspoon pepper

Dissolve yeast in warm water. Combine milk and melted butter in small saucepan and heat until lukewarm. Pour into mixing bowl. Add dissolved yeast, salt, and about 2 cups flour. Beat until smooth. Turn out onto a floured board and knead until smooth. Place in a greased bowl, cover, and let rise in a warm place until doubled in bulk — about 1 hour. Make filling. Mix melted butter, rice, haddock, and eggs in a bowl. Season with herbs, salt, and pepper.

Punch down dough, turn out onto a floured board, and knead until smooth. Roll out dough into rectangle 11x14 inches, or large enough to line a buttered shallow 2-quart or 9x13-inch baking dish or pan. Lay dough in baking dish, leaving enough lapping over edges to fold over top. Add filling, then fold dough over, and seal down center. Let rise 15 minutes. Brush with milk, and bake at 400°F. for 30 minutes, or until golden. Cut in squares. Serves 6.

Nadia Yovanovitch
Sherman Cooks!

Broiled Flounder Fillets

Flounder enhanced by bacon and onion and broiled to a golden brown. Garnish with lemon wedges and parsley sprigs for a festive platter. Serve with a green salad.

4 strips bacon
1 onion, chopped fine
¼ teaspoon salt
⅛ teaspoon pepper

3 pounds flounder fillets
paprika
2 tablespoons lemon juice
2 tablespoons butter

Fry bacon until crisp. Remove from pan and drain on paper. Sauté onion in bacon drippings until translucent. Crumble bacon, and combine with sautéed onion, salt, and pepper. Lay half the flounder fillets side by side on a broiler pan lined with foil. Spread bacon/onion mixture over fillets. Sprinkle with paprika and lemon juice. Place remaining fillets on top and dot with butter. Put under broiler about 6 inches from heat and broil until fish flakes — about 20 minutes. Check during broiling time, and add more butter dots if fish looks dry. Serves 4-6.

Camilla Lincoln
Los Angeles, CA

Festive Flounder Rolls

Looks very appetizing — and is! The tangy sauce alone is worth the effort.

3 tablespoons butter
12 ounces mushrooms, sliced
1 carrot, thinly sliced
4 scallions, cut in 1-inch pieces
1 clove garlic, chopped
½ teaspoon rosemary
2 tomatoes, seeded and chopped
¾ cup water
¼ cup dry white wine
1 pound flounder fillets, halved,
    rolled up, and held with
    toothpicks

1 teaspoon salt
⅛ teaspoon pepper
1 egg yolk
2 teaspoons cornstarch dissolved in
    2 tablespoons water
3 tablespoons butter
ripe olives, pitted and sliced, for
    garnish

(continued)

Melt 3 tablespoons butter in skillet and sauté mushrooms, carrot, scallions, garlic, and rosemary for 3-5 minutes. Add tomatoes and cook 3 minutes longer. Add water and wine. Bring to boil, then add flounder, salt, and pepper. Bring back to boil, turn down heat, cover, and simmer 7-8 minutes, or until fish flakes easily. Carefully dip out fish rolls with slotted spoon, and place on warm serving platter. Arrange vegetables attractively around fish rolls, and keep platter warm while you prepare the sauce. Strain cooking liquid into saucepan. Bring to boil, and boil until liquid is reduced to ⅔ cup. Turn heat to low. In bowl, combine egg yolk with water-cornstarch mixture. Stir a little of the reduced liquid into egg mixture, then beat warmed egg mixture into liquid in saucepan. Stir in 3 tablespoons butter, and cook over medium heat until sauce has thickened. Pour sauce over fish and vegetables. Garnish with olives. Serves 4.

Mark Bastian
Manchester, NH

Haddock Casserole

Haddock (or cod) fillets baked in pink shrimp sauce with a lightly seasoned crumb topping. For richer sauce, mix shrimp soup with 2-ounce can of tiny shrimp, rinsed and drained. Good with parslied boiled potatoes and a green vegetable. Quickly made and consumed.

2 pounds fresh haddock or cod
    fillets
10-ounce can condensed cream of
    shrimp soup
¼ cup butter

½ teaspoon grated onion
½ teaspoon Worcestershire sauce
¼ teaspoon garlic powder
1¼ cups crushed Ritz-type cracker
    crumbs

Arrange fish in single layer in buttered 7x11-inch baking dish. Spread shrimp soup over fish. Bake at 375°F. for 15-20 minutes. While fish is baking, melt butter. Add onion, seasonings, and cracker crumbs. Toss well to mix. Sprinkle crumb mixture over fish, return dish to oven, and bake for another 10 minutes, or until fish flakes easily and topping is lightly browned. Serves 4-6.

Linda Schaefer
Muskego, WI

Quenelles de Poisson (Fish Dumplings)

These really are not as complex as they may sound, being basically choux *paste (cream-puff dough) mixed with ground fish. A food processor grinds fish beautifully. Serve according to suggestions following the recipe.*

1 cup water	6 eggs
1¼ teaspoons salt	1½ pounds halibut, ground
10 tablespoons butter	¼ teaspoon pepper
1 cup sifted flour	¼ teaspoon nutmeg

Boil water and salt in a saucepan. Add 4 tablespoons butter and let it melt. Remove from heat, and add flour all at once, stirring with a wooden spoon to blend thoroughly. Return to moderate heat, and beat vigorously until mixture leaves sides of pan and forms a smooth, shiny ball. Transfer to mixing bowl. Add 4 eggs, one at a time, beating thoroughly after each addition. Add fish, pepper, and nutmeg and beat at high speed for 6 minutes. In separate bowl, cream remaining 6 tablespoons butter, then gradually beat creamed butter into fish mixture. Beat in 2 more eggs, one at a time. Spread mixture out on flat pan or cookie sheet, and chill 15 minutes in freezer or 6 hours or overnight in refrigerator.

Boil 4 inches of fish stock or salted water in roasting pan or large pot. Form cold mixture into small, sausage-shaped dumplings by taking for each a rounded tablespoon of mixture and rolling lightly by hand on floured board. Reduce stock or water to simmer and carefully slip in dumplings. Do not overcrowd, but poach in batches uncovered, for 20 minutes; then turn gently, and poach another 5 minutes. Remove with slotted spoon and drain on towel. Makes about 40 dumplings.

Serving Suggestions:

Place cooked dumplings on cookie sheet and sprinkle well with grated Swiss cheese and melted butter. Bake in upper third of 375°F. oven for about 25 minutes, or until cheese browns nicely. Garnish with paprika or fresh chopped parsley.

Lay a bed of chopped, cooked spinach in buttered baking dish. Arrange dumplings on top and cover with a cheese sauce, or with grated cheese and melted butter, and bake as above. Serve with broiled tomatoes or cold, sliced tomatoes.

Dumplings can be frozen by placing on a cookie sheet in a single layer. When frozen, pack in a container.

Irene K. Weddell
Sherman Cooks!

Salmon Mousse

This creamy-smooth mousse is firm but not gelatinous. Use either fresh or canned salmon.

1½ pounds fresh salmon, or 3 cups
    canned salmon, drained and
    flaked
2 tablespoons unflavored gelatin
⅓ cup cold water
¾ cup boiling water
1 cup mayonnaise
1½ tablespoons lemon juice

2 tablespoons minced onion
1 teaspoon Tabasco sauce
1 teaspoon paprika
1½ teaspoons salt
2 tablespoons finely chopped
    capers
1 cup heavy cream

If using fresh salmon, wrap in cheesecloth and poach in seasoned water for 40-45 minutes. Discard cheesecloth, skin and bone fish, then flake into bite-sized pieces. Set salmon aside. Soften gelatin in cold water. Add boiling water, and stir until gelatin has dissolved. Cool. Add mayonnaise, lemon juice, onion, Tabasco, paprika, and salt, and mix well. Refrigerate until mixture is the consistency of unbeaten egg whites. Add salmon and capers. Whip cream, and fold into salmon mixture. Pour into oiled 2-quart ring mold and chill 3-4 hours. Unmold and serve. Serves 8.

Williamsville Inn
Housatonic, MA
Cooking at Court

Sole Fillets in Creole Sauce

The sole flavors beautifully in this dish. Be sure to let the vegetables cook thoroughly to enrich the sauce.

4 tablespoons butter
1 onion, chopped
2 stalks celery, chopped
8-ounce can tomato sauce
½ teaspoon salt

½ teaspoon curry powder
⅛ teaspoon pepper
3 green peppers, chopped
2 pounds sole or flounder fillets

Melt butter in large skillet. Add onion and celery, and sauté until soft. Add tomato sauce, salt, curry powder, pepper, and green peppers and continue to cook over medium heat about 5 minutes. Place fillets over sauce in a single layer. Heat to boiling, then cover, and simmer gently for 15-20 minutes or until fish flakes easily. Transfer fish to a warm serving platter with a slotted spoon. Stir sauce, then pour over fish. Serves 6.

Je Me Souviens la Cuisine de la Grandmère

Fillet of Sole Baked with Potatoes and Mushrooms

An elegant arrangement of fish and potatoes with a rich and subtle flavor.

½ pound mushrooms, sliced
3 tablespoons butter
6 cooked potatoes, sliced thin
1½ teaspoons salt
½ teaspoon pepper
1 teaspoon paprika

⅔ cup white wine
1 cup sour cream
2 pounds fillets of sole
2 tablespoons chopped chives
parsley sprigs for garnish

Sauté mushrooms in 3 tablespoons butter and set aside. Butter 9x13-inch baking dish generously, and spread sliced potatoes over bottom. Distribute mushrooms evenly over potatoes. Sprinkle with half the salt, pepper, and paprika. Pour in wine. Distribute ½ cup of the sour cream evenly over mixture. Lay sole fillets on top, and season with remaining salt, pepper, and paprika. Sprinkle with chives. Top with remaining ½ cup sour cream. Bake at 350°F. for 30-40 minutes. Garnish with parsley. Serves 6-8.

Virginia Rogers
Portland, OR

Sole Rolls Filled with Roquefort Cheese and Shrimp

Serve when the boss and his wife come to dinner.

½ cup butter
2 ounces cream cheese
4 ounces raw, shelled shrimp, cut in small pieces
2 ounces Roquefort cheese, crumbled
1 tablespoon lemon juice
1 teaspoon chopped parsley
1 teaspoon chopped chives

dash Tabasco sauce
dash Worcestershire sauce
⅛ teaspoon pepper
4 fillets of sole, approximately 10 ounces each
1 egg, beaten
1 cup dry bread crumbs
¼ cup butter, melted
paprika

To make filling, combine first 10 ingredients, mixing well. Chill. Divide filling into four equal parts, and spread one part over each of the sole fillets. Roll up fillets, tucking in edges, and securing with toothpicks if necessary. Dip fillets in beaten egg, then in crumbs. Place rolls, close together, seam side down, in small buttered baking dish. Sprinkle melted butter and paprika over rolls, and bake at 375°F. for 15-20 minutes, until fish flakes. Serves 4.

Nicholas Jackson
Washington, DC

"Scalloped" Sole

A very unlikely marriage of ingredients that come together in wedded bliss! There are a few "parts" to putting this together, but actually it takes only about 30 minutes to prepare. It can all be done early in the day. Serve with rice.

½ cup minced celery
½ cup minced fresh parsley
½ cup minced onion
2 pounds sole or flounder fillets
½ cup milk
1 cup dry bread crumbs
7 tablespoons butter
salt
½ cup chopped walnuts
1 cup consommé
⅓ cup white raisins
2 tablespoons lemon juice
⅛ teaspoon cayenne pepper
⅛ teaspoon rosemary
1 pound scallops, bite-sized (cut up large scallops)
½ pound thinly sliced bacon
parsley for garnish

Mix celery, parsley, and onion. Spread evenly over bottom of a 9x13-inch or 10x12-inch baking dish. Set aside. Dip fish fillets in milk and then in dry bread crumbs. Melt 4 tablespoons of the butter in large skillet. Add fillets, and brown lightly on both sides. Place fillets on bed of chopped celery, parsley, and onion. Sprinkle with salt. Melt remaining 3 tablespoons butter in same skillet. Add walnuts, and brown lightly. Add consommé, raisins, lemon juice, cayenne, and rosemary. Bring mixture to boil, and spoon over fish. Wrap scallops in bacon, and fasten with toothpicks. Broil until delicately brown on both sides. Cool slightly, remove toothpicks, and arrange around fish fillets. Bake entire dish for 20 minutes at 375°F. Garnish with parsley. Serves 8.

Mary Todisco
Lancaster, CA

Swordfish with Mushroom Sauce

A tangy marinade pervades every fiber of the fish. A Yankee prizewinner.

2 pounds swordfish steaks
¼ cup Chablis or water
3 tablespoons lemon juice
1 clove garlic, minced

½ teaspoon each of salt, pepper,
  thyme, and oregano
½ pound mushrooms, sliced
3 tablespoons olive oil
parsley for garnish

Cut fish to serving size. Combine Chablis or water, lemon juice, garlic, salt, pepper, thyme, and oregano to form marinade. Place fish with marinade in plastic bag or container, close bag or container, and refrigerate for 2 hours, turning occasionally. Reserving marinade, barbecue or broil fish approximately 6-8 minutes per side. While fish is cooking, sauté mushrooms in olive oil. Add marinade to sautéed mushrooms, and simmer 1 minute. Place fish on platter, cover with mushroom sauce, and garnish with parsley. Serves 4-5.

David J. Robare
San Jose, CA

Swordfish with Wine and Sour Cream

In this simple sauce of sour cream and white wine, swordfish becomes a moist and succulent delight. Adding a little fresh chopped herb in season — dill, tarragon, or thyme.

2 pounds swordfish
salt and pepper to taste
4 tablespoons butter
2 teaspoons grated onion

½ cup white wine
1 chicken bouillon cube, crushed
1 tablespoon sour cream
¼ cup white wine

Lay fish in shallow baking dish. Sprinkle with salt and pepper, and dot with butter. Sprinkle with onion. Pour ½ cup wine over fish. Bake at 400°F. until tender, about 20-30 minutes, basting occasionally. Mix bouillon cube, sour cream, and ¼ cup wine in a small saucepan. Cook over medium heat until bouillon cube has dissolved, stirring occasionally. Lightly brown fish under broiler. Transfer to warm serving platter, and pour sauce over fish. Serves 4.

Mrs. Wayne K. Elliott
An Olde Concord Christmas

Mountain Trout

Plan on one trout per person, and you can adapt this recipe to serve as many as you'd like. There's nothing like the taste of the first trout of spring! Adjust cooking time to the size and number of fish you are preparing.

3 slices bacon
bacon drippings, or melted butter
6 trout
½ teaspoon salt
¼ teaspoon pepper
½ cup cornmeal

½ cup flour
4 tablespoons (or more) butter
½ teaspoon thyme
1 tablespoon lemon juice
2 tablespoons chopped parsley

Cook bacon until crisp. Drain on paper, and crumble when cool. Brush trout generously with bacon drippings (or melted butter). Sprinkle with salt and pepper. Mix cornmeal and flour, spread on breadboard, and roll trout in mixture until well covered. In large, heavy iron skillet, heat 4 tablespoons melted butter. Add trout and fry over medium heat, turning once, being careful to keep fish whole. Cook about 6 minutes per side, or until fish flakes easily with a fork. When both sides are browned, sprinkle trout with thyme. Set on absorbent paper for a minute or two, then transfer to a warm platter. Sprinkle with lemon juice, chopped parsley, and crumbled bacon. Serves 6.

Louise Mac Veagh
Harrisville, NH

CRAB, LOBSTER, AND SHRIMP

Crab-Broccoli Casserole

Easy to prepare, attractive, and aromatic. Serve with parslied rice.

12-ounce package frozen or 1
    bunch fresh broccoli spears
1 tablespoon butter
½ pound fresh mushrooms, sliced
1 pound crab meat
1½ cups sour cream

3 ounces blue cheese, grated
1 scant teaspoon garlic powder
¼ teaspoon salt
1 cup Ritz-type cracker crumbs
1 tablespoon butter, melted
paprika

Cook broccoli in slightly salted water until tender. Drain. Line a buttered 9-inch square baking pan with broccoli. Melt butter in skillet, and sauté mushrooms 3-5 minutes. In bowl, combine mushrooms with crab meat, sour cream, blue cheese, garlic powder, and salt. Spoon mixture over broccoli. Toss cracker crumbs with 1 tablespoon melted butter, and sprinkle over top. Sprinkle paprika over all. Bake at 375°F. for 25 minutes. Serves 4.

Hazel D. Little
Vienna, VA

Crab Cakes

A beautiful crisp brown when fried and very appealing. Vary by adding a little chopped onion or green pepper. Or mold into smaller rounds for an impressive hors d'oeuvre.

1 pound crab meat	1 tablespoon mayonnaise
1 teaspoon salt	1 egg, beaten
½ teaspoon pepper	⅔ cup cracker meal
1 teaspoon dry mustard	4 tablespoons cooking oil
1 tablespoon melted butter	

Combine all ingredients except oil in large bowl, and mix well. Mold into cakes, and fry in oil in a large skillet, adding more oil as needed. Serves 4-6.

Lillian Forsyth
Mifflinburg, PA

Crab-Stuffed Crepes

Fantastic crab-meat crepes to serve for dinner or brunch. You can prepare the crepes early in the day, stack, and refrigerate until ready to bake. Or freeze the crepes until needed.

Crepes:

1 egg	½ cup flour
pinch salt	2 tablespoons melted butter
¾ cup milk	melted butter for pan

Beat egg in bowl. Add salt, and continue beating as you add milk until well blended. Slowly beat in flour and butter. Beat until smooth. Heat a small cast-iron skillet or crepe pan, brush well with melted butter, and ladle in just enough batter to coat bottom thinly. Over medium heat, cook until upper side is no longer runny, then turn over and brown other side. Stack crepes on warm plate and set aside. Makes 8 crepes.

Filling:

1½ cups crab meat	1½ teaspoons paprika
½ teaspoon dry mustard	⅔ cup mayonnaise
1 teaspoon Worcestershire sauce	1 tablespoon chopped chives
2 tablespoons lemon juice	1 tablespoon grated Parmesan
1 teaspoon salt	cheese

Mix all ingredients except Parmesan cheese until well blended. Reserve one-fifth of filling. Place equal amount of filling in center of each crepe, roll up crepes, cut in half, and place in buttered 9x13-inch baking dish. Spoon a little of the reserved filling over each piece, and sprinkle with grated cheese. Bake at 325°F. for 8-10 minutes. Serves 4-6.

Henry Flory
Southern Pines, NC

Crab Mornay

A Mornay more cheesy than the usual, closely resembling Welsh Rabbit (Rarebit) in consistency. Serve over toast points or in patty shells.

1 cup finely chopped scallions	½ cup parsley
4 tablespoons butter	2 tablespoons sherry
2 tablespoons flour	1 teaspoon salt
1 pint heavy cream	1 pound crab meat
½ pound grated Jarlsberg cheese	

In large skillet, sauté scallions in butter. Add flour, and cook 3 minutes over medium heat until just bubbly but not brown. Stir in cream and cheese, mixing well. Add ¼ cup of the parsley, sherry, and salt, and simmer 10 minutes over low heat. Gently fold in crab meat. Garnish with remaining parsley. Serves 6.

Alma Wall
Ridge, MD

Newburg Sauce

This patrician version of the classic uses more eggs and sherry and less butter than the standard Newburg sauce. Enough sauce for 2 cups cooked lobster, crab, scallops, or shrimp. Heat seafood in sauce over hot water in double-boiler top (sauce will curdle if you let it boil), and serve over rice.

2 tablespoons butter	3 egg yolks, well beaten
½ cup dry sherry	½ teaspoon salt
1 cup heavy cream or half and half	¼ teaspoon paprika

Melt butter. Add sherry, and cook 2 minutes over medium-low heat. Then add cream. Pour cream mixture in slow stream into yolks, beating constantly. Place in top of double boiler and cook over low heat until sauce thickens, about 5 minutes. Continue stirring throughout cooking time. Season with salt and paprika. Makes 1½ cups sauce, enough to serve 4.

Louise Mac Veagh
Harrisville, NH

Sherried Lobster Almondine

Fine made with rock lobster too. Serve over hot rice or buttered noodles, with a crispy green salad. Can be prepared ahead and reheated in double boiler.

6 tablespoons butter
1 cup slivered, blanched almonds
3 tablespoons flour
½ teaspoon paprika
½ teaspoon salt

⅛ teaspoon pepper
2 cups milk
¼ cup sherry
1 pound cooked lobster meat (2 packed cups)

In double-boiler top, melt butter. Add almonds and brown lightly. Blend in flour and seasonings. Add milk and cook, stirring constantly, until thickened. Stir in sherry, and fold in lobster meat. Cook 15-20 minutes over hot water until heated through. Serves 4-6.

Elizabeth Bauer
Middleburg, VA

Coconut Butterfly Shrimp with Hot Mustard Sauce

A sweet-hot South Seas dish that can be made even hotter by adding red pepper flakes. Use unsweetened coconut, freshly grated if possible.

1 pound fresh shrimp
½ cup flour
1 teaspoon salt
(1 tablespoon red pepper flakes)
1 teaspoon dry mustard
2 eggs
¼ cup light cream
1½ cups shredded coconut

⅔ cup fine dry bread crumbs
cooking oil

Sauce:
⅓ cup dry mustard
1 tablespoon brown sugar
2 teaspoons lemon juice
¼ cup cold water

Leave tails on shrimp. Slit shrimp down the middle of the curved side with a sharp knife. Place on paper towel. Combine flour, salt, optional red pepper flakes, and dry mustard. In another bowl, beat together eggs and cream. In third bowl, combine coconut and crumbs.

Heat 2 inches cooking oil in heavy pan to 350°F. Dip each shrimp in cream mixture, then in flour mixture, again in cream mixture, then lastly in the coconut/crumb mixture. Cook a few shrimp at a time in hot oil for approximately 2 minutes, or until done. Drain well on paper towels. Keep warm while you make sauce.

Combine sauce ingredients and heat until sugar has melted. Serve hot with shrimp. Serves 4.

Franklin Jr. Woman's Club
GFWC-NHFWC Complete Menu Cookbook

Shrimp and Rice Casserole

A lovely light supper to serve with garden lettuce. For a stronger shrimp stock, cook shrimp in shells, then shell and devein before marinating.

1 quart water
2 ribs celery with leaves, cut up
½ green pepper, sliced
1 onion, thinly sliced
1 bay leaf
1 pound medium shrimp, fresh or
    frozen
½ cup white wine
1 cup raw rice
reserved shrimp stock

4 ounces water chestnuts, drained
    and thinly sliced
2 tablespoons butter
½ pound mushrooms, thinly sliced
4 ounces pimiento, cut into strips
1 tablespoon cornstarch
1½ cups chicken stock
salt and pepper
4 tablespoons butter
1 cup dry bread crumbs

In 2-quart saucepan, combine water, vegetables, and bay leaf. Bring to boil, and simmer over medium heat for 10 minutes. Dip out vegetables and bay leaf. Reserve vegetables; discard bay leaf. Add shrimp to cooking water, and bring to boil. Reduce heat to medium and simmer 3-4 minutes. Remove pot from heat, and let stand about 15 minutes. Shrimp are done when they turn pink and the tails are curled. Reserving cooking stock, drain shrimp. Place drained shrimp in bowl with white wine, and allow to marinate for 1 hour, turning occasionally. Cook rice according to package directions, using reserved shrimp stock as cooking liquid (add water if necessary to make up the required volume). Fold reserved chopped vegetables into cooked rice (first draining if necessary). Spoon rice into buttered 7x11-inch Pyrex casserole dish, and pat into flat layer covering bottom of dish. Sauté mushrooms in 2 tablespoons butter for 4-5 minutes. Drain shrimp, reserving marinade. Arrange shrimp in rows on top of rice bed. Top with water chestnut and mushroom slices, and decorate with pimiento strips.

Make sauce. Blend cornstarch with ½ cup of the chicken stock. Combine remaining chicken stock with reserved marinade in saucepan, and bring to boil. Stir in cornstarch mixture. Cook, stirring, over medium heat until sauce is smooth and thick (if too thick, thin with white wine). Add salt and pepper to taste. Pour sauce over ingredients in casserole dish. Melt 3 tablespoons butter, and stir into bread crumbs. Sprinkle buttered crumbs over top of casserole, and dot with remaining 1 tablespoon butter. Bake at 350°F. for 20-30 minutes, or until heated through. Serves 4-6.

Margaret Cross
Dublin, NH

Delta Shrimp

Fragrant in the cooking, delicious in the eating. Serve this Creole-type dish over hot buttered rice.

2 tablespoons cooking oil
1 onion, chopped fine
1 green pepper, diced
1 clove garlic, minced
½ teaspoon salt
⅛ teaspoon pepper

1-pound can tomatoes, undrained
1 bay leaf
2 whole cloves
1 pound shrimp, cooked and
    shelled

Heat oil in skillet, and sauté onion and green pepper until onion is tender. Add garlic, salt, pepper, tomatoes, bay leaf, and cloves. Bring to boil, reduce heat, cover, and simmer for 25-30 minutes. Take out bay leaf and cloves. Stir in shrimp and heat through. Serves 4.

Alma Britten
Savannah, GA

Outdoor-Grilled Shrimp Scampi

Leaving the shells on while grilling over coals prevents the shrimp from scorching and helps to keep them tender. You can do this inside too, under the broiler, but peel off shells before broiling in oven.

2 pounds jumbo shrimp, in shells
1 clove garlic, mashed
1 teaspoon black pepper

juice of 1 lemon
⅓ cup olive oil

Split each shrimp shell on underside down to tail with sharp knife, without cutting into meat. Place in bowl and add other ingredients. Stir well. Cover bowl, refrigerate, and let marinate, stirring occasionally, for 3 hours. Thrust skewers through shrimp and grill over coals, 6 inches from heat, for 15-17 minutes, turning frequently. Serve with garlic butter (see below). Serves 4.

Garlic Butter:
⅔ cup butter, melted
1 tablespoon lemon juice
1 teaspoon Worcestershire sauce

1 clove garlic, crushed
½ teaspoon Tabasco sauce
½ teaspoon salt

Mix all ingredients together. Pass as a dip for shrimp, or serve in individual bowls. Makes about 1 cup.

Marlene Ciodi
Phoenix, AZ

Shrimp de Jonghe

This is absolutely at its best with fresh herbs. The amounts given below are for dried tarragon, parsley, and chervil. Double those amounts if you are lucky enough to have access to the fresh herbs.

1 clove garlic, minced
½ teaspoon tarragon
½ teaspoon parsley
½ teaspoon chervil
½ teaspoon chopped shallot
½ teaspoon chopped onion
½ cup melted butter

1 cup soft bread crumbs
½ teaspoon salt
⅛ teaspoon pepper
⅛ teaspoon nutmeg
½ cup dry sherry
3 cups shelled, cleaned, cooked
   shrimp

Combine all ingredients except shrimp and toss well to mix. In each of six generously buttered ramekins, place layer of shrimp. Cover with layer of crumb mixture. Bake at 325°F. for 15-20 minutes, or until crumbs brown. Serves 6.

Faye Delay
Tacoma, WA

Wild Rice Seafood

Mayonnaise is the key to the moistness of this tasty and elegant mixture. You can economize by using the mixed wild and brown rice combination available in the supermarket.

1½ cups wild rice
1 pound mushrooms, sliced
3 tablespoons butter
1 green pepper, diced
1 cup diced celery
1 Bermuda onion, chopped
1 teaspoon Worcestershire sauce
1½ pounds cooked shrimp, lobster,

or crab meat, or all three,
   combined
1 teaspoon curry powder
1½ cups mayonnaise
1 teaspoon salt
½ teaspoon pepper
(½ cup water or seafood stock)

Cook rice according to package directions. Sauté mushrooms in butter. Mix all ingredients together lightly, adding optional water or stock only if mixture seems dry. Turn into buttered 3-quart casserole dish, cover, and bake at 350°F. for 45 minutes. Serves 8.

Mrs. Herbert Dalton
Cooking at Court

Shrimp Pie

From 1 to 10, this is an 11! You can use a 1-quart casserole dish instead of the individual ramekins, if you prefer. In that case, halve the pastry recipe.

Pastry:

2 cups flour
1 teaspoon salt

¾ cup lard or shortening
¼ cup water

Combine flour and salt. Measure, and set aside ⅓ cup of mixture. Cut in shortening to remainder of mixture until the texture of small peas. Add water to reserved ⅓ cup of mixture, and mix well. Blend with shortening mixture. Chill. Roll out as needed. Makes pastry enough for 2-crust pie, or for 4 ramekins, with a little left over.

Peg Rodenhiser
New Ipswich, NH

Filling:

1 pound shrimp
2 tablespoons butter
¼ pound mushrooms, sliced
1 onion, minced
3 tablespoons butter
3 tablespoons flour

2 cups milk
½ teaspoon salt
⅛ teaspoon pepper
1 tablespoon chopped parsley
1 cup diced cooked potato
1 cup cooked green peas

Boil shrimp in salted water for 3-5 minutes, or until just beginning to turn pink. Drain and set aside. In large skillet, melt 2 tablespoons butter. Add mushrooms and onion, and sauté until tender. Stir in shrimp. Remove from heat, and keep warm while you make sauce.

In saucepan, melt 3 tablespoons butter. Add flour, stirring until smooth and bubbly. Gradually stir in milk, salt, and pepper. Cook, still stirring, until sauce has thickened. Add sauce to shrimp mixture, then stir in parsley, potato, and peas. Pour into four buttered ramekins. Top each ramekin with pastry, leaving enough overlap so that edges can be fluted. Bake at 425°F. for 10-15 minutes, or until pastry is golden brown. Serves 4.

Noelle Green
Bethlehem, PA

CLAMS, OYSTERS, AND SCALLOPS

Baked Stuffed Clams

Serve these piping hot.

2 tablespoons butter
2 tablespoons flour
⅓ cup milk
salt and pepper
¼ cup chopped parsley
1 tablespoon finely chopped onion
¼ teaspoon paprika
⅛ teaspoon garlic powder

¼ teaspoon Worcestershire sauce
¼ teaspoon dry mustard
1 tablespoon lemon juice
two 6-ounce cans minced clams
juice from 1 can minced clams
1 cup bread crumbs
2 tablespoons butter

In medium saucepan, melt butter and stir in flour. Add milk, and stir until smooth and thickened. Add salt and pepper to taste. Stir in parsley, onion, paprika, garlic powder, Worcestershire sauce, mustard, and lemon juice. Add minced clams and juice from 1 can. Combine clam mixture with all but 3 tablespoons of the bread crumbs. Grease 12 clam shells (or small ramekins). Fill with clam mixture, and sprinkle with remaining bread crumbs. Dot with 2 tablespoons butter. Bake at 400°F. for 15 minutes. Serves 4-6.

Barbara Barbieri
West Hartford, CT

Escalloped Oysters

Amazing what just a tiny touch of Tabasco sauce can do.

3 cups coarse soda-cracker crumbs
6 tablespoons melted butter
36 oysters, shucked and drained
    (reserve liquor)
2 teaspoons salt

¼ teaspoon pepper
⅛ teaspoon Tabasco sauce
¼ cup oyster liquor
½ cup light cream

Toss crumbs with butter to coat evenly. Layer crumbs and oysters alternately in 7x11-inch baking dish, ending with crumbs. Sprinkle with salt and pepper. Combine Tabasco, oyster liquor, and cream, and dribble over top. Bake at 350°F. for 30 minutes. Serves 6-8.

Samantha Georges
Wilmington, DE

Potato Oyster Pie

Garnish with parsley sprigs, and serve with a green vegetable or a watercress salad for a supper fit for a king.

2 cups hot creamy mashed potatoes
24 shucked oysters with liquor
1½ tablespoons chopped red pepper, or pimiento
2 teaspoons minced onion
2 tablespoons butter, melted
4 teaspoons cornstarch, dissolved in 1 tablespoon oyster liquor

¼ teaspoon salt
½ teaspoon celery salt
⅛ teaspoon pepper
1 cup oyster liquor (add milk if necessary to make 1 cup)
1 tablespoon lemon juice
pinch mace

Butter a 9- or 10-inch Pyrex deep-dish pie plate, and arrange mashed potatoes in an even border around rim. Keep warm. Cook oysters in oyster liquor until edges just begin to curl. Drain oysters, reserving liquor. Keep warm. Sauté pepper or pimiento and onion in butter until tender. Stir in cornstarch dissolved in 1 tablespoon oyster liquor, salts, pepper, and reserved oyster liquor (with milk added if necessary to make 1 cup). Cook over medium heat, stirring, until mixture thickens and clears. Stir in lemon juice and mace, blending well. Fold in oysters, and spoon mixture into pie plate, inside potato ring. Place under broiler just long enough to brown potatoes lightly. Serves 4.

Jane H. Colley
Falls Church, VA

Oysters Rockefeller

In this classic American dish, spinach adds color and flavor to baked oysters. Garnish with lemon slices, and serve as an appetizer for twenty-four persons, or pig out on it for dinner with three other persons (with salad and toasted garlic bread).

24 shucked oysters (reserve deep halves of shells)
butter for shells
1 tablespoon grated onion
¼ cup cooked, drained spinach (¼ package frozen chopped spinach)
2 tablespoons butter

2 tablespoons chopped basil or parsley
salt, pepper, and paprika
4 strips bacon, cooked crisp, drained on paper, and crumbled
½ cup fine dry bread crumbs
butter dots

(continued)

Drain oysters well. Wash and dry reserved shells. Butter lightly, and place 1 oyster in each. Arrange shells in 10x15-inch jelly-roll pan. Sauté onion and spinach in butter over medium heat until onion is tender, and spinach begins to stick to pan. Stir in basil or parsley. Spoon a little spinach mixture over each oyster. Sprinkle oysters lightly with seasonings. Top with bacon and bread crumbs. Dot with butter. Bake at 450°F. for 8-10 minutes. Serves 4.

Sarah Delay
Portsmouth, NH

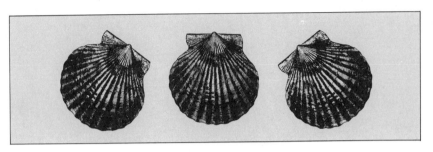

Baked Scallops with Sherry

Very expensive and utterly delicious. Could also be served in individual scallop shells or puff-pastry patty shells. For a thinner sauce, use only 3 tablespoons flour. The sauce is similar to a Newburg sauce.

2 pounds sea scallops
4 tablespoons butter
½ pound mushrooms, sliced
1 small onion, chopped
5 tablespoons flour
1 cup light cream

1 cup milk
½ cup reserved scallop liquid
½ teaspoon salt
¼ teaspoon pepper
½ cup sherry
½ cup dry bread crumbs

Rinse scallops well, and place in saucepan with water barely to cover. Bring to boil, reduce heat, and simmer 5 minutes. Drain, and reserve liquid. When scallops are cool enough to handle, cut them in half. Melt butter in large skillet. Add mushrooms and onion, and sauté, stirring, for about 5 minutes. Stir in flour as smoothly as possible. Gradually add cream, milk, and reserved scallop liquid. Season with salt and pepper. Add sherry. Cook sauce over low heat until bubbling and thickened. Stir in scallops, and transfer to a buttered 2-quart casserole dish. Sprinkle with bread crumbs. Bake at 350°F. for 25-30 minutes, or until crumbs are golden brown. Serves 6-8.

Opal Tucker
The Rockport Heritage Cookbook

CHAPTER SIX

Vegetable Dishes and Casseroles

Yankee's Good Neighbors have come up with a tempting array of interesting ways to cook vegetables. Many of these recipes can stand alone as a supper or lunch, or can be served with a dish selected from Chapter Two for a meatless lunch or dinner. Others harmonize particularly well with a meat, poultry, or seafood entrée.

Use fresh vegetables in season whenever possible, those from your own or a neighbor's garden will of course produce superior results, but the profusion of produce available year round in the supermarket and the excellent quality of most frozen or canned vegetables today mean that it is the rare vegetable recipe that cannot be put together at any time of year. No wonder we don't need those awful-tasting "spring tonics" any more!

Artichoke Supreme

Supreme it is, and hearty too. Serve instead of stuffing with roast chicken, or with cold sliced chicken and a green salad. A fine vegetarian entrée, as well. Just as good made without the onion.

two 6-ounce jars marinated
    artichoke hearts
(1 medium onion, chopped)
3 cloves garlic, chopped
4 eggs, beaten

¼ cup bread crumbs
¼ teaspoon pepper
1 teaspoon oregano
1 tablespoon chopped parsley
2 cups grated Cheddar cheese

Drain marinade from artichoke hearts into skillet. Chop artichokes and set aside. Heat marinade, add optional onion and garlic, and sauté until onion is tender. In separate bowl, combine eggs, bread crumbs, and seasonings. Fold in parsley and cheese, then artichokes and sautéed mixture, including marinade. Bake in 9-inch square baking dish at 350°F. for 30 minutes. Serves 6-8.

Isabelle R. Alter
Haverhill, MA

Asparagus Polonaise

Serve warm to flatter a main dish. If you feel like splurging, serve with a seafood Newburg. Or try it cold as a summer salad.

6 tablespoons butter
⅔ cup dry bread crumbs
2½ pounds fresh asparagus, or
    three 10-ounce packages
    frozen asparagus spears

2 strips bacon, fried crisp
2 tablespoons lemon juice
1 hardboiled egg, chopped
1 tablespoon chopped parsley
2 tablespoons butter, cut into dots

Melt butter in a skillet. Add bread crumbs, and sauté until just golden. Remove from heat. Steam fresh asparagus until tender, or cook frozen asparagus according to package directions. Drain. Layer warm asparagus in buttered 9x13-inch baking dish. Sprinkle with crumbled bacon, lemon juice, egg, parsley, and bread crumbs. Dot with butter, and heat briefly under broiler or in 450°F. oven until butter has melted. Serves 6.

Anna Michalska
Charleston, WV

Special Asparagus

The ingredients here bake together to form a creamy-rich sauce without any bother. If you don't have any ham around, use ¼ cup crumbled crisp bacon.

2 pounds fresh asparagus, or two
    10-ounce packages frozen
    asparagus spears
3 tablespoons butter

4 tablespoons grated Parmesan
    cheese
3 tablespoons cream
¼ cup finely chopped ham

(continued)

Cook fresh asparagus in boiling salted water until tender, about 8 minutes. Or cook frozen asparagus according to package directions. Drain. Lay spears in buttered 7x11-inch baking dish. Top with bits of butter and sprinkle with cheese. Pour cream over. Cover with chopped ham. Bake at 475°F. for 8 minutes, or until light brown. Serves 4.

Mrs. David Herdman
Fredericksburg, VA

How Long Do Vegetables Stay Fresh?

The following fresh vegetables should be used as soon after purchase as possible; asparagus, broccoli spears, corn on the cob (in husks), eggplant, and bean sprouts. Keep in the crisper drawer of the refrigerator for only 2-3 days. Never store fruits in the same drawer with vegetables, as ethylene gas given off by fruit will soften vegetables.

You can store string and wax beans, cauliflower, celery, lettuce, green onions, parsley, peas (in pod), peppers, spinach, summer squash, tomatoes, and watercress for up to a week in the crisper drawer. Before refrigerating greens, wash them well, remove tough stems and brown spots, dry, and wrap in a clean towel. Washed and crisped, the greens will be ready for use when wanted.

Stored in a cool, dark location, potatoes, sweet potatoes, turnips, and onions will keep well for up to 2 weeks. Do remember to store potatoes and onions in separate locations; the two vegetables interact to encourage softening and sprouting of each.

Baked Beans

Ginger, thyme, and parsley give these beans a different but very likable taste. Serve with ham or spicy German frankfurters, sautéed in butter. Purists will leave out the baking soda, mindful of the consequences!

1 pound beans, pea, yellow-eyed, or kidney	1 teaspoon dry mustard
(1 teaspoon baking soda)	¼ teaspoon pepper
½ cup sugar	2 teaspoons salt
3 tablespoons molasses	¼ teaspoon parsley flakes
1 tablespoon maple syrup	1 tablespoon tomato catsup
¾ teaspoon ginger	4 tablespoons butter
	¼ teaspoon thyme

Pick over beans carefully; wash beans, then soak overnight in water to cover. Next morning, drain, and cover with fresh water. Bring to a boil, then add optional baking soda. Boil 2-3 minutes and rinse once again. Place in 2-quart bean pot or casserole dish, and add rest of ingredients. Add hot water to just cover beans. Bake in 275°F. oven for 5-6 hours, adding hot water as needed to keep beans covered. Serves 8.

Mrs. J. Raymond Young
An Olde Concord Christmas

Bourbon Baked Beans

Easy to assemble, wonderful dish for a buffet or barbecue. Outstanding served with ham.

two 28-ounce cans baked beans
20-ounce can pineapple slices,
    drained (reserve syrup)
⅓ cup reserved pineapple syrup
½ cup brown sugar, firmly packed

⅓ cup bourbon whisky
¼ cup minced onion
1 tablespoon instant coffee
1 teaspoon dry mustard
6 slices bacon

In 9x11-inch casserole dish, combine beans, pineapple syrup, brown sugar, bourbon, onion, coffee, and mustard. Let stand at room temperature for 1 hour. Arrange bacon slices on top of beans, and pineapple slices on top of bacon. Bake uncovered at 375°F. for 1½ hours. Serves 8-10.

Frances Lonsky
Little Falls, NJ

Green Bean Casserole

The cornflakes toast up nicely to lend a crunchy contrast to the cheesy sour-cream sauce. But you could alway substitute croutons or bread crumbs instead.

2 tablespoons butter
2 tablespoons flour
1 teaspoon salt
¼ teaspoon pepper
1 teaspoon sugar
¼ teaspoon basil
1 teaspoon grated onion

1 cup sour cream
4 cups cooked, drained green beans
½ pound mild cheese, grated
2 cups crushed cornflakes
2 tablespoons butter, melted
paprika
chopped parsley

Melt 2 tablespoons butter in small saucepan. Stir in flour, salt, pepper, sugar, basil, onion, and sour cream. Stir constantly over medium-low heat until thick. Place beans in buttered 2-quart casserole dish, and fold in sour-cream sauce. Sprinkle cheese over top. Combine cornflakes and melted butter, and spread over top of beans. Sprinkle with paprika and parsley. Bake at 400°F. for 20 minutes. Serves 8.

Juanita H. DeHart
Cortland, NY

String Beans in Tomato Sauce

To satisfy that Italian-food urge without gaining the usual calories. The tomato sauce is actually like a spaghetti sauce. A good dish to serve hot with sliced cold meats.

1½ pounds fresh string beans
2 cloves crushed garlic
¼ cup chopped onion
5 tablespoons olive oil
16-ounce can Italian-style tomatoes
¼ teaspoon salt

⅛ teaspoon pepper
¼ teaspoon basil
1 teaspoon sugar
¼ teaspoon oregano
4-5 parsley sprigs

Cook beans in salted water for 10 minutes. Drain well and set aside. In dutch oven, sauté garlic and onion in olive oil. Drain tomatoes, then add to sautéed mixture. Add salt, pepper, basil, and sugar, and cook for 20 minutes. Add string beans, oregano, and parsley, then simmer for another 30 minutes, or until beans are tender. Serves 6.

Elsie Stupinsky
Bernardsville, NJ

Delicious Beets

Beets in pineapple sauce make an interesting and tangy side dish to complement ham or poultry.

2 tablespoons brown sugar
1 tablespoon cornstarch
¼ teaspoon salt
8-ounce can crushed pineapple,
    with juice

1 tablespoon butter
1 tablespoon lemon juice
1-pound can sliced or diced beets,
    drained

Combine sugar, cornstarch, and salt. Stir in pineapple and juice. Cook until thick. Add butter, lemon juice, and beets and heat 5 minutes more, or until beets are hot. Serves 4.

Jane Hanson
Boulder, CO

Grated Beets and Sour Cream

In this nifty invention, red pepper sparks beets with a brand new vitality.

12 beets, cooked and grated
½ teaspoon salt
1-2 medium sweet red peppers,
    minced

1 tablespoon lemon juice
½ cup sour cream
1 clove garlic
buttered bread crumbs

Mix beets with salt, red peppers, lemon juice, and sour cream. Pour into 1½-quart baking dish that has been rubbed with garlic. Top with bread crumbs. Bake in 350°F. oven for 20 minutes, or until heated through. Serves 8.

Norma Jones
The Rockport Heritage Cookbook

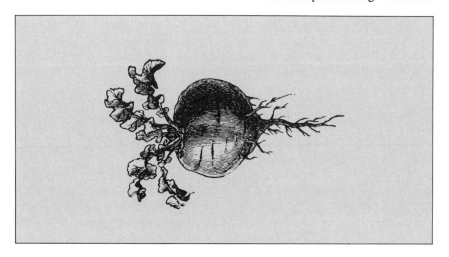

Ohio Beets and Apples

A novel blend of flavors that creates a brand new taste, this is very good and very pretty, with a bright red sauce.

2 medium apples, peeled, cored,
    and sliced
1-pound can sliced beets, drained
    (reserve juice)
3 tablespoons butter

1 tablespoon flour
½ cup reserved beet juice
1 tablespoon vinegar
1 teaspoon salt
½ cup brown sugar, packed

In buttered 1-quart casserole dish, layer apples and beets alternately. Melt butter in saucepan, and blend in flour. Stir in beet juice, vinegar, salt, and brown sugar. Bring to boil and allow to boil for 1 minute. Remove sauce from heat and pour over beets and apples in casserole dish. Bake at 350°F. for 25-30 minutes. Stir gently before serving. Serves 4.

Jane Hanson
Boulder, CO

Broccoli with Blue Cheese

Bored with broccoli? Here's a zippy version to serve with meat and potatoes. Don't use the mustard unless you prefer things really sharp.

10 ounces fresh or frozen broccoli
    spears
1 tablespoon butter
1 tablespoon flour
¼ teaspoon salt

½ cup milk
⅓ cup crumbled blue cheese
(2 teaspoons prepared mustard)
¼ cup grated Parmesan cheese

Cook broccoli in boiling salted water. Drain. In saucepan, melt butter. Blend in flour and salt; add milk immediately. Stirring often, cook to a boil. Stir in blue cheese and optional mustard. Add broccoli and heat thoroughly. Sprinkle with Parmesan. Serves 4.

Lucy Ackerman
Macungie, PA

Yogurt-Sauced Broccoli

A pretty dish when made with fresh broccoli cooked as below to preserve the green color. Similar in taste to broccoli Hollandaise, but with fewer calories.

3 egg yolks
½ teaspoon cornstarch
boiling water
2 teaspoons prepared mustard,
    preferably Dijon
1½ cups yogurt
1 garlic clove, mashed

1 teaspoon lemon juice
salt and pepper
4 quarts boiling water
2 teaspoons salt
2 pounds fresh broccoli, stems
    trimmed and peeled

Beat egg yolks with cornstarch until light yellow in double-boiler top. Pour boiling water into double-boiler bottom, enough to accommodate insertion of top into bottom without water boiling over — there is usually a line molded into the metal of the double-boiler bottom indicating this level; lacking this, use your judgement. To egg yolks, add mustard, yogurt, and mashed garlic clove. Put double boiler together, turn heat down to medium, and beat mixture constantly until it thickens enough to densely coat a wooden spoon. Beat in lemon juice, turn heat down to medium-low, and season to taste with salt and pepper.

Cook broccoli. In large pot, bring 4 quarts water to boil, and add salt and broccoli. Cook broccoli in boiling salted water until tender-crisp and still bright green — about 5 minutes. Drain off hot water from pot, and add cold water immediately to stop cooking process. Drain off cold water, lift out broccoli carefully, branch by branch, and place in 2- to 2½-quart ceramic or metal baking dish (you may want to lightly grease a metal dish), taking care to keep broccoli branches whole and to arrange them neatly. Pour sauce over broccoli and serve at once. Serves 4.

Lillie V. Brown
St. Louis, MO

Baked Cabbage

If you thought you didn't like cooked cabbage or that cabbage was only good for sauerkraut or cole slaw, wait until you taste this! Serve with roast pork, baked potatoes, and apple rings.

1 medium-sized cabbage, coarsely
   shredded
1 tablespoon sugar
2 tablespoons flour

1 cup heavy cream
salt and pepper to taste
4-6 slices bacon

Put cabbage in 7x11-inch baking dish. Mix sugar, flour, and cream, season to taste, and pour over cabbage. Place bacon slices on top to cover without overlapping. Bake, covered, at 350°F. for 40-50 minutes. Remove cover, and bake 15-20 minutes longer to crisp bacon. Serves 6.

Marguerite Munson
Madison, WI

Hot Slaw

A crunchy hot slaw to perk up any winter lunch or supper. Good served cold the next day, too.

1 medium cabbage head
5 strips bacon
¼ cup brown sugar, packed
½ teaspoon celery seeds

¼ teaspoon salt
½ teaspoon dry mustard
¼ cup vinegar

Shred cabbage and set aside. In a large skillet, fry bacon until crisp. Remove from pan and break into bits. Leave bacon grease in pan and add sugar, celery seeds, salt, mustard, and vinegar. Stir until hot, then add cabbage, turning and mixing well. Toss in bacon bits. Cabbage should be heated through but not really cooked. Serves 8.

Mrs. Lloyd Mitchell
Englewood, FL

Red Cabbage with Apples

Try serving this simple, and simply delicious version of the classic dish with the Russian Fish Pie on page 131.

2½ pounds red cabbage, shredded
¾ cup boiling water
6 apples, peeled, cored, and diced

¼ cup vinegar
⅓ cup brown sugar, packed
salt and pepper

Cook cabbage in boiling water for about 10 minutes. Add apples, and cook until slightly soft, but not mushy. Stir in vinegar, brown sugar, and salt and pepper to taste. Serves 6-8.

Jody Saville
Jaffrey, NH

Carrot Pudding Puff

Light, sweet, and airy vegetable course. Another Yankee prizewinner.

4 eggs, separated
½ cup sugar
1 cup grated raw carrot, firmly packed
¼ cup grated apple

¼ cup red wine
2 tablespoons lemon juice
½ teaspoon grated lemon peel
⅓ cup flour

Beat egg yolks with sugar. Add remaining ingredients except egg whites, and blend well. Beat egg whites until stiff, and fold into carrot mixture. Spoon into well-greased 1½-quart casserole dish. Bake at 375°F. for 35 minutes, or until golden brown. Serve immediately. Serves 6.

Barbara Wener
West Hartford, CT

Enlivening Beets and Carrots

Some people feel that plain boiled beets and carrots are dull — and they can be, if elderly. To add sparkle, use any of the following herbs alone, or in combination — but add gingerly, one at a time, and taste before adding anything else.

Beets: dill (weed or seeds); marjoram; pepper; nutmeg; ginger; celery seeds; vinegar; sugar; lemon or orange juice; sour cream *and* any of the above herbs (do not combine sour cream with vinegar, sugar, or citrus juice). Or glaze beets with orange juice mixed with a little marmalade and cinnamon; or mix the orange juice with chutney as a glaze.

Carrots: mint, often combined with vinegar and sugar (use a *little* of each); tarragon; rosemary; thyme; and parsley. The last four herbs mentioned should be used with melted butter — cook 1 teaspoon in 2 tablespoons melted butter and stir into cooked carrots. Or add herbs to cooking water. Glaze carrots with butter and brown sugar, spiced with nutmeg or cinnamon (a touch, only).

Carrots Vichy

Vermouth adds a nice touch of flavor to these lightly glazed carrots.

12 carrots, sliced in 1-inch diagonal
    pieces
1 teaspoon sugar
1 tablespoon butter

3 tablespoons white vermouth
salt
2 tablespoons chopped parsley

Cook carrots in salted boiling water about 10 minutes, or until tender. Drain. Return to skillet, and add sugar, butter, and vermouth. Salt to taste. Cook, uncovered, for 5 minutes. Top with parsley. Serves 6.

Mrs. James Andrews
Salem, NH

Cheese-Scalloped Carrots

Coin-sliced or slivered — however — these carrots in a mustardy cheese sauce are pretty and yummy. If you don't have celery seeds, use celery salt. Double the mustard if you serve this with beef for a spicy side dish.

6 medium carrots, pared, then
    sliced thin or slivered
1 small onion, minced
2 tablespoons butter, melted
2 tablespoons flour
½ teaspoon salt
⅛ teaspoon dry mustard

1 cup milk
pinch pepper
¼ teaspoon celery seeds
¼ pound Cheddar cheese, shredded
1 cup soft bread crumbs
2 tablespoons butter, cut into dots

Cook carrots in boiling salted water barely to cover, in covered pot until just tender. Drain. Sauté onion in melted butter until tender. Sift together flour, salt, and mustard; add onion, then milk. Cook, stirring, until smooth and thickened. Add pepper and celery seeds. In 1-quart buttered casserole dish, arrange layer of carrots, then scant layer of cheese. Repeat until all is used, ending with carrots. Pour on mustard sauce. Top with bread crumbs and butter dots. Bake at 350°F. for 25-30 minutes, or until bubbling and browned. Serves 4.

Marjorie Spaulding
Ladies Circle Community Baptist Church
Whitefield, NH

Company Carrots

Very rich, very good, and visually appealing. A grand party vegetable as it can be made ahead and reheated.

5 cups peeled, thinly sliced carrots
1 cup sour cream
3 ounces cream cheese, softened

2 tablespoons sliced green onion
½ teaspoon salt
½ teaspoon grated lemon peel

Cook carrots in boiling salted water for about 8 minutes. Drain. In 1-quart saucepan, combine sour cream, cream cheese, green onion, salt, and lemon peel. Stir in cooked carrots, and heat thoroughly. Serves 4-6.

Janice Ryzewski
Shrewsbury, MA

Italian Cauliflower

In tomato sauce, of course!

1 head cauliflower
3 tablespoons olive oil
1 clove garlic, minced
1 small onion, chopped fine
2 tablespoons chopped parsley
1 teaspoon basil

2 cups tomato sauce
salt and pepper
¼ cup grated Parmesan cheese
2 tablespoons dry bread crumbs
1 tablespoon butter, melted

Separate cauliflower into florets, and cook in boiling water for 15 minutes, or until tender. Drain. In olive oil, sauté garlic and onion until tender. Add parsley, basil, tomato sauce, and salt and pepper to taste. Simmer 10 minutes, stirring from time to time. Cover bottom of greased 2-quart baking dish with thin coating of sauce. Add cauliflower pieces, and cover with sauce. Combine cheese, bread crumbs, and butter and sprinkle over top. Bake at 425°F. for 10 minutes, or until bubbling and browned. Serves 6.

Veronica Marinaro
Quechee, VT

Curried Cauliflower

The subtle touch of curry adds character to a vegetable often bland. Be sure not to overcook the cauliflower.

1 head cauliflower, about 2 pounds with leaves	1 tablespoon chopped shallots
water to cover	1 teaspoon curry powder
¼ cup milk	½ cup heavy cream
½ teaspoon salt	salt and pepper
	1 tablespoon butter

Cut away leaves and core of cauliflower. Break into large florets. Put florets in saucepan, and add water to cover. Add milk and ½ teaspoon salt. Bring to boil, and cook 15-20 minutes, or until cauliflower is tender but not soft. Drain. Chop cauliflower pieces coarsely, then return to saucepan, and add shallots, curry powder, and cream. Season to taste with salt and pepper. Cook, stirring, over heat until piping hot. Stir in butter. Serves 4.

Je Me Souviens la Cuisine de la Grandmère

Celery Braised in Broth

Even elderly stalks are tasty prepared this way.

chicken broth	1 tablespoon chopped green onions
12 stalks celery, cut into 2-inch lengths	¼ cup butter, melted
	salt and pepper

Pour chicken broth into 1-quart saucepan to depth of 1 inch, and bring to boil. Add celery, cover pan, and simmer over medium heat until tender (10-15 minutes). Drain. Combine green onions with melted butter and mix into celery. Season to taste with salt and pepper. Serves 4.

Melissa Hawkins
Boston, MA

Chopped Celery

A very old, very good recipe for what is a sort of a celery relish. Serve with roast chicken or turkey.

1 bunch celery	1 egg, lightly beaten
¼ cup vinegar	½ teaspoon dry mustard
⅓ cup sugar	1 tablespoon grated onion

Wash celery, and put through grinder, leaves and all. Combine other ingredients, and mix well until sugar has dissolved. Pour over celery, and stir to blend. Keeps in covered jar in refrigerator a long time. Makes about 1 pint.

Mrs. Gertrude Fitts
Foxboro, MA

Corn Soufflé

An excellent soufflé with a delightfully "corny" taste. Use fresh corn cut from the cob, canned kernels (drained), or frozen kernels, thawed and drained.

1 teaspoon butter
2 tablespoons flour
1 cup milk
2 eggs, separated

2 cups corn kernels
1¼ teaspoons salt
few grains pepper

Melt butter, stir in flour, and gradually add milk. Cook, stirring, just to boiling point. Beat egg yolks until thick and light yellow, and mix with corn. Stir into white sauce, and season with salt and pepper. Remove from heat. Beat egg whites until stiff, and fold into corn mixture. Spoon into unbuttered 1-quart baking dish. Bake 30 minutes at 350°F. Serves 6.

Peggy Shortlidge
N. Swanzey, NH

Corn, Okra, and Tomatoes

Equivalent amounts of frozen corn and okra can be substituted for fresh, if completely thawed before use.

1 large onion, chopped
2 tablespoons oil
2 cups fresh okra, cut into 2-inch
    pieces
2-3 fresh tomatoes, cut into 2-inch
    pieces

2 cups fresh-cut corn kernels
1 teaspoon salt
½ teaspoon pepper

In large iron skillet, sauté onion in oil. Add okra and cook about 5 minutes, stirring well. Add tomatoes, corn, salt, and pepper. Cover tightly, and simmer 15-20 minutes. If necessary, add a little water to prevent sticking. Serves 8.

Mrs. W. O. Scott, Jr.
Pensacola, FL

Dilled Baby Limas

Lima beans in a creamy sauce herbed with chives and dill weed.

½ cup sour cream
2 teaspoons chopped chives
½ teaspoon dill weed

10-ounce package frozen baby lima
    beans
pepper

In double-boiler top, covered, heat sour cream, chives, and dill weed together over boiling water. Cook beans, drain, and stir into sauce. Season with pepper to taste, and heat through. Serves 4.

Barbara T. Hudson
Baltimore, MD

Lima Beans in Tomato Sauce

Serve with a green salad and rolls for a meatless meal.

2 tablespoons butter
1 large onion, chopped
1 green pepper, chopped
1 clove garlic, chopped
2 cups tomato puree
¼ teaspoon basil

1 teaspoon Worcestershire sauce
salt and pepper
2½ cups fresh or frozen lima
    beans, cooked and drained
3 ounces Parmesan cheese, grated
1 tablespoon butter

Melt 2 tablespoons butter, and sauté onion, green pepper, and garlic until onion is tender. Add tomato puree and seasonings, and simmer for 20 minutes. Pour sauce over beans. In buttered 1½-quart casserole dish, place a layer of beans and sauce. Cover with one-third the grated Parmesan. Repeat this process twice more. Dot with butter. Bake at 350°F. for 20 minutes, or until heated through and bubbling. Serves 6.

Sarah Bauhan
Boston, MA

Glazed Onions and Carrots

A delicate and handsome dish to grace a roast. To save time, you can use frozen pearl onions, which need not be parboiled.

1 pound small white onions
1 pound baby carrots, scraped and
    trimmed
½ cup butter

4 tablespoons sugar
1 cup chicken broth
salt and pepper

In separate saucepans, cook onions and carrots in boiling salted water to cover for about 10 minutes. Slip skins off onions, and drain onions on paper towel. Drain carrots. Melt butter in large skillet. Add vegetables, and toss over medium heat until butter is absorbed. Sprinkle with sugar, and cook, stirring frequently, until vegetables are glazed and sugar is beginning to caramelize (10-15 minutes). Add broth, cover pan, reduce heat to low, and simmer 30 minutes. Uncover pan, turn heat up to medium, and cook until sugar is caramelized and all liquid is evaporated — about 10 minutes. Season and serve. Serves 8.

Philip Bourassa
Atlanta, GA

Onions au Gratin

Prepare this ahead, but hold back the bread crumbs and cheese until ready to bake. Onions become sweeter when baked.

2 sweet Spanish onions (3-4 inches in diameter)
1 beef bouillon cube
¾ cup boiling water
¼ teaspoon thyme
¼ teaspoon salt
⅛ teaspoon pepper
1 tablespoon butter, cut into dots
½ cup bread crumbs
2 tablespoons butter, melted
¼ cup grated sharp Cheddar cheese

Peel and thickly slice onions. Arrange in an 8-inch square baking dish, overlapping slices. Dissolve bouillon cube in boiling water, add thyme, and pour over onions. Sprinkle with salt and pepper, and dot with butter. Cover and bake at 400°F. for 20 minutes. Toss bread crumbs in melted butter, stir in cheese. Sprinkle over onions. Return to oven, and bake, uncovered, 10 minutes longer, or until crumbs are crisp and golden. Serves 4.

Mrs. Leroy Sawtell
Cooking at Court

Mushrooms

When you buy fresh mushrooms in a closed plastic container, and do not plan to use them immediately, store in a porous container (there are holed containers on the market especially for mushrooms), or simply transfer the mushrooms to a paper bag, wrap the bag in a damp towel, and refrigerate. When you are ready to use the mushrooms, as you should be within a few days, wash each mushroom carefully, to remove any earth still adhering. Do not soak, as soaking will leach out the flavor. Occasionally, a recipe will direct you to skin the mushrooms. This is a thankless task, and indeed unnecessary with the mushrooms available in the market today. You should, however, cut out any soft spots and wash the mushrooms; discard all limp mushrooms.

Peas à la Bonne Femme

Cooked in a bacon-and-onion sauce.

2 tablespoons butter
12 small white onions
2 slices bacon, diced
4 teaspoons flour
1 cup chicken broth

3 pounds fresh green peas, shelled,
   or two 10-ounce packages
   frozen peas (do not thaw)
salt and pepper

Melt butter in large skillet over medium-high heat. Brown onions slowly all over, about 6-8 minutes. Add bacon and sauté until crisp. Stir in flour, slowly add chicken broth, and mix until smooth. Cook, stirring constantly, until thickened. Reduce heat to medium-low, cover skillet, and simmer 10 minutes until onions are tender-crisp. Add peas, cover skillet, and simmer 8-10 minutes for fresh peas, or 5-7 minutes for frozen. Break up frozen peas after 2 minutes' cooking. Season to taste with salt and pepper. Serves 6.

Je Me Souviens la Cuisine de la Grandmère

Petits Pois

Serve in patty shells for a luncheon entrée, or as a side dish with roast lamb or beef. In season, use ¾ pound garden peas instead of the frozen.

2 tablespoons butter
2 onions, minced
10-ounce package frozen peas
2 lettuce leaves
salt and pepper

1 tablespoon chopped parsley
⅛ teaspoon nutmeg
½ teaspoon sugar
(8-10 small cubes ham)
¼ cup water

Melt butter in dutch oven, and sauté onions. Add peas and lettuce and cook over low heat, covered, for 10 minutes. Sprinkle with seasonings and sugar, then add optional ham and water. Cover, and cook 10-15 minutes longer over low heat, stirring occasionally, until peas are tender but still green. Serves 4.

Je Me Souviens la Cuisine de la Grandmère

Italian Stuffed Pepper

For extra body, add ½ cup grated Mozzarella cheese to the bread-crumb mixture.

4 large green peppers
2 cups bread crumbs
¼ cup water
4 anchovies, chopped
2 tablespoons chopped parsley

12 stuffed olives, chopped
1 garlic clove, minced
½ cup olive oil
(1 teaspoon capers)

(continued)

Cut out tops of peppers, remove seeds, and rinse. In a mixing bowl, combine remaining ingredients except for ¼ cup of the olive oil. Stuff mixture into peppers. Stand them in a small baking pan, and drizzle with remaining olive oil. Bake at 325°F. for 45 minutes. Serves 4.

H. Raineri
Sherman Cooks!

Baked Two Potatoes

Sweet potatoes and cheese confer glorious golden color and taste upon these stuffed baked potatoes.

6 medium baking potatoes
¼ cup butter
4¾-ounce jar strained sweet
potatoes

salt and pepper
4 ounces Cheddar cheese, shredded

Bake potatoes at 400°F. for 1 hour. Cut in half lengthwise, scoop out potato from shells, and mash. Add butter and stir until melted. Add sweet potatoes, salt, and pepper. Mix well. Spoon mixture back into shells, and top with cheese. Bake at 400°F. for 15-20 minutes, or until cheese is golden and potatoes are heated through. Serves 6-8.

Mrs. Margaret Skinner
Carlstadt, NJ

Dusty Potatoes

In texture similar to French fries, but far superior in taste. The touch of nutmeg is fantastic. Can be reheated, wrapped in foil.

6 large baking potatoes
2 cups fine dry bread crumbs
¾ teaspoon nutmeg

1 cup butter, melted
salt and pepper

Peel potatoes and cut each into 8 long wedges. Mix bread crumbs and nutmeg. Dip potato wedges in melted butter, then roll in bread crumbs. Arrange in single layer on lightly greased cookie sheet. Sprinkle with salt and pepper. Bake at 350°F. for about 1 hour, or until brown and crisp. Drizzle with melted butter just before serving. Serves 6-8.

Dianne Stillings
New York, NY

Oven-Fried Potatoes

Baking time will depend somewhat on the way in which you cut the potatoes. Thick wedges will take twice as long as thin ones.

6 medium potatoes	½ teaspoon salt
¼ cup vegetable oil	¼ teaspoon garlic powder
1 tablespoon grated Parmesan cheese	¼ teaspoon paprika
	¼ teaspoon pepper

Scrub potatoes and cut into wedges (approximately six per potato). Combine remaining ingredients and mix well. Arrange potatoes in a 9x13-inch baking dish. Brush with oil mixture and bake at 375°F. for 30-60 minutes. Turn potatoes halfway through baking time. Serves 6.

Deb Christensen
Brookline, NH

Italian Potatoes

A kind of layered potato pizza. Great for lunch or buffet supper.

1 tablespoon cooking oil	1 cup shredded Provolone cheese
5 potatoes, peeled and sliced ¼ inch thick	½ teaspoon oregano
1 onion, sliced	1½ teaspoons salt
3 medium tomatoes, sliced	⅛ teaspoon pepper
½ cup grated Parmesan cheese	3 tablespoons butter

Oil a 2½- to 3-quart, flattish casserole dish. Arrange a layer of potatoes, a layer of onion, and a layer of tomatoes. Sprinkle with both cheeses, oregano, salt and pepper. Repeat, ending with potatoes, seasoning, and cheese. Dot with butter. Bake, uncovered, at 400°F. for 45 minutes. Serves 8.

Dorothy Butler
Guilford, CT

Potatoes Margaret

Sour cream makes the difference — gives a nice tang. Buttery crumbs toast on top. Good side dish for any meat, poultry, or fish entrée.

1 cup sour cream
½ cup milk
1 tablespoon minced onion
5 cups sliced, cooked (5-6 medium)
  potatoes
salt and pepper

1 tablespoon butter
2 tablespoons fine fresh crumbs
  (2 slices bread crumbed in
  blender)
paprika
parsley sprigs for garnish

Combine sour cream, milk, and onion. Place half the potatoes in greased 7x11-inch baking dish. Sprinkle generously with salt and pepper. Add half the sour-cream mixture. Repeat layers. Melt butter, add crumbs, and toss to mix well. Sprinkle over potatoes, then sprinkle paprika over crumbs. Bake at 350°F. for 20-25 minutes. Garnish with parsley. Serves 6.

Peg Rodenhiser
New Ipswich, NH

Potato-Mushroom Pie

Grand for company, it actually looks like a pie when served.

3 medium baking potatoes
¼ cup milk
1 egg
1 tablespoon butter
¾ teaspoon salt
¼ teaspoon baking powder
⅛ teaspoon pepper
½ cup chopped onion

4 tablespoons butter
8 ounces fresh sliced mushrooms
2 tablespoons chopped parsley
¼ teaspoon thyme
¼ teaspoon salt
dash pepper
¼ cup grated Cheddar cheese
paprika

Peel and quarter potatoes. Boil in salted water until tender; drain. Mash, then beat until smooth. Add milk, egg, 1 tablespoon butter, ¾ teaspoon salt, baking powder, and ⅛ teaspoon pepper. Continue to beat until well mixed and fluffy. In small skillet, sauté onion in 4 tablespoons butter until translucent. Add mushrooms, and cook 3-5 minutes. Add parsley, thyme, ¼ teaspoon salt, and dash pepper. Butter an 8-inch pie pan. Spread 1½ cups of potato mixture over bottom and up sides of pan. Spoon mushrooms over potatoes in even layer, then top with remaining potatoes, bringing top layer of potatoes right out to pan edges to seal. Bake at 400°F. for 15 minutes. Sprinkle with cheese and paprika, and bake 4 minutes more. Serves 6.

Campbell Greeff
Greenwich, CT

Potato and Onion Cake

A different kind of scalloped potato without the sauce. Very onion-y!

1½ pounds potatoes	¼ pound butter
3 onions	salt and pepper to taste

Wash potatoes and slice paper-thin under cold water. Peel and slice onions. Butter shallow casserole dish and line with buttered aluminum foil. Cover bottom with a layer of potatoes, then alternate layers of onions and potatoes, finishing with a layer of potatoes. Season with salt and pepper, then dot with butter. Cover with foil and put in a preheated 350°F. oven for 1 hour. Increase oven temperature to 400°F., and bake another 20-30 minutes. During the last 10 minutes, remove the top foil and let brown. Serves 6.

Dianne Stillings
New York, NY

Norwegian Spinach Potatoes

Mashed potatoes and spinach flavored with onion and dill weed make a very attractive vegetable dish with a brand new taste. Two and two in this case equals six! The recipe is easily halved or doubled and freezes well.

6 large potatoes	2 teaspoons minced onion
¾ cup milk, or half and half	1½ teaspoons dried dill
4 tablespoons butter, softened	10-ounce package frozen chopped
2 teaspoons salt	spinach, partially cooked and
1 teaspoon sugar	well drained
¼ teaspoon black pepper	

Boil potatoes until tender. Remove skins. Mash, and mix in milk, butter, salt, sugar, and pepper. Beat until light and fluffy. Add onion, dill, and spinach, and mix well. Turn into shallow, greased 2-quart casserole. Bake at 350°F. for 30 minutes, or until piping hot. Serves 6-8.

Salem Junior Women's Club
GFWC-NHFWC Complete Menu Cookbook

Brandied Pumpkin Butter

Spread on bread like apple butter, serve in a bowl with the Thanksgiving turkey, or give small jars as Christmas presents. Jars should be kept refrigerated. Use either canned or fresh cooked pumpkin.

3 cups cooked, mashed pumpkin	½ teaspoon cinnamon
3 tablespoons butter	¼ teaspoon mace
½ teaspoon salt	1½ tablespoons brown sugar
¼ teaspoon pepper	⅔ cup brandy
½ teaspoon cloves	

(continued)

Place all ingredients together in *large* saucepan (mixture tends to spatter while cooking), and cook slowly over low heat, stirring often, until mixture thickens enough to hold together like apple butter. Serves 6.

Sandra Lindsay
Hartford, CT

Creamed Madeira Spinach

Absolutely delicious and quickly assembled. Goes nicely with most meat, poultry, or fish. Excellent with Pineapple Chicken and Brown Rice (page 75).

three 10-ounce packages frozen
   chopped spinach
1½ tablespoons butter
6 tablespoons heavy cream

¼ teaspoon nutmeg
½ teaspoon salt
pinch pepper
3 tablespoons Madeira wine

Cook spinach as directed on package. Drain and press out all water. Combine spinach with 1½ tablespoons butter, cream, nutmeg, salt, and pepper. Add Madeira. Serves 4-6.

Susan Shattuck
Valhalla, NY

Creamed Spinach with Mushroom-Stuffed Eggs

A good meatless lunch or supper, served with fresh French or Italian bread and butter. Three 10-ounce packages frozen chopped spinach may be used instead of the fresh. If you use dried parsley flakes, use only a teaspoonful.

½ clove garlic, crushed
½ cup minced onion
1 cup minced mushrooms
1½ tablespoons butter
½ teaspoon salt
⅛ teaspoon pepper
⅛ teaspoon nutmeg
6 hardboiled eggs
2 teaspoons butter

2 tablespoons cream
1 tablespoon minced fresh parsley
paprika or cayenne pepper
three 10-ounce bags fresh spinach
½ cup water
1 tablespoon butter
½ cup sour cream
¼ teaspoon salt
⅛ teaspoon pepper

Sauté garlic, onion, and mushrooms in 1½ tablespoons butter until soft. Put into bowl and stir in salt, pepper, and nutmeg. Shell the eggs and cut into halves lengthwise. Add egg yolks to mixture in bowl. Add 2 teaspoons butter, cream, and parsley, and mix well. Stuff egg whites with mixture, and sprinkle with paprika or (*lightly*) with cayenne pepper. Cook spinach, covered, in water for 10 minutes, or until tender. Drain and press dry. Chop fine, then drain and press dry again. Mix spinach with 1 tablespoon butter, sour cream, salt, and pepper. Place in 1½-quart casserole dish, and top with stuffed egg halves. Bake at 350°F. for 15-20 minutes, or until heated through. Serves 4-6.

Elizabeth Bauer
Middleburg, VA

Acorn Squash and Apples

Very attractive harvest supper dish; the green of the rind contrasts beautifully with the orange pulp and white apple slices sprinkled with nutmeg. Easily multiplied.

1 acorn squash	2 medium apples
water	2 tablespoons sugar
1 teaspoon cinnamon	⅓ cup water
1½ teaspoons nutmeg	2 tablespoons butter

Cut squash in half lengthwise, and remove seeds. Place cut-side down in shallow baking dish. Add water to about ½ inch up sides of dish. Bake at 350°F. for 30-45 minutes (depending on size of squash) until just tender. Place squash halves skin side down in buttered baking dish. Pierce squash pulp all over with fork. Sprinkle with cinnamon and a little nutmeg. Core, peel, and slice apples. Cook in saucepan with sugar and ⅓ cup water until slightly soft — about 5-7 minutes. Spoon apples into squash cavities. Dot with butter, and sprinkle with remaining nutmeg. Return to oven and bake at 350°F. for 15-20 minutes. Serves 2.

Mrs. Stuart Anderson
Brookfield, CT

Creoled Summer Squash

Prepare early in the day, then bake just before serving time. Eggplant or zucchini work just as well in this recipe.

2 cups sliced summer squash	1 teaspoon salt
3 tablespoons butter	1 tablespoon brown sugar
3 tablespoons flour	½ bay leaf, crumbled
2 cups chopped tomatoes (or canned, undrained)	2 whole cloves
1 small onion, chopped	1 cup croutons
1 green pepper, chopped	2 tablespoons butter, melted

If squash is large, or if you are using eggplant, peel slices and parboil for 5 minutes. Drain. Layer in buttered 9x13-inch baking dish or 1½-quart casserole dish. In large saucepan, melt 3 tablespoons butter and stir in flour. Cook, stirring, about 1 minute, then add tomatoes, onion, green pepper, salt, brown sugar, bay leaf, and cloves. Continue stirring as you cook sauce for 5 minutes. Pour sauce over squash and mix lightly. Toss croutons with 2 tablespoons melted butter to coat evenly, then spread over squash. Bake at 350°F. for 30 minutes. Serves 6-8.

Mrs. Roger Butler
Cooking at Court

Cranberry Squash

Another colorful dish perfect for Thanksgiving dinner. Can be prepared in advance and refrigerated, then baked just before serving time. Again, easily multiplied.

1 butternut squash	¾ cup cranberries, halved
1 egg, beaten	salt and pepper
1-2 tablespoons sugar	¼ teaspoon nutmeg
2 tablespoons butter, melted	

Peel squash, and cut into large chunks. Cook in boiling salted water until soft. Drain and mash (you should have approximately 2 cups mashed squash). In a large bowl, combine squash, beaten egg, sugar, 1 tablespoon melted butter, and cranberries. Season with salt and pepper to taste. Transfer to 7x11-inch buttered casserole dish, and drizzle remaining butter over top. Sprinkle with nutmeg. Bake at 400°F. for 45 minutes. Serves 6-8.

Mrs. Raymond Wolcott
Cooking at Court

Baked Tomatoes with Special Stuffing

A far cry from the usual bread-stuffed tomatoes, these are filled with a most appetizing mixture of tomato, spinach, onion, mushrooms, and cheese. Choose tomatoes that are a little under-ripe; they hold up better during baking.

6 tomatoes	2 generous tablespoons sliced,
1½ tablespoons butter	sautéed mushrooms (or half a
¼ cup chopped onion	drained 4-ounce can)
¼ cup chopped fresh parsley	¼ cup cooked, drained spinach
¾ cup packed fresh bread crumbs	⅛ teaspoon nutmeg
½ teaspoon basil	1 teaspoon sesame seeds
½ teaspoon salt	¼ cup grated Parmesan cheese
black pepper to taste	butter dots
dash Tabasco sauce	

Cut top slice off each tomato, and remove tomato core. Scoop out pulp and ribs. Chop this coarsely and reserve. Drain tomato cases upside down on plate. Melt butter, and sauté onion lightly. Add reserved tomato pulp and remaining ingredients except butter dots, and simmer until well blended — about 10 minutes. (If there is any excess liquid, boil it off by raising heat briefly to high, watching carefully.) Remove from heat. Pack mixture firmly into tomato cases. Stand tomatoes upright in buttered baking dish just large enough to hold them comfortably. Place a small dot of butter on top of each. Bake at 350°F. for 30 minutes, or until tomatoes are soft, and heated through. Serves 6.

Christina Myrtle
Cleveland, OH

Tomatoes and Mushrooms

Onions, too — a different and enticing vegetable side dish. Or, add ½ cup heavy cream to mixture, heat through, taking care not to boil, and serve over toast as an opulent breakfast or brunch. Sprinkle with bacon as for side dish.

4 slices bacon, cooked crisp
¼ cup butter
⅔ cup minced onion
12 ounces mushrooms, sliced
3 large tomatoes, peeled and cut
    into chunks

1 teaspoon salt
¼ teaspoon pepper
¼ cup chopped fresh parsley

Drain bacon on paper and discard fat. Melt butter in same skillet, and sauté onion lightly. Add mushrooms and cook until brown. Add remaining ingredients, and cook at simmer for 10-15 minutes. If the dish still has too much liquid (you don't want a watery dinner plate), turn heat to high, and boil down, watching carefully, and stirring. Turn into serving dish and sprinkle with crumbled bacon. Serves 4-6.

Carrie Schulz
Madison, WI

Chinese Vegetables

Cook fresh vegetables only until tender-crisp to preserve taste and crunchiness. Serve with rice and roast pork, or over Chinese noodles with bratwurst.

½ cup beef broth
2 cups fresh cauliflower florets
2 cups fresh broccoli florets
½ cup sliced celery
2 tablespoons finely diced ginger
    root
10-ounce package frozen snow
    peas, thawed and drained
½ cup thinly sliced red pepper
12 whole mushrooms, sliced thin

¼ head cabbage, shredded
2 tablespoons Tamari soy sauce
8-ounce can bamboo shoots,
    drained and diced
8-ounce can water chestnuts,
    drained and sliced thin
1 medium onion, sliced thin and
    separated into rings
half a 1-pound can bean sprouts,
    drained and rinsed

Bring broth to boil in wok or large, heavy skillet over high heat. Add cauliflower and broccoli florets, celery, ginger, snow peas, and red pepper. Cook, stirring, for 2-3 minutes. Add mushrooms and cabbage and continue to cook and stir for 1-2 minutes. Stir in remaining ingredients and cook for 1 minute more over high heat, still stirring. Reduce heat to low, and simmer for 1 minute. Serve immediately. Serves 8-10.

Margaret Campbell
Buffalo, NY

Vegetable Motley

A colorful and tempting vegetable dish, fancy enough for a dinner party and easy enough for everyday. An exciting meld of flavors.

½ pound mushrooms, sliced
1 onion, thinly sliced and separated into rings, or 4-5 small white onions, peeled and thinly sliced
4 tablespoons butter, melted
1 medium red pepper, seeded and coarsely chopped

10-ounce package frozen peas, thawed and drained
2 tablespoons sherry
½ teaspoon marjoram
½ teaspoon nutmeg
salt and pepper to taste

In 10-inch skillet, sauté mushrooms and onion(s) in butter until just tender. Add chopped pepper, peas, sherry, and spices. Simmer 15-20 minutes, stirring occasionally. Serves 4.

Lucy Grey
Northfield, VT

Vegetables and Noodles

Add some cooked chicken or tuna for a one-dish meal.

2 tablespoons butter
8-ounce package egg noodles
3¼ cups chicken broth
¼ teaspoon garlic powder
salt and pepper to taste
2 medium tomatoes, peeled and cut in wedges

2 medium zucchini, thinly sliced
1 cup sliced mushrooms
1⅓ cups shredded Mozzarella cheese

Melt butter in large skillet. Add uncooked noodles and brown lightly, stirring frequently. Add chicken broth, garlic powder, salt, and pepper. Bring to a boil, then add vegetables. Simmer, covered, for 15-20 minutes, or until noodles and vegetables are tender. Toss cheese with noodles. Serves 6.

Janice Ryzewski
Shrewsbury, MA

Italian Stuffed Zucchini

Anchovy-flavored stuffing and tomato sauce.

4 slices bacon	½ teaspoon salt
2 slices bread	2 teaspoons oregano
milk to cover	¼ teaspoon black pepper
1 pound zucchinis, unpeeled	1 egg, beaten
4 mushrooms, chopped	2 cups tomato sauce
4 anchovy fillets, chopped	¼ cup dry bread crumbs
4 tablespoons grated Parmesan cheese	butter dots

Cook bacon until crisp, and drain on paper. Tear bread into pieces and place in large measuring cup with milk to cover. Let soak 10 minutes, then wring out and discard milk, and place bread in large bowl. Cook zucchinis in boiling salted water for 3-4 minutes. Drain. Cut in half lengthwise, and scoop out pulp. Place pulp in bowl with bread, and add mushrooms, anchovies, 2 tablespoons of the cheese, salt, oregano, pepper, and egg. Stir well to mix. Fill zucchini shells with mixture. Arrange in lightly greased baking dish, and cover with tomato sauce. Combine remaining 2 tablespoons cheese with bread crumbs and sprinkle over filled zucchinis. Dot with butter, and bake at 350°F. for 35-40 minutes. Serves 4.

Veronica Marinaro
Quechee, VT

Zucchini-Potato Latkes

Vegetable pancakes that are terrific with a dollop of sour cream or applesauce — or both! Enough here to serve six generously.

3 eggs, beaten	2 pounds zucchinis
1 teaspoon cooking oil	2 large potatoes
½ cup flour (approx.)	1 medium onion, grated
½ teaspoon salt	oil for frying
¼ teaspoon pepper	

In large bowl, beat eggs with oil, flour, salt, and pepper. Cut zucchinis in half, and scoop out seeds. Grate. Turn into sieve and press to remove as much liquid as possible. Peel potatoes (if done ahead, drop into cold water containing a little lemon juice). Grate, and remove moisture by pressing against sieve or squeezing in clean dish towel. Add immediately to egg mixture to prevent discoloration. Add onion. Press zucchini once more, and add to batter. If needed, add up to ¼ cup more flour. In large heavy skillet, heat oil almost to smoking. With a serving spoon, spoon up a round portion of batter and flatten in skillet. Brown, turn, and brown second side, about 1 minute on first side, less on second. Keep warm until ready to serve. Makes 18 pancakes.

Clara Zunt
Parma Heights, OH

CHAPTER SEVEN

Breads and Breadstuffs

Home-baked goods — breads, rolls, coffee cakes, pastries, biscuits, the lot — are unequalled for flavor and aroma, wholesomeness and economy. Commercially baked products are comparatively quite expensive. You can bake three loaves of bread for the price of one from the supermarket. Pre-packaged goods may have chemical additives to prolong shelf life, and often carry extremely high levels of sodium. When you bake at home, *you* control the ingredients; it's possible, for example, to cut the salt content by half (important for those who must reduce sodium intake) and still have eminently delectable results. Professionally baked items come into your house in a box or bag or in a frozen state. Home-baked breadstuffs fill your home with aroma and anticipation as they are whisked from the oven and set on a rack to cool.

When you give a gift of home-made bread, the recipient knows you really care. You have donated your own creativity, time, and effort. When swamped with requests for that dinner-roll recipe after a home or communal meal, there is the satisfaction and pleasure of being able to share a good experience. And there are none so willing to share their recipes, experiences, and expertise as those who do their own baking.

YEAST BREADS

There are experienced cooks as well as those new to cooking who are apprehensive about baking with yeast doughs. There seems to be something intimidating or mystifying about the process. Of course, there *is* a wonderful mystery about baking. The transformation of a sticky mass of flour and liquid into a supple, smooth, elastic ball of dough and further into the finished product of loaves, rolls, or pastries *is* somewhat awe-inspiring! But the basics are easy and few, and there is no area of cooking that allows as much room for variation and creativity as that of baking. For information and tips on baking with yeast, see the following, "Five Things to Keep in Mind," and "Baking Tips," on page 190.

FIVE THINGS TO KEEP IN MIND ABOUT YEAST BREADS

Don't Kill the Yeast!

Yeast is a living plant organism. Since this is the stuff that is going to make your bread rise, it's essential to treat it properly. The recipes in this book call for active dry yeast, which should be stored in the refrigerator or freezer, but must be brought to room temperature before use. Dissolve it in water heated to a temperature of 105-115°F. A lower temperature will retard yeast growth — a higher temperature will kill it. If you are an experienced baker and can judge this safe temperature range by touch, fine. But if you're new to yeast baking, or just like to be sure, test the water with a candy or instant meat thermometer. Aim for a reading of 110°F., which falls right in the middle. (If you choose to substitute compressed yeast, dissolve it in lukewarm water, about 90°F.) Active dry yeast packages are stamped with an expiration date; try to use them before that date. Sometimes, yeast remains active even after the specified date. To test, or proof, the yeast, dissolve a package in ¼ cup warm water, and then add a teaspoon of sugar. This gives the yeast plants something immediate to feed upon. If you see foaming and bubbling after 5 or 10 minutes, the yeast is still active. Many bakers choose to proof the yeast each time they bake.

You Need to Knead

Kneading accomplishes the twofold purpose of distributing the yeast throughout the dough and activating the gluten in the flour. (Gluten is the protein in flour that makes dough elastic.) You can't really over-knead, but under-kneading can result in inferior bread. To knead, fold the dough in half toward you, press the doubled dough with knuckles and the heels of your hands, rotate the dough a quarter-turn, and repeat. If dough gets "bucky," i.e. develops folds that remain during kneading, slam it down hard a couple of times to relax it. Kneading bread dough is a great exercise for body and mind. As you knead, you use not only your hands, but your arms, shoulders, and torso as well. You have kneaded long enough when the dough is no longer sticky, springs back when pinched, and feels velvety smooth and slightly sweaty.

Don't Rush the Rise

Dough should not rise too fast or too much. The most important thing about letting yeast dough rise is that it not be rushed. Given optimum conditions, it will probably rise in the time indicated in many of the recipes. Yeast doughs rise best at temperatures of 75° to 85°F., and they dislike drafts. If you have a cold house, a gas oven with a pilot light is a good spot to set the dough to rise, as is an electric oven, preheated on the lowest setting for a minute and then turned off. (Repeat after an hour or so if the oven chamber cools down.) You can also set two pots of water boiling on the stove, and set the bowl of dough to rise between the pots. Or you can set the bowl of dough on the upper oven rack and put a pan of hot water on the shelf beneath it. A bowl of dough set to rise out in the room should be bundled with towels to keep off drafts. When you perceive that the dough has doubled in mass or bulk, you can test it by pressing your fingertips slightly into the dough. If the indentations remain after 10 minutes, the dough has risen enough.

To punch down the dough, plunge your fist into the center of the risen dough. This releases large pockets of gases. You can then either shape the dough into a ball and let it rise again in the bowl (for finer texture and improved flavor), or you can shape it into loaves or rolls for a final rise.

If you can't get to the dough when it's ready, and it does rise too much, all is not lost. Punch it down, knead it, and set it to rise again. Dough is very forgiving.

Is a Good Shape Important?

Not critical, but your home-baked bread is going to taste fantastic, so don't you want it to look great too? A good method of shaping dough to fit loaf pans is to roll it into a rectangular shape (about 12x18 inches for a 9x5-inch pan) with a rolling pin. This helps force out remaining air bubbles which could result in holes in the baked bread. Then roll up from the short end as tightly as possible, pinch the seam, turn the ends under, and pinch to seal them as well. Place seam-side down in the greased loaf pan, making sure the

(continued)

ends of the loaf touch the ends of the bread pan (this helps support the dough as it rises). A free-form oblong loaf can be made by rolling up the dough from the longer side and setting it on a baking sheet to rise. A round loaf is formed by kneading the dough into a smooth ball and pinching the underside firmly together.

Don't Underdo a Good Thing

Use the times in the recipes as a guide. Look for a nicely browned loaf that has shrunk slightly from the sides of the pan. Further test by turning the loaves out of the pans and tapping the bottoms with your fingertips. The loaves should sound hollow. Remove at once to a rack to cool, or put the loaves back directly on the baking shelf for a few minutes to crisp the bottom crust. Do not wrap until cooled completely, as loaves packaged while still warm readily develop mold. Well-wrapped in plastic bags, bread may be stored in breadbox, refrigerator, or, for longer periods (1-3 months) in the freezer.

See also Baking Tips, page 190.

Linda Bensinger
Dublin, NH

ALL-PURPOSE YEAST BREADS

Black Pepper Cheese Bread

Wonderfully textured and flavored bread. Also good toasted.

½ teaspoon dry mustard	2 packages active dry yeast
½ teaspoon warm water	2 tablespoons sugar
6-6½ cups flour, divided	2 tablespoons cooking oil
1 tablespoon salt	2 eggs
1 tablespoon coarsely ground black pepper, divided	1½ cups shredded Cheddar cheese melted butter
1¾ cups warm milk	kosher salt

Combine mustard and water; set aside for 10 minutes for flavor to develop. Combine 3 cups of the flour with salt and 2 teaspoons black pepper; set aside. In electric-mixer bowl, place warm milk and yeast; stir until dissolved. Mix sugar, oil, eggs, and mustard mixture. Gradually beat in flour/pepper mixture. Increase speed to medium and beat 2 minutes. Stir in cheese. With wooden spoon stir in remaining 3 cups flour, or enough to make stiff dough. Turn dough onto floured board. Knead until smooth and elastic, about 10 minutes, adding more flour if needed. Place in lightly greased bowl, turning to grease top. Cover and let rise in warm place until doubled in bulk, about 1 hour. Punch down dough; divide into two equal pieces. Knead until smooth. Place each piece in greased 9x5-inch loaf pan. Cover with light, damp towel; allow to rise in warm place until doubled in bulk, about 1 hour. Brush loaves with melted butter; sprinkle with remaining black pepper and dust with kosher salt. Bake in 375°F. oven until bread is golden and sounds hollow when tapped, about 50-55 minutes. Turn out of pans; cool on wire rack. Makes two 9x5-inch loaves.

Mrs. Nelda Young
Jacksonville, FL

Dilly Batter Bread

Lovely, fragrant round loaves with a piquant flavor. Good with a hearty soup or stew or a luncheon of chicken salad. Batter bread dough is not kneaded.

2 tablespoons butter
2 tablespoons chopped onion
1½ cups milk
2 tablespoons sugar
1 teaspoon salt
2 packages active dry yeast

½ cup warm water
1½ teaspoons crushed dried dill weed
2 teaspoons dried parsley
4½ cups flour

In small saucepan, melt the butter over medium heat, and sauté onion until tender. Add milk, sugar, and salt, and heat until warm (105-115°F.), stirring to dissolve sugar and salt. In mixer bowl, dissolve yeast in warm water. Add milk mixture, dill weed, and parsley. Add flour gradually, and beat until batter is smooth. Cover bowl, set in warm, draft-free spot, and allow batter to rise until doubled in bulk, about 1 hour. Stir down batter and turn into two greased 1½-quart casserole dishes. Let rise for 30 minutes. Bake in 350°F. oven for 30-45 minutes, or until nicely browned and hollow-sounding when tapped. Turn out of dishes and cool on racks. Makes 2 round loaves.

Cathy J. Demberg
Catskill, NY

Quick Oatmeal Molasses Bread

Close-grained and somewhat chewy, with a definite molasses taste. It's quick because there's only one rise.

1 cup rolled oats
½ cup wheat germ
3 tablespoons shortening
3 teaspoons salt
¾ cup molasses

3 cups boiling water
2 tablespoons brown sugar
2 packages active dry yeast
½ cup warm water
7 cups flour

Combine first five ingredients, then stir in boiling water. Let cool until warm. Combine brown sugar and yeast in pint measuring cup with warm water. Let stand 10 minutes until foamed to top of cup. Stir into molasses mixture, then beat in flour, 2 cups at a time, until you have a sticky, roll-like dough. Grease your hands well and knead in bowl for 8-10 minutes, or until dough is shiny — granules in dough are oatmeal. Turn into two greased 9x5-inch loaf pans, and allow to rise until doubled in size. Bake in 350°F. oven for 45 minutes, or until done. Makes two 9x5-inch loaves.

"Charley"
Avon, CT

Poppy-Seed Batter Bread

Soft, moist, and loaded with poppy seeds. A very special flavor in an easy, no-knead bread.

1 cup warm water	2 teaspoons salt
1 package active dry yeast	3½-4 cups flour
2 tablespoons butter	1 egg white
2 tablespoons poppy seeds	1 tablespoon water
2 tablespoons sugar	poppy seeds

In large mixing bowl, sprinkle yeast on warm water, let stand a few minutes, and stir until dissolved. Add butter, poppy seeds, sugar, and salt. Stir in 2 cups of the flour, and beat until well blended. Stir in enough additional flour to make a soft dough. Cover, and let rise in warm place until doubled in size, about 1 hour. Stir down. Spread evenly in greased 9x5-inch loaf pan. (This is best accomplished by using buttered fingers.) Let rise uncovered in warm place until dough just barely reaches top of pan, 20 minutes or so. (Do not allow to rise above top edge.) Beat together egg white and water and brush gently on top of loaf. Sprinkle with poppy seeds. Bake at 375°F. for about 30 minutes, until loaf sounds hollow when tapped. Makes one 9x5-inch loaf.

Catharine Bellinger
Hummelstown, PA

Polish Dark Rye Bread

An heirloom recipe from Poland featured at the 1983 Connecticut Jubilee, a free summer series of ethnic festivals held at the Old State House in Hartford.

2 cups milk, scalded	½ cup warm water
2 tablespoons butter	4 cups rye flour
2 tablespoons sugar	2½ cups whole-wheat flour
1 teaspoon salt	2 tablespoons caraway seeds
1 package active dry yeast	(melted butter)

Pour scalded milk over butter, sugar, and salt in large bowl; stir. Cool. Dissolve yeast in warm water. Add softened yeast and 3 cups of the rye flour to milk mixture. Beat thoroughly; then beat in remaining rye flour. Cover and let rise in warm place until doubled in bulk. Turn onto well-floured surface. Knead in whole-wheat flour and caraway seeds. Knead until dough is smooth. Divide dough in half and shape into two round or oblong loaves. Place loaves in greased pans. Cover and let rise in warm place until doubled in bulk. Bake at 450°F. for 15 minutes; reduce heat to 350°F., and bake 35-40 minutes longer. For a tender crust, brush with melted butter 5 minutes before done. Makes 2 large loaves.

Joan Z. Godlewski
The Connecticut Jubilee Bread Cookbook

Sheepherder's Bread

Moist and chewy, somewhat coarse in texture. Fun to serve at a buffet supper with cold cuts, chili, cheese, and what-have-you. Present the round loaf on a big bread board. Cut the bread in half, place cut-side down, and let people slice to suit their appetites. Use stone ground flour, if available, for best flavor.

1 package active dry yeast	½ cup cooking oil
2 cups warm water	2 teaspoons salt
¼ cup sugar	7 cups flour (approx.)

In large bowl, dissolve yeast in water. Stir in sugar, and let stand 10-15 minutes until bubbly. Add oil, salt, and 4 cups of the flour. Mix well. Mix in additional flour to form stiff dough. Turn out onto floured surface, and knead until smooth and elastic. Place in greased bowl, turn to grease top, cover, and let rise in a warm spot until doubled, about 1 hour. Punch down, shape into smooth ball, and place in greased 5-quart dutch oven. Cover, and allow to rise until top of dough is just about even with top edge of dutch oven. Preheat oven to 375°F. Grease lid of dutch oven well, and set in place over dough. Bake 10-15 minutes, until dough begins to push up the lid. Remove lid, and continue baking 30-35 minutes longer, until golden brown and hollow-sounding when tapped. Turn out onto rack to cool. Makes 1 loaf, 10 inches in diameter and 6 inches high, equal to two 9x5 loaves.

Joyce Brandt
Fennimore, WI

Mae's Shredded-Wheat Bread

Even the satiny beige dough smells great. Slightly sweet — good for toast or sandwiches.

2 cups boiling water	3 tablespoons butter
2 large shredded-wheat biscuits	1 package active dry yeast
2 teaspoons salt	¼ cup warm water
¼ cup sugar	6-7 cups flour
¼ cup molasses	

Pour boiling water over shredded wheat in large bowl. Add salt, sugar, molasses, and butter. Stir well and cool to lukewarm. Dissolve yeast in ¼ cup warm water. Let stand 5 minutes, and add to shredded-wheat mixture. Stir in enough flour to make a stiff dough. Turn out onto floured board and knead well, until smooth and elastic. Place in greased bowl, turn, cover, and let rise in warm draft-free place until doubled, about 1 hour and 30 minutes. Punch down, divide in half, and form into two loaves. Place in two greased 9x5-inch loaf pans, cover, and let rise until doubled, 45 minutes to 1 hour. Bake in 375°F. oven about 30 minutes, or until loaves sound hollow when tapped. Turn out onto wire rack to cool. Makes two 9x5-inch loaves.

Linda Long
Reading, MA

Sugar and Spice Bread

Pretty loaves that are subtly spiced and not too sweet, with a fine, almost cake-like texture. Especially good toasted.

2 packages active dry yeast
½ cup warm water
1½ cups milk
½ cup butter
⅓ cup sugar
1 teaspoon salt
2 eggs

1 egg, separated
1 teaspoon cinnamon
¼-½ teaspoon nutmeg
5½-6½ cups flour, divided
1⅓ cups wheat germ
1 tablespoon wheat germ

In large bowl, sprinkle yeast on warm water. Let stand a few minutes, then stir to dissolve. Heat milk, butter, sugar, and salt until warm. Add to yeast mixture. Stir in 2 eggs and one yolk, cinnamon, nutmeg, and 3 cups of the flour. Beat until well blended. Stir in 1⅓ cups wheat germ and remaining flour to form a soft dough. Knead on floured surface until smooth and elastic, about 10 minutes. Place in greased bowl, turn to grease top, cover, and let rise until doubled, about 1 hour. Punch down; divide dough in half. Divide each half into two ropes. Twist together and fit in greased 9x5-inch loaf pans by tucking ends under. Cover and let rise until doubled, 45-50 minutes. Brush with beaten egg white, and sprinkle with 1 tablespoon wheat germ. Bake at 350°F. for 35-45 minutes, until loaves sound hollow when tapped. Cover with foil last 10 minutes to prevent over-browning. Remove from pans and cool completely on rack. Makes two 9x5-inch loaves.

Lucy and Sarah Grandchamp
Coventry, RI

White Bread

Perfect firm-textured white bread for sandwiches or toast. Do not allow to rise too fast, or the texture will be affected.

½ cup milk
3 tablespoons sugar
3 tablespoons butter
2 teaspoons salt

1½ cups warm water
1 package active dry yeast
6-7 cups flour (approx.)

Combine milk, sugar, butter, and salt in 1-quart saucepan, and heat to warm, stirring to dissolve butter. In warmed mixing bowl, combine warm water and yeast. Let stand a few minutes, then stir to dissolve yeast completely. Add milk mixture to bowl, along with enough of the flour to make a stiff dough. Turn onto floured board, and knead until smooth and elastic. Place dough in greased bowl, turn to grease top, cover, and allow to rise until doubled in bulk, about 1 hour. Punch down dough and divide in half. Form into two loaves and place in greased 9x5-inch loaf pans. Cover, and allow to rise again until doubled, about 1 hour. Bake in 375°F. oven for 30 minutes, or until loaves sound hollow when tapped. Remove from pans and cool completely on racks. Makes two 9x5-inch loaves.

Kitty Deardorff
Harrisburg, PA

Whole-Wheat Bread

Dark and dense with a nutty-sweet flavor. Makes knockout toast and grilled sandwiches. White flour may be substituted for up to half the total amount of whole-wheat flour.

2 cups warm water
1 tablespoon brown sugar
2 packages active dry yeast
¾ cup powdered milk
⅓ cup brown sugar, packed

2 teaspoons salt
⅓ cup cooking oil
6-7 cups whole-wheat flour
butter

In large warmed mixing bowl, combine warm water, 1 tablespoon brown sugar, and yeast. Stir to dissolve, and allow to stand and bubble about 10 minutes. Add powdered milk, ⅓ cup brown sugar, salt, and oil to the bowl, with enough flour to make a stiff dough. Turn out onto floured board, and knead until smooth and elastic. Place dough in greased bowl, turn to grease top, cover, and let rise in a warm spot until doubled, about 1 hour. Punch dough down and divide in half. Shape each half into loaf and place in greased 9x5-inch pans. (Or shape dough halves into two round loaves, and place on a greased baking sheet.) Allow loaves to rise until doubled, approximately 30 minutes. Preheat oven to 400°F. and bake bread for 15 minutes. Reduce heat to 350°F., and bake about 30 minutes longer, until loaves sound hollow when tapped. Turn loaves out onto racks immediately, butter top crusts, and allow to cool completely before slicing. Makes two 9x5-inch loaves.

Lee Schaefer
New Berlin, WI

SWEET YEAST BREADS AND COFFEE CAKES

Sweet yeast-raised breads are a real treat, well worth the extra effort involved (as compared with quick breads). Make any one of these innovative delights for a group occasion — neighborhood coffee, community breakfast, or brunch — or for Christmas presents, and your fate is sealed. You'll have to go on making it forever! Perhaps, if you are lucky, you'll just be pressed for the recipe. See Baking Tips on page 190 if you are new to baking. Even experienced bakers may well find a time-saver here.

Almond Kringle

Sweet and altogether irresistible. You can use a 12-ounce can of "Solo" almond filling rather than making your own.

Dough:
4 cups unbleached flour
3 tablespoons sugar
1 teaspoon salt
1 cup butter, softened slightly
3 eggs, separated
1 cup milk, scalded

1 package active dry yeast

Filling:
½ cup butter, softened
1 cup sugar
7 ounces almond paste
3-4 tablespoons milk

In large bowl, blend flour, sugar, and salt on low speed of electric mixer. Add butter in 1-tablespoon chunks, and cut in, using low speed. In small bowl, beat egg yolks lightly. Cool milk to lukewarm, add yeast, and stir to dissolve. Add yolks. Add to butter mixture. Mix on low speed until soft dough forms. Do not overbeat. Put dough in clean dry bowl. Cover with plastic wrap (right down on surface of dough), and refrigerate overnight or up to 48 hours.

Make filling. In mixing bowl, cream butter and sugar until fluffy. Beat in almond paste a little at a time, and then add milk. Beat until smooth. Makes enough filling for all four kringles.

Divide dough into quarters. Work with one part at a time, keeping the others refrigerated. On lightly floured board or pastry cloth, roll dough into 8x20-inch rectangle, with 8-inch end facing you. Spread filling down center 3 inches of dough to within an inch of each end.

In dry, grease-free bowl, beat egg whites until stiff. Spread one quarter of the beaten whites evenly over kringle filling. Fold one long edge over filling, then the other, so that there is a 1½-inch overlap of dough covering filling. Brush surfaces to be joined with water to seal overlap. Gently lift kringle and

(continued)

place seam-side down on ungreased baking sheet, carefully bending it into a crescent. With sharp knife, cut slit down center of top crust, end to end. Cover with towel and let rise for 30 minutes. Repeat procedure above for each of the other three kringles. After each has risen for 30 minutes, bake kringles in 375°F. oven for 18-20 minutes. Prepare icing while kringles bake.

Icing:

1½ cups confectioner's sugar
2-3 tablespoons milk

¼ teaspoon vanilla
sliced or slivered almonds

In mixing bowl, beat together all ingredients except almonds to form thin icing. As you take each kringle from oven, gently press sides in over filling with clean hot pad or paper toweling (they will open as they bake due to the action of the beaten egg white). Spread with icing while hot. Sprinkle almonds down center. Makes 4 kringles.

Ann Brandt
Fennimore, WI

BREAD STARTER WITH HOPS

This was what great-grandmother had to use to raise her bread. Uniform, commercially available yeast was undreamed of then.

½ cup hops
2 cups hot water
1 potato (size of an egg)

1 tablespoon flour
1½ teaspoons sugar
1½ teaspoons salt

Brew hops in water for 20 minutes. Drain, reserving liquid. Grate potato, and pour hops liquid over it. Add remaining ingredients. Let set until mixture becomes sour and bubbly (ferments). Use 1 cupful to make bread.*

Grace Hornberger
Macungie, PA

* Use 1 cup for each package active dry yeast.

Cranberry Bread

Both tangy and sweet. Studded with cranberries and nuts and drizzled with glaze, it's a festive holiday treat.

juice of 2 medium oranges (reserve 2-3 tablespoons for glaze) plus water to total ⅔ cup liquid
¾ cup butter
1 cup rolled oats, quick or regular
1 cup sugar
4 teaspoons salt
grated rind (zest) of 2 medium oranges
½ cup warm water
½ teaspoon sugar

3 packages active dry yeast
2 large eggs
1 cup chopped walnuts
6½ cups flour (approx.)
2 cups chopped fresh cranberries
melted butter

Glaze:

1 cup confectioner's sugar
1 tablespoon butter, softened
orange juice

Place ⅔ cup orange juice/water with butter in small saucepan, and heat just to boiling. Pour over oats, sugar, salt, and orange rind in a large bowl. Mix well, and allow to cool to warm. Combine warm water, sugar, and yeast in 2-cup measuring cup or bowl. Let sit for a few minutes, stir to dissolve yeast completely, then let stand until foaming. Add yeast, eggs, nuts, and 2 cups of the flour and mix well by hand or machine. Stir in about 4 more cups of flour. Scrape mixture (it will be sticky) out onto lightly floured board, and knead in small amounts of additional flour as needed. Knead until dough is elastic and only slightly sticky. Place dough in a greased bowl, turn to grease top, cover, and put in warm, draft-free place to rise until nearly doubled, 1½-2 hours.

Punch down dough, and transfer to a larger bowl. Knead in chopped cranberries, a little at a time, until well incorporated into dough. Turn dough out onto floured board and divide into quarters. Roll each quarter into a rope about 10 inches long. Twist each pair of ropes together, fold ends under, and place in two well-greased 9x5-inch loaf pans. Brush tops of loaves with melted butter, and let rise in warm place until almost doubled. Bake 15 minutes at 375°F., cover loosely with aluminum foil, and continue baking about 30 minutes longer until loaves sound hollow when tapped lightly. (Bottoms and sides of loaves have a tendency to burn, so do not overbake.) Remove from pans and cool completely on racks. Combine confectioner's sugar, butter, and reserved orange juice to make a thin glaze. Drizzle glaze over cooled loaves. Makes two 9x5-inch loaves.

Grace Hornberger
Macungie, PA

·Heckman·

Aunt Milly's Currant Bread

Great texture and flavor are developed from the sponge step and multiple risings. Give loaves of this unusual bread as Christmas gifts, and advise the recipients it is best toasted. Freezes well.

1 medium potato, peeled	2 teaspoons salt
1⅓ cups water	3 tablespoons shortening
1 tablespoon sugar	1½ cups dried currants
1 package active dry yeast	⅔ cup sugar
8 cups flour (approx.)	⅓ cup butter, melted
1⅓ cups milk, scalded	

Simmer the potato in water until tender. Drain water into large bowl. Mash or rice potato, and add to bowl. Stir in 1 tablespoon sugar, and let mixture cool to warm. Sprinkle yeast over and allow to dissolve. Stir in 1 cup of the flour, cover bowl, and let mixture stand about 30 minutes, until bubbly. Combine scalded milk, salt, and shortening, and stir to dissolve. When milk mixture has cooled to warm, add to yeast sponge. A couple of cups at a time, stir in about 6 more cups flour to make a stiff dough. Turn dough out onto floured board, and knead in additional flour until dough kneads easily without sticking. Knead until smooth and elastic. Put dough in greased bowl, turn to grease top, cover, and let rise in a warm spot until doubled. Punch down dough. (At this point, if you have the time, allow dough to rise again in bowl until doubled, as this makes the texture and flavor even better.) Transfer dough to a larger bowl. Combine currants, sugar, and melted butter. Knead gradually into dough in bowl until well incorporated. (Dough will feel sticky at this point.) Cover bowl, and allow to rise until doubled.

Punch down dough, and turn out onto lightly floured board. Pat a little flour onto dough to make it easier to handle. Divide dough into quarters and shape into loaves. Place in greased 4x8-inch loaf pans. Let rise until doubled, brush with melted butter, and bake at 375°F. for 20-30 minutes, until loaves sound hollow when tapped. Remove from pans and cool on racks. Makes four 8x4-inch loaves.

C. Irene Schovel
Hegins, PA

BAKING TIPS

1. For bread baking, use unbleached all-purpose or bread flour rather than bleached.

2. Store whole-wheat flour and wheat germ in the refrigerator or freezer; higher fat content affects keeping quality.

3. Flours like rye and soy are used in combination with wheat flour because they lack sufficient gluten.

4. Rule of thumb: Usually a ratio of 3:1 (cups of flour to liquid) is needed to produce bread dough; this results in a 1-pound loaf, approximately.

5. Humidity can affect the ability of flour to absorb liquids; you may need more flour on damp days.

6. To dissolve active dry yeast, sprinkle it over warm water and allow it to stand 3-4 minutes before stirring. "Warm" water should be 105-115°F.

7. 1 package active dry yeast equals 1 scant tablespoon (2½ teaspoons) dry yeast or one ⅔- or ⅗-ounce cake of compressed yeast.

8. Larger quantities of active dry yeast can be stored in the freezer for long periods of time and will remain free-flowing; fill a small jar and keep it in the refrigerator for regular use.

9. A new strain of dry yeast has been developed which is supposed to cut rising time by 50%; check manufacturers' instructions for use.

10. Save the water in which you have boiled potatoes, and use it in bread baking; potato water aids yeast action, improves keeping quality, and adds moistness, compared to bread made with plain water.

11. Scalding milk was always done to kill bacteria which could hinder yeast action, so unless you're using raw milk straight from the cow, it's only necessary to heat to warm when using pasteurized milk, dried milk solids, or canned milk, but scalding does help melt fat.

12. Kneaded dough is greased to keep a dry crust from forming, which would prevent the dough from rising.

13. Stoneware, ceramic, or glass bowls are better for rising than metal or plastic because they retain warmth.

14. Choose a rising bowl that is about twice the volume of the unrisen dough.

15. A deep rising bowl with a smaller diameter is better because the dough doesn't have to work as hard to rise.

16. If dough is very elastic and difficult to work with, let it rest, covered, 10-15 minutes; this allows the gluten to relax.

17. Very soft doughs can be chilled to facilitate their handling.

18. Braid soft doughs by starting in the middle and working toward each end.

19. Cover freshly baked loaves with a clean dish towel to soften crusts.

20. If you slice a loaf of bread before freezing, you'll always be able to get a slice or two without thawing the whole loaf.

21. Make your own croutons from heels of loaves and leftover rolls. Dice bread, spread on baking sheet, place in 250°F. oven until crisp; sprinkle or toss croutons with desired flavorings (butter, herbs, cheese, etc.).

22. The dough for rolls, sweet rolls, coffee cakes, etc. is softer than bread dough. Use just enough flour to prevent sticking. Less kneading is required. Bake rolls apart for crusty sides and touching in the pan for soft sides.

23. Here's how to make the various different shapes of rolls.

Bowknots: Roll dough into rectangle about ⅜ inch thick and 10 inches long on one side. Cut 10-inch strips about ¾ inch wide. Roll each strip lightly and tie into loose bow.

Butterhorns or Crescents: Roll dough out into circle ¼ inch thick. Cut wedges (pizza cutter works well), then roll up wedges, starting at wide end. Tip of rolled wedge should be on underside. Curve rolled wedges slightly for crescents.

Cloverleaves: Put three small balls of dough in each greased muffin cup.

Clusters: Make balls of dough, put in round cake pans.

Fan Tans: Cut strips of dough about 1½ inches wide. Stack strips six high, and cut into 1½-inch lengths. Stand on cut edges in muffin cups.

Parker House: Roll out dough about ½ inch thick. Cut with 2-inch round cookie cutter, and fold over in half, moistening bottom half with damp pastry brush, so fold will hold.

24. To cut butter into a dry mixture, cut softened butter into quarter-tablespoons, then beat with electric mixer on low until well blended.

25. For best results, have eggs at room temperature.

Linda Bensinger
Dublin, NH

Delicate Pastry

The name says it all. While the finished product looks fancy and complicated, it's unbelievably easy to do. Serve at breakfast, brunch, or church coffee hour.

1 package active dry yeast
¼ cup warm water
1 teaspoon sugar
2 cups flour
½ teaspoon salt
¾ cup butter
2 eggs, separated

¼ teaspoon cream of tartar
½ cup sugar
1 teaspoon pure vanilla extract (or almond extract)
½-1 cup chopped nuts (walnuts, pecans, or almonds)
confectioner's sugar

Dissolve yeast in warm water, add 1 teaspoon sugar, and set aside for 10 minutes. Combine flour and salt in mixing bowl, and cut in butter as for pie crust, until mixture looks like coarse meal. Stir in egg yolks. Pour this mixture over pastry mixture, and stir with fork. Divide dough in half. On floured board or pastry cloth, roll each half into 9x13-inch rectangle.

Make meringue. Beat egg whites until frothy, then add cream of tartar. Add sugar gradually as you continue to beat egg whites until stiff. Mix in vanilla (or almond) extract. Spread half the meringue on each rectangle of dough, and sprinkle each with ¼-½ cup chopped nuts. Roll up from long side like a jelly roll. Pinch ends. Put seam-side down on lightly greased baking sheet. Leave several inches of space between pastries as they will expand while baking. Cut lengthwise down the center of each pastry, cutting through all but the bottom layer. Bake at 375°F. for 22 minutes. Press edges down over filling, and carefully remove from baking sheet and sprinkle with confectioner's sugar. Makes 2 pastries, each about 13 inches long by 3 inches wide.

Mrs. Grace Chatterton
Portland, OR

Schneken

This German delicacy (the name means "snails") somewhere between Danish and puff pastry is flaky, sweet, and crunchy. After baking, schneken can be frozen, wrapped in wax paper and placed in box. To thaw, unwrap, place on plate, and leave uncovered on counter for a short while.

½ pound sweet butter, softened
5 egg yolks
¾ cup evaporated milk
4⅓ cups flour
1 package active dry yeast
¾ cup finely chopped nuts
1½ cups sugar

extra sugar

Glaze:
1½ cups confectioner's sugar
½ cup water
few drops vanilla

(continued)

Make dough a day ahead, and refrigerate overnight. Cream butter and beat in egg yolks, one by one. Add evaporated milk. In separate bowl, combine 3 cups of the flour and yeast. Add this mixture gradually to butter mixture while beating. Work in remaining flour by hand, since it will be a very hard dough. Place dough in bowl, and flatten dough smooth. Cover with plastic wrap, right down on top of dough. Cover bowl with lid or plate and refrigerate overnight.

Next day, combine ½ cup of the chopped nuts with 1 cup of the sugar. On a pastry board or cloth, arrange sugar/nut mixture in a 6-inch circle, and place half the dough on top. Refrigerate remaining dough until needed. Roll out dough, keeping sugar/nut mixture underneath. Sprinkle extra sugar over dough to coat the upper surface. Roll dough as thin and as long as possible, which can be a slightly sticky process. Beginning with long edge, roll up dough as tightly as possible. Carefully cut into ½-inch slices, and place about 1 inch apart on lightly greased cookie sheet. Repeat the process with remaining chopped nuts, sugar, and dough. Allow to rest uncovered in a draft-free spot for an hour. Bake at 350°F. for 10-12 minutes, or until golden. Do not allow to brown. Remove from baking sheet, and when still slightly warm, brush with glaze. Makes about 6 dozen.

Dina M. Thomas
Lanoka Harbor, NJ

Swedish Coffee Braids or Loaves

The distinctive taste of cardamom is subtle in this fine-textured, sweet bread. Plain or toasted, it's a real treat.

2 cups milk	1 package active dry yeast
¾ cup butter	¼ cup warm water
1 cup sugar	½ teaspoon salt
8 cardamom seeds, shelled and	7-8 cups flour
pulverized (equals	
approximately ½ teaspoon	
ground cardamom)	

Heat milk, then add butter, sugar, and cardamom. Cool to lukewarm. Dissolve yeast in ¼ cup warm water. Add to first mixture. Add salt and enough flour to make a stiff dough. Knead until smooth and elastic. Put in greased bowl, turn to grease top, cover, and let rise until doubled, about 90 minutes. Punch down. Knead again, and divide dough in half. For braids, divide each half into thirds, and roll each third into a rope. Braid, and place braids on lightly greased baking sheet. For loaves, form each half into a loaf, and place each in greased 9x5-inch loaf pan. Let rise again until doubled, about 45 minutes. Bake at 350°F. for about 40 minutes, until golden brown and hollow-sounding when tapped. Remove from baking sheet or pans, and cool completely on racks. Makes two braids or two 9x5-inch loaves.

Joan Knutson Lund
Dublin, NH

Streusel Coffee Cake

Moist, crumb-topped yeast cake made plain or with blueberries or apples. You'll love all the variations for breakfast or coffee klatsch.

1 package active dry yeast
¼ cup warm water
½ cup butter, softened
¾ cup sugar
2 teaspoons salt
2 eggs
1 cup warm mashed potatoes
4 cups flour

Streusel Topping:
1 cup flour
1 cup sugar
½ cup butter, softened
(blueberries)
(melted butter)
(thinly sliced apples)
(cinnamon)

Soften yeast in warm water and set aside. Cream butter and sugar until light and fluffy. Beat in salt, eggs, and mashed potatoes. Add softened yeast, and stir to blend. Gradually add flour, beating to form stiff dough. Turn into greased bowl, grease top of dough, cover, and let rise until doubled, about 2 hours. (Or, refrigerate to rise overnight.) Punch down, divide dough in half, and knead each half for several turns on lightly floured board until smooth. Cover and let rest 10 minutes. Press each half into greased 9-inch square pan.

Make streusel topping by mixing flour with sugar, and cutting in butter to form crumbs. For plain coffee cake, sprinkle topping over dough, and let rise until almost doubled. Bake at 350°F. for 20 minutes. Makes two 9-inch square coffee cakes.

Blueberry variation: Sprinkle dough with fresh (or frozen without syrup and thawed) blueberries. Press them lightly into dough. Top with streusel and let rise until almost doubled. Bake.

Apple variation: Brush top of dough with melted butter and let rise until almost doubled. Gently press thin, pared apple slices into dough. Top with streusel and sprinkle with cinnamon. Bake.

Sandra Taylor
Austin, TX

YEAST ROLLS, BUNS, AND A PIZZA

Hard-to-find recipes for items one often wishes to make from scratch — hamburger rolls (the real thing), hard rolls, sweet rolls, (including that Philadelphia classic, sticky buns), and even homemade pizza dough — along with superb dinner rolls that can make your reputation overnight. Again, see Baking Tips on page 190 for useful advice.

Carrot Cloverleaf Rolls

Pale-orange rolls flecked with bits of carrot and slightly sweet. A handsome dinner roll.

4 medium carrots, cooked, drained *well,* and mashed (about 1 cup)
1 package active dry yeast
¼ cup warm water
½ cup milk

½ cup brown sugar, packed
¼ cup butter
1-2 teaspoons salt
5-6 cups flour
melted butter

Put mashed carrots in bowl, and cool until warm. Combine yeast and warm water, let stand a few minutes, and stir to dissolve yeast completely. Set aside. Heat milk, brown sugar, butter, and salt to warm. Add this mixture and dissolved yeast to mashed carrots. Mix well. Add enough flour to make a stiff dough, turn out onto lightly floured surface, and knead well. Place in greased bowl, turn once, cover, and let rise until doubled, about 1 hour. Punch down, let rest 10 minutes. Divide dough into 24 equal parts. Shape each part into three small balls. Place each set of these small balls in one cup of a greased muffin pan. Let rise again until almost doubled — about 30-45 minutes. Bake in 375°F. oven for 15-20 minutes. Brush tops with melted butter. Cool on racks. Makes about 2 dozen rolls.

Barbara Sedlak
Wauwatosa, WI

Sticky Buns

Marvelous texture. A gooey enough confection to satisfy any sweet tooth. Serve with tea, for "coffees," or as a delicious surprise at dinner. Wonderful split, toasted, and drenched with melted butter.

1 package active dry yeast
½ teaspoon sugar
½ cup warm water
¾ cup milk, scalded and cooled to
    lukewarm
3½ cups flour, divided
½ cup granulated sugar
½ cup butter, softened
1 teaspoon salt

1 cup brown sugar, packed
1½-2 teaspoons cinnamon
(1 cup chopped pecans, slivered
    almonds, or raisins)

Icing:

1 egg white
2 cups sifted confectioner's sugar
½ teaspoon pure vanilla extract
milk as needed

Dissolve yeast and ½ teaspoon sugar in warm water in large bowl. Let stand until bubbly. Stir in lukewarm milk. Stir in 1 cup of the flour. Cover and let rise 30 minutes. Stir in ½ cup sugar, ¼ cup of the butter, salt, and 2 more cups flour. Turn dough onto lightly floured surface. Knead in remaining ½ cup of flour. Knead until smooth and elastic, about 10 minutes. Put in greased bowl, turn dough to grease top, cover bowl, and let rise in warm place until doubled, about 1 hour. Roll dough on lightly floured surface into 12x18-inch rectangle. Spread with remaining butter. Mix brown sugar and cinnamon together. Sprinkle on top of butter. Sprinkle optional nuts or raisins over dough. Roll up, beginning at longer edge. Cut into eighteen 1-inch slices. Butter two round 9-inch or two square 8-inch pans. Place nine rolls in each pan. Let rise until doubled, 30 minutes to 1 hour. Heat oven to 350°F. Bake rolls 20 minutes. Invert immediately onto serving plate. Combine icing ingredients and spread on rolls while still hot. Cool. Makes 18 sticky buns.

Colleen Selmer
Jaffrey, NH

Crusty Casserolls

No-knead dinner rolls with buttery bottoms and crusty tops. Wonderful, and a snap to make. A Yankee prizewinner.

⅔ cup milk
1 tablespoon sugar
½ teaspoon salt
6 tablespoons butter, melted

1 package active dry yeast
⅓ cup warm water
2 cups sifted flour

(continued)

Scald milk. Stir in sugar, salt, and 1 tablespoon of the butter. Set aside to cool. In large bowl, sprinkle yeast over water and stir to dissolve. Stir in lukewarm milk mixture and flour. Beat until smooth and elastic — about 50 strokes. Brush top lightly with a little melted butter. Cover with plastic wrap or damp towel, and let rise in warm place until doubled in bulk — about 25 minutes. Pour half of remaining melted butter into shallow 1½-quart casserole dish or 9-inch square baking pan. Stir dough down. Drop by large tablespoons into melted butter in casserole dish or pan. Spoon remaining butter over rolls. Cover, and let rise until doubled — about 25 minutes. Bake in 400°F. oven for 20-25 minutes, or until done. Serve in casserole dish or pan, slightly warm. Makes about 16.

Mrs. M. E. Rowland
Westlake, OH

Clustered Cinnamon-Nut Rolls

Sweet and tender pull-apart yeast rolls with a sparkling hint of lemon are encased in a crispy sugar/nut coating. For lemon-nut rolls, simply omit the cinnamon.

1 cup milk	2 eggs, lightly beaten
½ cup butter	grated rind of 1 lemon
½ cup sugar	5⅓ cups flour
1½ teaspoons salt	⅔ cup butter, melted
2 packages active dry yeast	1⅓ cups sugar
½ cup warm water	1 cup finely chopped nuts
1 teaspoon sugar	1 tablespoon cinnamon

Heat milk, butter, ½ cup sugar, and salt in saucepan until butter is melted. Cool to lukewarm (105-115°F.). In 2-cup measure dissolve yeast in warm water, add 1 teaspoon sugar, and let stand 5 minutes. Combine milk mixture and yeast in large bowl. Add eggs and lemon rind. Mix thoroughly. Beat in approximately 5 cups of flour. Turn out onto floured surface, and knead until smooth and elastic, adding a little additional flour if necessary. (Do not use too much flour; try to keep dough soft.) Place in greased bowl, turn to grease top, cover, and place in a warm, draft-free spot to rise until doubled in bulk — 1 hour to 1 hour and 30 minutes.

Punch dough down, and cut into quarters. Divide each quarter into 12 equal pieces. Shape each piece into a ball. Place melted butter in small bowl. Combine sugar, nuts, and cinnamon in another small bowl. Dip each ball of dough into melted butter, then roll in sugar/nut mixture. (Using a pair of forks for the butter dip and a separate pair for the sugar/nut mixture works well and keeps fingers clean.) Place 16 balls in each of three greased 9-inch round or 8-inch square pans, starting at outer edges and working toward center. Let rolls rise until almost doubled — about 30-60 minutes. Bake at 375°F. for 15-20 minutes, until just lightly browned. Cool in pans on racks. Serve in pans, or invert rolls onto a plate, then invert again onto a serving plate. (Rolls separate *very* easily.) Makes 48 rolls (3 pull-apart coffee cakes).

Pearl Just
Wauwatosa, WI

Delicious Rolls

Brown-sugar sweetness and cornmeal crunch make these rolls really special. When they taste them, people invariably say, "These are delicious rolls!" For a slightly softer dough, add the optional egg.

½ cup cornmeal
½ cup rolled oats
½ cup brown sugar, packed
2 teaspoons salt
3 tablespoons butter

1½ cups boiling water
1 package active dry yeast
¼ cup warm water
(1 egg, lightly beaten)
5 cups flour (approx.)

Put the cornmeal, oats, brown sugar, and salt in mixing bowl. Melt butter in boiling water and pour over mixture in bowl. Stir, and let cool to warm. Dissolve yeast in warm water, and stir in. Add flour to make a rather stiff dough (add optional egg if desired); knead until smooth and elastic. Put into greased bowl, turn to grease top, cover with plastic wrap, and let rise in warm place until doubled — about 1 hour and 30 minutes. Punch down, and let rise a second time until doubled in bulk — about 60 minutes. Form into rolls of desired shape (page 191). Place on lightly greased baking sheets, and let rise until doubled — about 30-60 minutes. Bake at 350°F. about 15 minutes, until just lightly browned. Reheat to serve. Makes about 3 dozen rolls.

Mrs. Joseph Tschetter
Whitehall, WI

Dinner Rolls

Chilling makes it possible to handle this very soft dough with ease, and the rolls that result are incredibly light and buttery.

1 cup milk
2 tablespoons sugar
1½ teaspoons salt
¼ cup butter
1 package active dry yeast

¼ cup warm water
1 egg, beaten
3½ cups sifted flour
butter

Heat milk just to boiling. Stir in sugar, salt, and butter. Cool to lukewarm. Dissolve yeast in warm water. Pour milk mixture into bowl, and add yeast. Add beaten egg, and mix. Stir in flour. Place dough in greased bowl; brush top with melted butter. Cover bowl and put in refrigerator. Chill the dough for at least 2 hours, or overnight. Scrape dough out onto lightly floured surface, sprinkle with a little flour to prevent sticking, and roll out to approximately ¼-inch thickness. Cut with round cookie cutter. (Knead scraps together, roll out, and repeat). Place small pat of butter just off-center on each circle of dough; fold in half. Place rolls in two greased 7x11-inch baking pans, allowing some room for the dough to expand. Let rise until doubled, about 1 hour. Bake at 350°F. for 15-20 minutes. Makes about 2 dozen rolls.

Colleen Selmer
Jaffrey, NH

Pizza Dough

A soft crust with the freshest possible pizzeria flavor. If you prefer your pizza thick, make one crust rather than two.

1 cup water
2 tablespoons butter
1 teaspoon sugar
1 teaspoon salt
1 package active dry yeast
3 cups flour

olive oil
shredded Mozzarella cheese
(other toppings — sausage or
    hamburger bits, green peppers,
    mushrooms, *et al.*)

In 2-quart saucepan, heat water, butter, sugar, and salt. Stir until butter has melted. Cool slightly until temperature on candy thermometer is 105-115°F. Sprinkle yeast over mixture, allow to sit for several minutes, then stir to dissolve completely. Stir in flour. Turn dough onto lightly floured board, and knead briefly until smooth and elastic. Grease 2-quart bowl with olive oil, put dough in, and turn to grease top. Cover, and put in a warm place to rise until doubled — about 45 minutes. Punch dough down, and divide in half. Roll out on lightly floured surface to form one or two pizza crusts — use round pans 12-14 inches in diameter, or 10x15-inch rectangles. Do not be afraid to roll dough thin. Place dough in oiled pans (use olive oil). Add sauce (see below), shredded mozzarella cheese, and your favorite toppings. Prepare and bake first pizza. While this is baking, prepare the second pizza. Bake at 450°F. on lowest rack of oven for approximately 15-20 minutes. Length of baking time will depend on amount of topping. Watch closely after 12-15 minutes. Bake until hot and bubbling. Makes 2 thin pizzas, or 1 thick one.

Pizza Sauce:
6-ounce can tomato paste
8-ounce can tomato sauce

1½ teaspoons Pizza or Italian
    seasoning*
3-4 teaspoons sugar

Mix all ingredients well, and let stand to allow flavor to develop while dough is rising. Enough sauce for 2 pizzas. Spread on dough.

Linda Bensinger
Dublin, NH

*An excellent blend is available from The Spice House, 1102 N. 3rd Street, Milwaukee, Wisconsin 53202, which sells spices, herbs, and seasonings by mail. Send $1.00 for price list.

Hamburger Buns

Real *hamburger buns, but far better than those you can buy. Texture is like fresh home-made bread.*

1½ cups scalded milk	¼ cup warm water
¼ cup butter	1 egg, lightly beaten
2 tablespoons sugar	5½ cups flour (approx.)
1 teaspoon salt	(sesame seeds)
1 package active dry yeast	melted butter

Combine milk, butter, sugar, and salt and let cool to warm. Dissolve yeast in warm water and add to milk mixture. Add egg. Stir in the flour gradually to form a soft dough. Use only enough flour to enable you to knead dough. Put in greased bowl, turn to grease top, cover, and let rise in a warm spot until doubled. Toss dough *gently* on floured board; handling as little as possible, sprinkle with flour. Pat dough out to about ½-inch thickness. Cut with a 3-inch round cutter. (A clean tin can, ends removed, works beautifully.) Place on lightly greased baking sheet, and let rise, uncovered, until doubled. Sprinkle with sesame seeds if desired. Bake in 400°F. oven for about 15 minutes, until lightly browned. Remove to rack and brush tops with melted butter. Makes about 18 buns.

Barb Schneider
Des Plaines, IL

Hard Rolls

Golden-crusty outside, soft and steaming inside. Once they have cooled, reheat them briefly to recapture these features.

1 package active dry yeast	¾ cup warm water
¼ cup warm water	4 cups flour
2 egg whites	1 egg yolk mixed with 1 tablespoon
1 tablespoon sugar	cold water
1 teaspoon salt	(sesame seeds or poppy seeds)
2 tablespoons cooking oil	

Dissolve yeast in warm water and set aside. Beat egg whites in mixer bowl until frothy. Beat in sugar, salt, oil, ¾ cup warm water, dissolved yeast, and 1 cup of the flour. Stir in 2 more cups flour, and mix well. At this point, scrape dough onto floured board, and knead in the fourth cup of flour, a little at a time. Eventually all flour will be absorbed, and dough will become smooth and elastic. Place dough in ungreased 2-quart bowl, cover, and let rise until doubled — 45 minutes to 1 hour. Punch down, and let rise again, covered, until doubled — about 30 minutes.

(continued)

Turn risen dough out onto lightly floured board. Divide into 12 equal pieces, and form each piece into ball or cylinder. Place on greased baking sheet, flatten each roll slightly, and let rise, uncovered, until doubled — you can then slash rolls shallowly with sharp knife if desired. Brush with egg-yolk glaze. Sprinkle liberally with optional seeds, or leave plain. Place pan of hot water on lower shelf of oven. Preheat oven to 375°F., and place baking sheet on top shelf of oven, above pan of water. Bake 30-60 minutes. Longer baking time forms thicker crusts on rolls. Makes 12 rolls.

Loretta Shaefer
Milwaukee, WI

Seven-Day Refrigerator Rolls

A nice soft dinner roll, slightly sweet. If kept below 45°F., the dough can be stored in the refrigerator up to one week. Grand for a large family that likes freshly baked rolls daily.

2 packages active dry yeast	⅔ cup shortening
1 cup warm water	2 eggs, beaten
1 teaspoon sugar	10 cups flour (approx.)
2 cups milk	(beaten egg white)
3 teaspoons salt	(sesame or poppy seeds)
¾ cup sugar	(melted butter)

Combine yeast, warm water, and 1 teaspoon sugar in bowl. Stir, and let stand about 10 minutes. Scald milk, and dissolve in it salt, ¾ cup sugar, and shortening. Cool to lukewarm and add yeast in bowl. Add the eggs and about half the flour. Beat smooth. Add enough additional flour to make a dough somewhat softer than bread dough. Knead until smooth and elastic. If desired, store dough immediately in refrigerator in greased bowl for later use. Grease top of dough, and cover with plastic wrap or double thickness of wax paper.

Or, at this point, let all or part of the dough rise, covered, in warm place until doubled. Punch down. Shape into rolls (cloverleaf or cluster are good — see page 191), and let rise again. If you like seeded rolls, brush top of dough with optional beaten egg white and sprinkle with optional sesame or poppy seeds. Or bake rolls plain, and brush with melted butter when done. Bake at 375°F. for about 15 minutes, or until lightly browned. To use dough from refrigerator, shape rolls as desired, and allow to rise until doubled before baking. Makes about 5 dozen rolls, depending on size and shape.

Joyce Brandt
Fennimore, WI

Cinnamon Swedish Crescent Rolls

Dainty sweet rolls that rise once in the refrigerator and once in the oven. Shaping the rolls is the only thing that takes any time at all — but they're worth the effort.

3 packages active dry yeast
1 cup warm milk
1 teaspoon sugar
4 cups flour
1 cup shortening
½ cup sugar

1 teaspoon salt
2 eggs, well beaten
½ cup butter
1 cup sugar
1 tablespoon cinnamon

Dissolve yeast in warm milk, add 1 teaspoon sugar, and set aside to foam up. In large bowl, cut flour, shortening, ½ cup sugar, and salt together as you would for pie crust. Combine eggs with yeast mixture, and add to ingredients in large bowl. Cover, and refrigerate for at least 4 hours, or overnight. Then melt butter. Combine the 1 cup sugar and cinnamon. Cut dough into quarters. Work with one section at a time, and keep the rest refrigerated.

On floured pastry cloth, roll out each section into a circle like a pie crust, about ⅛-¼ inch thick. Transfer circle of dough to cutting board by rolling it around your rolling pin. Brush with one quarter of the melted butter and sprinkle with one quarter of the cinnamon/sugar mixture. Cut each circle into 16 wedge-shaped pieces. Roll up each piece, starting at wide end. Tip of rolled wedge should be on underside. (Work quickly. Dough gets harder to handle as it warms.) Place on ungreased baking sheet. Curve each roll slightly to form a crescent. Bake at 350°F. for 15-20 minutes. (Watch closely so they don't burn.) Glaze if desired with vanilla or orange icing. Makes 64 small sweet rolls.

Janice Ryzewski
Shrewsbury, MA

QUICK BREADS AND OTHER BREADSTUFFS

So named because they are speedy and easy, quick breads do not use yeast, and are neither kneaded nor risen. The recipes for breads, coffee cakes, muffins, biscuits, etc. which follow use either baking powder or baking soda, beaten eggs and/or egg whites, and other combinations of leavening agents.

Quick breads are characteristically cracked on top. There really doesn't seem to be anything one can do to avoid it, so don't fret. The good taste won't be affected. If you've ever had trouble getting quick breads out of the pan in one piece (even if you've greased and floured and allowed 10 minutes' cooling time before attempting to remove them), try this. Cut pieces of wax paper to fit the bottoms of the pans. Grease the pans, lay in the wax paper, and grease it as well. Freshly baked quick breads crumble easily. For easier slicing, cool for several hours or bake the day ahead.

QUICK BREADS

Fresh Apple Bread

Sweet, dark, and densely moist bread that keeps well and freezes well. Any time of day, you'll scarcely be able to leave this alone.

3 eggs, well beaten
¾ cup cooking oil
¼ cup apple juice or cider
2 cups sugar
2 teaspoons vanilla
3 cups flour
2 teaspoons baking soda

½ teaspoon salt
2 teaspoons cinnamon
3 cups coarsely chopped, peeled, cored apples (about 3 large)
1 cup chopped nuts
(1 cup raisins)

Combine eggs, oil, apple juice or cider, sugar, and vanilla in mixing bowl and beat well. Add dry ingredients, and mix thoroughly. Fold in apples, nuts, and optional raisins. Pour into two greased 9x5-inch loaf pans, or a well-greased 12-cup Bundt pan. Bake at 350°F. for 50-60 minutes. Cool in pans for 5-10 minutes, then turn out to cool on racks. Makes two 9x5-inch loaves or one large Bundt cake.

Rachel Stapp
Vandalia, IL

Apricot Nut Bread

Pretty, jewel-like slices to serve with the meat course as well as with tea. Butter the loaf all over when it comes from the oven to make it shiny.

6-ounce package dried apricots, coarsely chopped (about 1 cup)
⅔ cup water
1 egg, well beaten
1 cup buttermilk
3 tablespoons butter, melted
½ teaspoon vanilla

2½ cups flour
¾ cup sugar
4 teaspoons baking powder
½ teaspoon baking soda
1 teaspoon salt
¾ cup coarsely chopped cashews, or other nuts

Simmer apricots in water 10 minutes, or until most of the water is absorbed. Drain, and set aside to cool. In large bowl, combine egg, buttermilk, melted butter, and vanilla with apricots, blending well. Sift dry ingredients together, and add nuts. Gradually add to mixture in bowl, and beat well. Turn into greased and floured 9x5-inch loaf pan. Bake at 350°F. for about 1 hour and 15 minutes. Turn out of pan, and cool on rack. Makes one 9x5-inch loaf.

Marie O'Dell
Ottawa, IL

Banana Bread

Just right — sweet and moist but not heavy.

3 medium bananas
¾ cup sugar
1 egg, well beaten
¼ cup shortening
2 cups flour

½ teaspoon salt
1 teaspoon baking soda
1 teaspoon baking powder
½ cup chopped pecans, or other
    nuts

Crush bananas, and add sugar, egg, and shortening. Mix well. Sift together dry ingredients, and stir into banana mixture. Add nuts. Bake 1 hour at 325°F. in greased 9x5-inch loaf pan. Makes one 9x5-inch loaf.

Joy Harvey
Newark, NY

Jean's Buttermilk Coffee Cake

As light and buttery a coffee cake as ever you'll eat. Eat one cake right away, and freeze the other for later.

3 eggs, separated
¼ teaspoon cream of tartar
2½ cups sugar
¾ cup butter
1½ teaspoons baking soda
1¼ cups buttermilk

2¾ cups flour
1 teaspoon vanilla

Crumb Topping:
½ cup flour
¼ cup sugar
2 tablespoons butter

Beat egg whites until frothy. Add cream of tartar. While continuing to beat, gradually add ½ cup of the sugar. Beat until stiff peaks form. Set aside. Cream butter and remaining 2 cups sugar. Beat in egg yolks, one at a time. Dissolve soda in buttermilk, and add alternately with flour to creamed mixture. Add vanilla. Gently fold in beaten egg whites.

Combine topping ingredients in small bowl. Spread batter into two greased and floured 9-inch square cake pans. Sprinkle topping evenly over batter. Bake at 350°F. for 30-40 minutes, until cake tests done. Makes two 9-inch square coffee cakes.

Margaret S. Kerstetter
St. Andrew Episcopal Church
John Harris Doll Club
Harrisburg, PA

Corn Bread with Leeks and Poppy Seeds

An unusual, interesting, and good corn bread. It's moist, crunchy, and mildly pungent.

1 cup chopped leeks (white part, washed well)
2 tablespoons butter
1 egg, beaten
1 cup milk
¼ cup cooking oil
1 cup cornmeal
1 cup flour

2 teaspoons baking powder
½ teaspoon baking soda
¼ cup sugar
½ teaspoon salt
1 teaspoon dried dill weed
⅛ teaspoon black pepper
⅓ cup poppy seeds

Sauté leeks in butter until soft and transparent. Set aside. Combine egg, milk, and oil, and blend well. Mix together cornmeal, flour, baking powder, baking soda, sugar, salt, dill weed, and pepper. Combine liquid and dry ingredients. Add poppy seeds and sautéed leeks, stirring just enough to mix. Pour into greased 9x5-inch loaf pan. Bake at 350°F. about 45 minutes, or until loaf is lightly browned and tests done. Serve warm. Makes one 9x5-inch loaf.

Dorothy Butler
Guilford, CT

Holiday Gift Loaf

Leavened solely by eggs, this looks a little like a fruit cake when sliced, but its flavor is quite different.

½ cup butter, softened
1½ cups confectioner's sugar
5 eggs, separated
grated rind of 1 lemon
grated rind of 1 orange
½ teaspoon cream of tartar

1½ cups sifted flour
¾ cup slivered glacé cherries
   (approx. 7½-ounce container)
½ cup slivered almonds
¾ cup mini chocolate chips

Lightly grease and flour 9x5-inch loaf pan. Cream butter with ½ cup of the sugar. Beat in egg yolks, one by one. Add grated rinds. In separate bowl, beat egg whites with remaining sugar and cream of tartar until stiff. Fold into first mixture. Fold in flour, cherries, almonds, and chocolate chips. Spread batter in prepared pan, making slight depression in center. Bake at 350°F. for 50-60 minutes, or until cake tests done. Cool on rack. Wrap in foil, or keep in tightly covered container. Makes one 9x5-inch loaf.

Beverly Everett
Danville, VT

Christmas Nut Loaf

A real all-NUT loaf, with some dates for moistness, cherries for color, and just enough other ingredients to hold 1½ pounds of nuts together. Because loaves freeze well, you can make them in advance of the holidays, when walnuts and pecans are more reasonably priced.

¾ cup flour
¾ cup sugar
1 teaspoon baking powder
½ teaspoon salt
1 pound dates, pitted and cut-up
½ pound pecan halves

1 pound walnut halves
6-ounce jar maraschino cherries,
    drained and chopped
4 eggs (or 3 extra large)
1 teaspoon vanilla

Sift flour, sugar, baking powder, and salt together. Add dates, nuts, and cherries. Stir well to coat nuts and fruit with flour. Beat eggs with vanilla, and stir into dry mixture. Put into two greased and floured 8x4-inch loaf pans, and bake at 325°F. for 35-40 minutes, or until knife inserted in center of loaf comes out clean and loaves are lightly browned. Makes two 8x4-inch loaves.

Mrs. Floyd Fischer
West Palm Beach, FL

Peanut Butter Bread

Make snack or dessert sandwiches by spreading slices of this bread with your favorite jelly or jam. For extra nutrition, add optional wheat germ to batter.

¾ cup peanut butter
¼ cup cooking oil
1 egg, beaten
1 cup milk
2 cups flour

1 teaspoon salt
1 tablespoon baking powder
⅔ cup sugar
(½ cup wheat germ)

Combine peanut butter, oil, egg, and milk in large mixing bowl. Add dry ingredients. Beat at medium speed of mixer for about 1 minute to thoroughly blend ingredients. Spoon batter into greased 9x5-inch loaf pan. Bake at 350°F. for 50-55 minutes. Cool slightly, and turn out on rack to cool completely. Wrap and store in cool place. (Bread slices more easily the second day.) Makes one 9x5-inch loaf.

Ann Brandt
Fennimore, WI

Pear Pecan Bread

Pears and cinnamon are a natural combo — the addition of cardamom makes this excellent sweet bread unusual. Serve thin slices at tea or coffee gatherings.

1 cup sugar
½ cup cooking oil
2 eggs
¼ cup sour cream
1 teaspoon vanilla
2 cups flour
1 teaspoon baking soda
½ teaspoon salt

¼ teaspoon cinnamon
¼ teaspoon ground cardamom
½ teaspoon finely grated lemon
    peel
1½ cups coarsely chopped peeled
    pears
⅔ cup coarsely chopped pecans

Combine sugar and oil in large bowl, and beat well. Add eggs, one at a time, beating well after each addition. Mix in sour cream and vanilla. Sift together flour, soda, salt, cinnamon, and cardamom; add to batter, and beat well. Stir in lemon peel, pears, and pecans. Spoon batter into greased and floured 9x5-inch loaf pan. Bake at 350°F. for 1 hour to 1 hour and 10 minutes, or until bread tests done. (Tent with aluminum foil near end of baking time if sides of loaf are browning too much.) Turn out onto rack and cool completely before slicing. Makes one 9x5-inch loaf.

Norma Duer
Fletcher, OH

Prune Nut Bread

An excellent prune loaf — slightly chewy with a nice crisp crust to it.

1 cup sugar, brown or white
2 tablespoons shortening
1 egg
16-ounce jar canned prunes
    (reserve juice)
prune juice (add water, if necessary,
    to bring volume up to ½ cup)

1 cup buttermilk or sour milk
1 teaspoon baking soda
½ teaspoon baking powder
1½ cups white flour
1 cup whole-wheat flour
1 cup chopped walnuts or pecans

Cream sugar and shortening. Beat in egg. Pit and cut up prunes. Combine prune juice and buttermilk or sour milk. Sift together baking soda, baking powder, and white flour. Stir in whole-wheat flour. Combine prunes and nuts with 1 cup of the dry ingredients. Add liquid and dry ingredients alternately to creamed mixture, mixing well. Stir in prunes and nuts. Pour into two greased 8x4-inch loaf pans. Bake at 350°F. for 45 minutes. Remove from pans, and cool on racks. Makes two 8x4-inch loaves.

Mildred E. Brown
Contoocook, NH

Pumpkin Bread

As perfectly spiced as a Thanksgiving pumpkin pie. An exceedingly moist loaf with a crisp crust.

3 cups sugar
1 cup cooking oil
1-pound can pumpkin
4 eggs, beaten
3½ cups flour
2 teaspoons baking soda
2 teaspoons salt

1 teaspoon baking powder
1 teaspoon cinnamon
1 teaspoon nutmeg
1 teaspoon allspice
½ teaspoon ground cloves
⅔ cup water

Combine sugar, oil, pumpkin, and eggs in large bowl of mixer. Beat until light and fluffy. Mix dry ingredients together, and add them alternately with the water to pumpkin mixture. Mix until well blended. Turn into two greased and floured 9x5-inch loaf pans, and bake approximately 1 hour and 20 minutes at 350°F. Cool in pans 10 minutes, then turn out onto racks and cool completely. Makes two 9x5-inch loaves.

Sharon Smith
Peterborough, NH

Rhubarb Bread

A perfect blend of tart and sweet flavors is achieved in this quick bread. The crumbled sugar and butter topping melts into a glaze as the loaves bake.

1½ cups light brown sugar, packed
⅔ cup cooking oil
1 egg
1 cup buttermilk
1 teaspoon salt
1 teaspoon baking soda
1 teaspoon vanilla

2½ cups flour
2 cups diced rhubarb
½ cup chopped walnuts
¼ cup sugar
1 tablespoon butter, softened
(1 teaspoon cinnamon)

Combine brown sugar with oil, and beat until smooth. Stir in egg, buttermilk, salt, baking soda, vanilla, and flour. Blend just until moistened. Fold in rhubarb and nuts. Pour into two greased 8x4-inch loaf pans. Combine sugar, butter, and optional cinnamon until crumbly. Sprinkle evenly over batter. Bake at 350°F. for 50-55 minutes, or until bread tests done. Turn onto rack and cool. Makes two 8x4-inch loaves.

Marie O'Dell
Ottawa, IL

Zucchini Maple Bread

A unique zucchini bread. Good slathered with cream cheese.

2½ cups flour
½ cup sugar
½ cup real maple syrup
3½ teaspoons baking powder
1 teaspoon salt
grated rind of 1 orange

3 tablespoons cooking oil
½ cup plain yogurt
½ cup orange juice
1 egg
1 cup chopped nuts
1 cup finely chopped zucchini

Place all ingredients except nuts and zucchini in a large bowl, and mix at medium speed until well blended. Fold in nuts and zucchini. Pour into greased 9x5-inch loaf pan. Bake at 350°F. for 55-60 minutes, or until toothpick comes out clean. Makes one 9x5-inch loaf.

Mrs. Lorraine Hulst
New Haven, VT

Cherry-Almond Coffee Cake

Slightly extravagant, but worth it when you want a treat with a really special flavor. To make it look as yummy as it tastes, drizzle a thin confectioner's sugar glaze over the cake and decorate with candied cherries and slivered almonds.

½ cup butter
½ cup shortening
1½ cups sugar
1½-2 teaspoons almond extract
4 eggs
3 cups flour

1 teaspoon salt
1 teaspoon cream of tartar
½ teaspoon baking soda
½ cup sour cream
1 cup chopped almonds
12-ounce jar cherry preserves

Cream together butter, shortening, sugar, and almond extract. Add eggs, one at a time, beating well after each. Add dry ingredients, and beat thoroughly. Stir in sour cream, almonds, and cherry preserves. Mix well. Spread in two greased 9x5-inch loaf pans, or fill a well-greased 12-cup Bundt pan about two-thirds full. Bake excess batter in muffin cups. Bake at 350°F. for 45-55 minutes (muffins 15-20 minutes), until loaves or cake test done. Cool 10 minutes. Remove from pan(s) and cool completely on racks. Makes two 9x5-inch loaves or 1 Bundt cake plus several muffins.

Linda Bensinger
Dublin, NH

OTHER ASSORTED BREADSTUFFS

> Muffins, biscuits, popovers, Scottish oatcakes and scones, and a sesame cocktail cracker.

Bran Muffins

These muffins are very dark and rise evenly rather than rounding up high. To vary, add raisins or blueberries (fresh or frozen) to taste.

1 cup flour
2 cups bran
1 rounded teaspoon baking soda
¼ teaspoon salt

½ cup molasses
1 tablespoon butter
1½ cups milk (whole or skimmed)

Combine flour, bran, baking soda, and salt in bowl. In saucepan, heat molasses and butter just until mixture foams — watch closely so that it does not boil over. Add to dry ingredients. Add milk. Stir to blend. Spoon into greased or paper-lined muffin pans. Bake 20-22 minutes at 375°F. Makes 12 muffins.

Mrs. E. R. Hibbard
Portland, ME

Sesame Corn Muffins

Extra crunch thanks to the sesame seeds and wheat germ, and less crumbly than the usual cornmeal muffins. If you don't have buttermilk, add 2 tablespoons vinegar to 2 cups fresh milk.

½ cup flour
⅓ cup sugar
1 teaspoon salt
1¼ teaspoons baking soda
2 cups cornmeal

1 cup wheat germ
½ cup sesame seeds
⅔ cup cooking oil
3 eggs
2 cups buttermilk

Combine all dry ingredients in a large bowl and mix thoroughly. Add oil, eggs, and buttermilk. Stir well. Fill well-greased or paper-lined muffin cups one-half to two-thirds full. Bake at 375°F. for about 20 minutes. Makes about 18 muffins.

Gretchen S. Dale
Barrington, RI

Orange Muffins

The diced oranges and almonds settle down into the batter during the baking of these pretty butter-yellow muffins.

2 cups sifted flour
⅔ cup sugar
1 tablespoon baking powder
¼ teaspoon allspice
⅔ cup shortening
⅓ cup butter, softened
4 eggs, beaten

½ cup milk
½ cup orange juice
1 teaspoon grated orange rind
½ cup diced orange sections, fresh
    or canned
¼ cup sliced almonds
(sugar or cinnamon-sugar)

Mix flour, sugar, baking powder, and allspice in large bowl. Add in order, stirring after each addition: shortening, butter, eggs, milk, orange juice, and orange rind. Spoon batter into greased or paper-lined muffin cups to two-thirds full. Top each with orange sections and almonds. Sprinkle with optional sugar or cinnamon-sugar for extra sweetness. Bake at 350°F. for 25 minutes. Makes 16-18 muffins.

Jean Brownlee
Victorville, CA

Tropical Isle Muffins

Bright, sweet, and sunny muffins to serve for breakfast on a cold winter morning.

1 egg
½ cup milk
¼ cup cooking oil
½ cup sugar
1½ cups flour
2 teaspoons baking powder

½ teaspoon salt
¾ cup crushed pineapple, drained
¼ cup maraschino cherries,
    drained and chopped
⅓ cup flaked coconut
(sugar)

Beat egg, and stir in milk and oil. Add remaining ingredients, and stir until just blended. Fill greased or paper-lined muffin cups three-quarters full. Sprinkle tops with sugar if desired. Bake in a 400°F. oven for 15-20 minutes. Makes 12-16 muffins.

Bonnie Berrett
Jaffrey, NH

Melt-in-Your-Mouth Biscuits

Flaky-tender biscuits to accompany a main course or to become individual strawberry shortcakes.

2 cups flour
¾ teaspoon salt
4 teaspoons baking powder
½ teaspoon cream of tartar

1¾ teaspoons sugar
½ cup shortening
⅔ cup milk

Sift flour, salt, baking powder, cream of tartar, and sugar three times. Cut in shortening until mixture resembles coarse meal. Do this with pastry blender, two knives, or your fingers. Make a well in center of flour mixture, and add milk all at once. Stir with fork until dough follows fork around the bowl. Turn out onto floured board, and knead gently. Roll out to a thickness of ½-¾ inch. Cut with biscuit cutter, place on ungreased baking sheet, and bake at 450°F. for 8-12 minutes. Makes about 9 biscuits.

Peg Rodenhiser
New Ipswich, NH

Butterscotch Rolls

Fine biscuit dough spread with butter and brown sugar, rolled up, then baked in slices like cinnamon yeast rolls. Quickly made.

2 cups flour
4 teaspoons baking powder
2 teaspoons sugar
½ teaspoon salt
½ teaspoon cream of tartar

½ cup butter
⅔ cup milk
½ cup butter, softened
1 cup light brown sugar, packed
½ teaspoon cinnamon

Stir together flour, baking powder, sugar, salt, and cream of tartar. Cut in butter until particles are fine. Add milk. Mix with fork to form soft dough. Turn out on lightly floured surface. Knead about 10 times or until smooth. Roll into a 12x9-inch rectangle. Spread with half of the soft butter (¼ cup). Combine half the brown sugar (½ cup) with the cinnamon, and sprinkle evenly over butter. Roll up, jelly-roll fashion, from the 12-inch side. Use the remaining butter and brown sugar to put 1 teaspoon butter and 2 teaspoons brown sugar in each of 12 muffin cups. Cut the rolled-up dough into twelve 1-inch slices. Place dough slices, cut-side up, in muffin cups. Bake in a preheated 400°F. oven for about 17 minutes, or until rich golden brown. Immediately invert on wire racks to cool. Makes 12 sweet rolls.

Dorothy Steller
Little Falls, NJ

Scottish Oatcakes

You can substitute shortening, but these definitely have more flavor and character made with lard. Similar in texture to shortbread or a Chinese almond cookie; oatcakes are grand served with fruit — soup, platter, or salad.

3 cups quick rolled oats
3 cups flour
1 cup sugar
2 teaspoons salt
1 teaspoon baking soda

1½ cups lard, cut in pieces
¾ cup ice-cold water
about 1 cup extra rolled oats,
    ground fine in blender or food
    processor

Combine first five ingredients in large bowl. Cut in lard or shortening until coarse crumbs are formed. Add cold water, a tablespoon or two at a time, tossing with a fork as you would for pie crust. When all water has been added, gather dough into ball and divide in half, then divide each half into quarters. Form each of the eight pieces into a ball, and roll in ground oatmeal. Sprinkle pastry cloth or board with ground oatmeal; roll out each ball of dough into circle about ¼-⅜ inch thick. Sprinkle ground oatmeal over dough. Cut circle into 8 wedge-shaped pieces. Place on ungreased baking sheets and bake at 350°F. for 15-17 minutes, or until light brown. Bottoms will be golden. Remove from sheet and cool on racks. Makes 64 oatcakes.

Thelma M. Sawyer
Grafton, NH

Popovers

This recipe produces an elegant popover, high, handsome, and crisp, but not dry.

1 cup sifted flour
½ teaspoon salt
3 eggs

1 cup milk
1 tablespoon butter, melted

Beat all ingredients together until smooth. Grease well ten heat-resistant glass custard cups (5-ounce size). Fill cups one-third full of batter, and place on a baking sheet, allowing space between cups. Bake at 400°F. for 45 minutes, or until golden brown, firm, and crusty. Makes 10 popovers.

Arlene M. Kotterman
Lafayette, IN

Griddle-Baked Scones

Pronounced "scons" in Scotland, scones are closely related to the American baking powder biscuit. Here is a scone baked on top of the stove! Serve warm with lots of butter. Cooled scones can be split and toasted.

2 cups flour
1 teaspoon baking powder
1 teaspoon baking soda
⅓ cup sugar
¼ teaspoon salt

1 egg, beaten
3 tablespoons butter, melted and
    cooled
⅔ cup milk
(½-⅔ cup dried currants or raisins)

Mix all ingredients together well. Divide dough into quarters. Drop each quarter in turn on well-floured board, and liberally dust top of dough with flour. Pat dough into circle ½ inch thick. Cut circle into quarters. Carefully lift each piece to an ungreased skillet or griddle which has been preheated on low heat. Bake scones 10 minutes on one side; turn, and bake another 2-5 minutes on the other side. They should be golden brown when done. Makes 16 scones.

Doris Manning
Bridgeport, CT

Whole-Wheat Scones

Excellent for breakfast with jam or marmalade, split and toasted for lunch with cheese or peanut butter, or buttered as a satisfying accompaniment to soup. Quick and simple whenever you need a hearty bread pronto. The most time involved is in preheating the oven!

2 cups whole-wheat flour
1 teaspoon cream of tartar
1 teaspoon baking soda

½ teaspoon salt
½ cup butter
¾ cup milk

Stir dry ingredients together. Cut in butter with pastry blender or two knives until mixture forms pea-sized crumbs. Stir in milk just until moistened. Divide dough in half. On greased baking sheet, pat each half into circle 6-8 inches in diameter and about ½ inch thick. Bake at 400°F. for about 15 minutes. Remove from sheet, and cut each round into quarters. Serve immediately, while hot or, once cooled, split and toasted. Makes 8 scones.

Catharine Bellinger
Hummelstown, PA

Sesame Thins

Ultra-thin, crisp, flavorful crackers to nibble, dip, or serve with soups. Cool baked crackers completely, then wrap in plastic and store in air-tight tins.

1¾ cups flour
½ cup cornmeal
½ teaspoon baking soda
½ teaspoon salt
¼ cup butter, softened

½ cup water
2 tablespoons vinegar
¼ cup butter, melted
2 tablespoons sesame seeds

Measure flour, cornmeal, baking soda, and salt into large bowl. Cut in butter until mixture resembles coarse crumbs. Stir in water and vinegar. With hands, knead until well blended. Divide dough into eight equal parts. One part at a time, on lightly floured board or pastry cloth, roll dough paper thin. Using a pizza cutter, pastry wheel, or knife cut rectangular, square, or triangular shapes, as you prefer. With pancake turner place pieces of dough 1 inch apart on ungreased cookie sheets. Brush lightly with melted butter, and sprinkle with sesame seeds. Press seeds down with pancake turner. Bake at 375°F. for 8-10 minutes until lightly browned. Cool. Store in tightly covered container for up to a week. Yield depends on size you cut crackers to, but recipe easily makes 8-10 dozen crackers.

Bonnie Berrett
Jaffrey, NH

CHAPTER EIGHT

Salads, Dressings, *et al.*

This chapter is divided up into Fresh Vegetable and Fruit Salads; Pasta and Main-Dish Salads; Molded and Frozen Salads; and finally Dressings *et al.*, including two old-fashioned beverages: Raspberry Shrub and Haymaker's Switchel.

Other dressings may be found with specific salad recipes.

FRESH VEGETABLE AND FRUIT SALADS

From *A* for Asparagus to *V* for Vegetables — a most interesting and imaginative group of recipes.

Asparagus, Carrot, and Mushroom Salad

With a touch of onion, too. Mrs. Oyler serves this with Tomato Soup Dressing (page 240).

3 cups 2- or 3-inch lengths of fresh asparagus (or broccoli)
4 medium carrots, pared and slivered

2 small white onions, peeled and sliced thin
1 cup fresh tiny button mushrooms

Blanch asparagus (or broccoli) in boiling salted water for 2 minutes. Cook carrot strips in salted boiling water until *almost* tender. Drain asparagus and carrots, and place in salad bowl with onions, and mushrooms. Toss with dressing. Chill several hours. Serves 4-6.

Martha Sharp Oyler
Anderson, IN

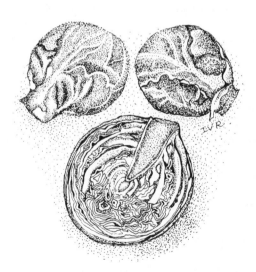

Broccoli Toss

A very pretty, very good, and most original salad with a wonderful texture — a Yankee prizewinner.

2 tablespoons cider vinegar
3 ounces cream cheese
2 tablespoons sugar
dash pepper
⅛ teaspoon garlic salt
¼ teaspoon salt
1 tablespoon prepared mustard
1 egg

2 tablespoons salad oil
6 cups chopped fresh broccoli
2 tablespoons chopped red onion
⅓ cup raisins
6-8 slices bacon, fried crisp and
     crumbled
4 large fresh mushrooms, sliced

Combine the first 8 ingredients in a blender and whirl. Add salad oil and whirl again. Chill. Combine remaining ingredients in bowl. Pour chilled dressing over and toss vigorously to mix well. Serves 8.

Roberta C. Gilbert
Lebanon, PA

Inspiration Salad

A cabbage-carrot salad with a spicy maple-soy dressing. Serve with hot spaghettini, or Chinese noodles (the kind that come in hanks, like yarn) for a meatless meal with oriental dash. Clover heads can be found at natural-food stores. (Or pick red clover blossoms from a field, and dry them.)

Salad:
¼ head cabbage, shredded
3 large carrots, pared and chopped
½ onion, finely chopped
3 tablespoons dried clover heads
10 dates, pitted and chopped
10 walnuts, halved

Dressing:
3 tablespoons mayonnaise
pinch tarragon

2 tablespoons cream (or 1
     tablespoon each of cream and
     sour cream)
½ inch fresh ginger root, chopped
     fine
1 tablespoon shoyu (soy) sauce
¼ teaspoon black pepper
1½-2 tablespoons real maple syrup
¼ of one anise star

Combine salad ingredients, and toss together in bowl. Combine dressing ingredients, mix well, pour over salad, and toss. Serves 4.

Mollie Thoron
London, GB

Hungarian Beet Salad

A colorful salad with just the hint of a bite. The hardboiled eggs make a pretty garnish.

4-5 large fresh beets
2 tablespoons white vinegar
2 tablespoons water
1 teaspoon salt
1 tablespoon sugar

½ teaspoon caraway seeds
1 teaspoon horseradish
4 hardboiled eggs, sliced or
    quartered

Cook, skin, and slice beets. Combine all other ingredients except eggs, mix well, and pour over beets. Let stand several hours, turning occasionally. Garnish with egg slices or quarters. Serves 4.

Jane Hanson
Boulder, CO

Cole Slaw

Classic in its simplicity.

½ cup cider vinegar
sugar
1 head cabbage (1½-2 pounds)

1 cup heavy cream
black pepper

To cider vinegar in measuring cup, add sugar until the ⅞ point is reached. Heat in saucepan until sugar melts. Cool. Shred cabbage. Whip cream until thick. Mix sugar mixture with whipped cream, and pour over cabbage. Sprinkle with a little black pepper, and serve. Serves 6.

Mrs. Elliot Fansler
Towson, MD

Confetti Cole Slaw

Shredded cabbage, carrot, onion, and green pepper in a mayonnaise dressing.

½ cup mayonnaise
3 tablespoons salad oil
2 tablespoons cider vinegar
2 tablespoons sugar
¼ teaspoon salt
½ teaspoon garlic salt

½ teaspoon celery salt
1 medium cabbage, shredded
1 onion, chopped
1 green pepper, cored and cut into
    fine shreds
1 tablespoon dill weed

In large covered jar or blender combine mayonnaise, oil, vinegar, sugar, and salts. Shake or blend well. Combine vegetables and sprinkle with dill. Pour dressing over vegetables and let stand at least 1 hour before serving. Toss often to distribute dressing. Serves 6.

Linda Long
Reading, MA

Chilled Chick Pea and Rice Salad

Another colorful salad with a new and original flavor. Allow 3-4 hours in the refrigerator for flavors to meld together properly.

2 cups drained chick peas
2 cups cooked brown rice
2 cups diced green peppers
2 medium tomatoes, cut into coarse
    dice
½ cup diced red onion

4 tablespoons olive oil
4 tablespoons wine vinegar
½ teaspoon dill weed
⅛ teaspoon pepper
(¾ teaspoon salt)

Combine all ingredients in large bowl, and toss well. Chill 1 hour, and toss again. Then toss hourly two-three times, and once again just before serving. Serves 4-6.

Janice E. Stoddard-McRae
Wakefield, MA

Cucumber Salad

Cucumber slices in a sweet-sour dressing with a fillip of other vegetables, sliced, diced, and shredded.

¼ cup sugar
½ teaspoon salt
½ cup white vinegar
½ cup water
2 teaspoons salad oil

2 cucumbers, thinly sliced
1 onion, thinly sliced
2 teaspoons diced green pepper
2 teaspoons carrot shreds
1 stalk celery, thinly sliced

Dissolve sugar and salt in vinegar. Add water and oil, and shake well to blend. Combine vegetables in bowl, pour dressing over them, and toss. Serves 4.

Mrs. Anna Morley
Carney's Point, NJ

Fruit Cocktail Supreme

Melon balls, grapes, grapefruit and orange sections, pineapple, apples, raspberries, and banana slices. Serve in a glass bowl for a summer dessert, or on lettuce with cottage cheese as a salad. Use fresh raspberries if possible.

1 cup watermelon balls
1 cup seedless green grapes
½ cup cantaloupe or honeydew
    balls
8-ounce can crushed pineapple,
    with juice
sections from 1 pink grapefruit
sections from 1 large navel orange
    (cut sections in half)

2 medium McIntosh apples, cored
    and diced (skin on)
10 large purple grapes, halved
    lengthwise and seeded
½ cup raspberries (or half a 10-
    ounce package frozen, drained)
1 banana, peeled and sliced
shredded coconut

Place all fruits in glass bowl, and toss gently. Chill 45 minutes in refrigerator. Sprinkle shredded coconut over top just before serving. Serves 8.

Lauralee Clayton
The Rockport Heritage Cookbook

Fruit Salad with Honey-Lime Dressing

Melons, papaya, and banana in a sweetly tart dressing; another refreshing fruit concoction to serve either as salad or, with vanilla cookies or pound cake, as dessert.

Dressing:
¼ cup honey
2 tablespoons fresh lime juice
½ teaspoon ground fresh ginger
    root

Fruit:
4 cups watermelon balls

1 cantaloupe, cut into melon balls
1 large, ripe papaya, peeled and
    cubed
3 bananas, peeled and sliced
lime wedges for garnish

Make dressing by combining ingredients and mixing well. In bowl, combine watermelon and cantaloupe balls, papaya cubes, and dressing. Toss gently. Cover, and refrigerate for 3-4 hours. Take from refrigerator, and stir in bananas. Garnish with lime wedges. Serves 8-10.

Mrs. Anne Seile
Sisters, OR

Green and White Salad

A pretty and adaptable salad — those who cannot eat onion or green pepper can make it without either and still have a winner (but you have to like all the other vegetables!). When first you try it, you may think it shy on dressing. Not so. There is just enough to lightly coat each crisp chunk, and that is how it should be. Makes enough for a crowd — so halve the recipe for home use.

Salad:
1 medium head cauliflower
1 bunch broccoli
10-ounce package frozen peas
½-1 large green pepper, diced
1 large onion, diced
3-4 stalks celery, diced

Dressing:
⅓ cup mayonnaise
2 tablespoons sugar
1 teaspoon salt
½ teaspoon pepper

Cut cauliflower into florets. Then cut florets into small pieces. Do the same for the broccoli, including a small portion of the stems. Thaw peas just enough to separate. (DO NOT COOK PEAS.) Place all vegetables into large bowl.

Mix together dressing ingredients, stirring to blend well. Stir into salad and toss well. Serves 16.

Deb Christenson
Brookline, NH

Lettuce and Sweet Onion Salad

Quickly made and wonderful. Try different kinds of lettuce — butterhead or black-seeded Simpson in season, for choice. Or oak-leaf, or red, or . . .

1 head lettuce
¾ cup heavy cream
4 tablespoons sugar or honey
2-3 tablespoons vinegar

½ teaspoon salt
dash pepper
1 Spanish or Bermuda onion

Wash lettuce, tear into bite-sized pieces, wrap in clean towel, and crisp in refrigerator for an hour or so. Combine cream, sugar or honey, vinegar, salt, and pepper in jar, and mix well. Take lettuce from refrigerator, put in salad bowl, add onion, cut into small pieces, pour dressing over, and toss well. Serves 6.

Melia Baughman
Hanover Center Cooks

Lettuce and Spinach Salad

A Caesar-type salad, made with spinach and two different kinds of lettuce in a lemon-cheese-egg dressing spiced with Worcestershire sauce. To serve fewer than 14, beat together all dressing ingredients except croutons, place in bottle, close tightly, and refrigerate. Use dressing and greens as needed. Will keep 3-4 days.

Greens:
2 heads Romaine lettuce
1 head Boston lettuce
half a 10-ounce package fresh
  spinach leaves

Dressing:
1 cup garlic oil*
1 egg

juice of 3 lemons
1 tablespoon salt
1 tablespoon freshly ground black
  pepper
1 tablespoon Worcestershire sauce
6 tablespoons grated or ground
  Romano or Romanella cheese
1 cup toasted croutons

Separate lettuces into leaves, wash well, and tear into largish pieces. Wash spinach well, and remove tough stems. Spin or pat dry, wrap all together in clean towel or towels, and place in refrigerator for 1-2 hours to crisp.

Take crisped greens from refrigerator and place in bowl. Pour garlic oil over greens. Break egg over center of salad, then pour lemon juice over all. Add remaining ingredients, and toss well from bottom. Serves 14.

Bev Pryor
The Well Tempered Kitchen

*To make garlic oil: add 8-12 chopped or crushed garlic cloves to 2 cups salad oil, and let sit at room temperature for at least 24 hours before using. Use only the oil, adding fresh oil to the bottle as used.

Pea and Peanut Salad

A clever combination of ingredients, easy to do. The peanuts add taste and texture. Use within 24 hours, as the peanuts will tend to soften after this, and the crunch of the salad is lost.

two 10-ounce packages frozen peas
4 cups boiling water
8 ounces dry, roasted peanuts

1 cup finely chopped celery
1 small white onion, chopped fine
2 cups sour cream

Defrost peas, and pour boiling water over them. Let cool, then drain. Combine peas with all other ingredients, mixing well. Chill in refrigerator for at least 2 hours. Serve on lettuce. Serves 8-10.

Martha Sharp Oyler
Anderson, IN

Portsmouth Salad

Lettuce, potatoes, cheese, and hardboiled eggs in a terrific dressing.

1 clove garlic
1 tablespoon cream
yolks of 3 hardboiled eggs, mashed
¼ pound Roquefort cheese,
   crumbled
1 tablespoon salt
1½ teaspoons dry mustard
¾ teaspoon black pepper
¾ teaspoon paprika
3 tablespoons Worcestershire sauce
3 tablespoons cream
4 tablespoons tarragon vinegar
3 tablespoons olive oil
whites of 3 hardboiled eggs,
   minced
3 heads lettuce, washed, torn, and
   crisped in refrigerator
3 boiled potatoes, sliced

Crush garlic in large bowl with 1 tablespoon cream. Discard garlic. Add egg yolks, cheese, salt, mustard, pepper, and paprika. Mix well. Add Worcestershire sauce and 1 tablespoon of the 3 tablespoons cream, and work to a smooth paste. Beat in remaining 2 tablespoons cream gradually, until all is smooth. Then beat in vinegar and finally olive oil, beating until dressing is light and foamy. Add minced egg whites, lettuce, and potatoes, and toss to mix well. Correct seasoning if desired. Serves 12.

Mrs. Frederic Gooding
An Olde Concord Christmas

Bill's Rolled Potato Salad

The test report said this potato salad was scintillating, *a word not normally applied to potato salads. It applies to this one!*

3 medium potatoes, peeled, cooked,
   and mashed (you should have
   3 cups)
⅓ cup mayonnaise
1 teaspoon salt
2 tablespoons chopped onion
½ teaspoon paprika
3 eggs, hardboiled and chopped
1 cup cottage cheese, drained in
   sieve
2 tablespoons mayonnaise

Combine cold mashed potatoes, ⅓ cup mayonnaise, salt, onion, paprika, and chopped eggs. Pat into a 9x12-inch rectangle on tin foil. Combine cottage cheese with 2 tablespoons mayonnaise. Spread over potato mixture to within 1 inch of edges. Roll up from 9-inch side, and chill. Slice to serve. Serves 4-6.

Bev Everett
Danville, VT

Spinach and Bacon Salad

Spinach and lettuce (substitute any kind of lettuce, including iceberg, for the red leaf lettuce) in an innovative dressing featuring mustard, poppy seeds, and cottage cheese.

1 pound fresh spinach
1 head red leaf lettuce
½ pound bacon
¼ cup sugar
1 tablespoon onion juice
1 cup salad oil

⅓ cup cider vinegar
1 tablespoon poppy seeds
1 teaspoon salt
1 teaspoon dry mustard
¾ cup large-curd cottage cheese

Wash and drain spinach; remove stems, and tear leaves into large pieces. Wash and drain lettuce, and tear into small pieces. Dry with paper towels, wrap spinach and lettuce in clean towel, and refrigerate while you make the rest of the recipe. Cook bacon until crisp; drain on paper. Make dressing by combining all remaining ingredients, and mixing well together. Place crisped greens in salad bowl, and crumble bacon over greens. Add dressing just before serving, and toss well. Serves 8.

Virginia Thaemert
Barrington, IL

Spicy Spinach Salad

Fresh spinach and mushrooms with water chestnuts and sesame seeds in a tangy dressing.

Salad:
10-ounce package fresh spinach
8 ounces fresh mushrooms, cleaned
   and sliced
8-ounce can water chestnuts,
   drained and sliced thin
2 tablespoons sesame seeds,
   toasted

Dressing:
⅓ cup salad oil
¼ cup lemon juice
2 tablespoons soy sauce
1 teaspoon dry mustard
1 teaspoon salt
⅛ teaspoon Tabasco sauce

Wash spinach and mushrooms well. Remove stems from spinach leaves, and tear into bite-sized pieces. Slice mushrooms.

Make dressing by combining all dressing ingredients and beating well together. Place salad ingredients in bowl, pour dressing over, and toss well to mix. Serves 6.

Jane Hanson
Boulder, CO

Super Sprout Salad

Colorful (green and red and white), crunchy (florets, lettuce, and sprouts), and smoo-ooth (avocados and yogurt), this is a salad to add to the repertoire of any vegetarian — or anyone else. Serve with dressing of 1 pint plain yogurt mixed with ½ teaspoon sugar.

1½ cups alfalfa sprouts
½ cup other sprouts
1 or 2 avocados, peeled, then sliced
   or chopped
2-4 tomatoes, cut into small wedges

4-6 leaves Romaine lettuce or fresh
   spinach, torn into small pieces
½ cup coarsely chopped cauliflower
   or broccoli florets

Place all ingredients together in large bowl and toss to mix well (amount of avocado, tomato, and greens depends on *size*). Serve with yogurt (as above) or other dressing. Serves 8-10.

Jane Hanson
Boulder, CO

Herbed Cherry Tomatoes

Serve marinated tomatoes cold on a bed of lettuce, or drain, and pop into roasting pan 5 minutes or so before you take out any roast meat or poultry. Or pass with toothpicks as an hors d'oeuvre.

1 pint cherry tomatoes
¼ cup minced parsley
¼ cup salad oil
3 teaspoons vinegar

½ teaspoon basil
½ teaspoon oregano
½ teaspoon salt
½ teaspoon sugar

Halve cherry tomatoes and place in bowl. Combine all other ingredients, and mix well, in blender or electric mixer — or the old way, by vigorous stirring and shaking. Pour over tomatoes. Serves 4 as salad.

Pat Black
The Rockport Heritage Cookbook

Stacked Tomato Salad

Couldn't be easier. Serve on lettuce as salad, or as is for a cold vegetable.

4 large tomatoes
¼ cup chopped fresh parsley
1 clove garlic, minced
1 teaspoon sugar
¼ teaspoon pepper

1 teaspoon salt
⅓ cup salad oil
2 tablespoons vinegar
1 teaspoon Dijon mustard

Peel tomatoes by dipping for a minute or so in boiling water, then removing peel. Slice each tomato crosswise into 3 or 4 slices. Reserve, ready to restack, while you make dressing. Combine in jar or small mixer bowl all other ingredients and shake or beat well to blend. Pour about 1 teaspoon over each layer of tomato as you restack them, topping each completed stack with another teaspoon of dressing. Place in 1-quart baking dish or bowl, and refrigerate for 1-2 hours, basting with dressing occasionally. Serves 4.

Katherine Bombara
Simsbury, CT

Swedish Vegetable Salad

For those who prefer their vegetables crisp, we suggest that carrots, peas, and beans be just very lightly parboiled.

Salad:
1½ cups diced cooked carrots
1½ cups cooked green peas
1½ cups cooked, sliced green beans
1½ cups sliced raw cauliflower
½ cup chopped onion

½ cup chopped celery
14-ounce can artichoke hearts,
    drained and quartered
⅔ cup sharp French dressing

Combine vegetables, and toss in French dressing. Marinate overnight. Drain.

Dressing for Swedish Salad:
¾ cup mayonnaise
¼ cup chili sauce
2 teaspoons dill weed

1 teaspoon salt
⅛ teaspoon pepper
1 tablespoon lemon juice

Mix all Dressing for Swedish Salad ingredients together, and blend thoroughly. Pour over salad, toss well, and chill for 1-2 hours before serving. Serves 8-10.

Mrs. James R. DeGolier
Middleton, WI

Vegetable Salad with Sharp Dressing

Spinach, cauliflower, broccoli, and mushrooms in an oil and vinegar dressing honed with mustard and horseradish.

½ pound fresh spinach
1 cup cauliflower florets
1 cup bite-sized pieces fresh
   broccoli
3 tablespoons olive oil
3 tablespoons wine vinegar
2 teaspoons horseradish

2 teaspoons prepared mustard
1 teaspoon sugar
1 teaspoon each of salt and garlic
   powder
⅛ teaspoon pepper
1 cup sliced fresh mushrooms

Wash spinach, remove stems, and tear leaves into bite-sized pieces. Combine in salad bowl with cauliflower and broccoli. Mix well together all other ingredients except mushrooms, to make dressing. Marinate mushrooms in dressing for 1 hour. Drain, reserving dressing, and add mushrooms to vegetables in bowl. Then pour dressing over, and toss well. Serves 4-6.

Elsie Stupinsky
Bernardsville, NJ

PASTA AND MAIN-DISH SALADS

Great combinations of chicken, fish, sea food, eggs, and cheese with vegetables and/or pasta to grace a summer buffet, or other occasion.

Chicken Salad with Grapes

A bit of work and a bit of money, but worth it for special gatherings. You can add up to another cup almonds, and vary the amount of grated onion, to taste. Easily halved or quartered.

8 cups cooked, diced chicken
20 ounces water chestnuts, drained
   and sliced
2 pounds seedless grapes, halved
2 cups diced celery
2 cups slivered almonds, toasted

3 cups mayonnaise
2 tablespoons soy sauce
1 tablespoon curry powder
2 teaspoons to 2 tablespoons grated
   onion, to taste
paprika

Mix all ingredients except paprika, and chill several hours. Serve on a bed of lettuce, and sprinkle with paprika. Serves 16.

Barbara Johnson
Athens, GA

Macaroni Salad

Notable for its cheese-and-sour-cream dressing.

1 cup raw macaroni
2 hardboiled eggs, sliced
¾ teaspoon salt
½ teaspoon pepper
2 tablespoons chopped green
    pepper

2 tablespoons chopped pimiento
2 tablespoons chopped celery
2 tablespoons sweet relish
1 cup grated cheese
¾ cup sour cream

Cook macaroni and drain. Add remaining ingredients in order given, and toss to mix well. Serves 4-6.

Mrs. Spencer Ham
Campton, NH

Rotini Salad

A gourmet pasta salad. Mixture will thicken as it chills.

2 cups mayonnaise
1 cup water
½ cup vinegar
1 cup sugar
½ teaspoon celery salt
½ teaspoon celery seeds
1 teaspoon turmeric

¼ teaspoon pepper
½ cup chopped onion
½ cup chopped celery
1 pound rotini, cooked *al dente* and
    drained
2 hardboiled eggs, chopped

Mix mayonnaise with water, vinegar, sugar, and seasonings in electric mixer until well blended. Add onion and celery, and blend well by hand. Pour dressing over hot cooked rotini, and add chopped eggs. Refrigerate overnight. Serves 6-8.

Joan Michaels
Wolcott, CT

Seafood and Pasta Shells

A brilliant idea for a buffet.

1 pound medium pasta shells	⅓ cup olive oil
7-ounce can tuna fish	(1 small onion, chopped)
9-ounce can crab meat	3 stalks celery, chopped
1 pound small shrimp, cooked, cooled, and halved	1½-2 cups mayonnaise
	4 hardboiled eggs, sliced
salt and pepper	4 medium tomatoes, sliced
2 tablespoons white vinegar	fresh parsley sprigs

Cook pasta shells, drain, and cool. Place tuna, crab meat, and shrimp in large bowl. Add pasta shells, salt and pepper, vinegar, oil, optional onion, and celery. Toss all together, then add enough mayonnaise to bind. Garnish with egg and tomato slices and parsley sprigs. Serves 8-10.

Elsie Stupinsky
Bernardsville, NJ

Spinach and Shrimp Chef's Salad

Serve with jellied consommé and rolls or French bread for a cool but filling summer meal.

10-ounce bag fresh spinach	½ cup slivered cooked ham slices
small head buttercrunch or Bibb lettuce	½ cup diced Colby, longhorn, or other mild cheese
4 hardboiled eggs, chopped	1 cup croutons
6 ounces fresh mushrooms, sliced thinly lengthwise	salad dressing (creamy Italian, Caesar, or Roquefort)
two 4½-ounce cans small shrimp, drained and rinsed	

Stem spinach leaves, and wash well. Dry, and wrap in clean towel. Tear lettuce leaves, wash, and wrap in clean towel. Refrigerate spinach and lettuce for 2 hours to crisp. Then place in salad bowl. In separate bowl, toss together chopped eggs, mushrooms, shrimp, ham, and cheese. When well mixed, add to salad bowl and toss again. Top with croutons. Add dressing, and toss before serving. Or, if you will be serving the salad a second time, pass dressing separately. Serves 4-6.

James R. Henry
Florissant, MO

Salads, Dressings, et al. / 231

Hot or Cold Tuna Potato Salad

Serve this salad hot, or cold on Bibb lettuce — a hearty meal either way.

½ cup diced onion or thinly sliced
    green onions
½ cup chopped celery
½ cup cooked green peas
7-ounce can tuna fish, drained and
    flaked

½ cup mayonnaise
6 small new potatoes, boiled and
    quartered
4 hardboiled eggs, sliced
6 slices bacon, cooked and drained

Combine onion, celery, peas, tuna, and mayonnaise with hot potatoes. Toss. Garnish with egg slices, and crumble bacon over top. Serves 4.

Adele Bourne
Moorestown, NJ

MOLDED AND FROZEN SALADS

Attractive and novel inventions to grace your dinner table, these are arranged from vegetable/protein salads to fruit salads.

Dried Beef and Celery Mold

A substantial salad that makes a fine summer luncheon or supper.

3-ounce package lemon gelatin
1¼ cups boiling water
1 cup salad dressing (Miracle
    Whip type)
2½ ounces dried beef, minced

2 tablespoons chopped green
    pepper
4 hardboiled eggs, chopped
2 tablespoons chopped onion
¾ cup chopped celery

Mix gelatin and boiling water, and stir until gelatin has dissolved. Chill until jelly-like, then whip hard. Beat in salad dressing. Fold in remaining ingredients, and pour into large mold (6-8 cups). Serves 6.

Nina A. Nelson
Ortonville, MN

Molded Broccoli Salad

Bright green and yellow salad that adds a festive note to any meal. Use real mayonnaise if possible.

two 10-ounce packages frozen
    chopped broccoli
6 hardboiled eggs
1 envelope plain gelatin
¼ cup cold water
10-ounce can consommé, heated
    but not boiled

¾ cup mayonnaise
1½ teaspoons salt
2 teaspoons lemon juice
4 teaspoons Worcestershire sauce
(pimiento strips)

Cook broccoli until just tender, and drain well. Mash 4 of the 6 eggs with potato masher or in food processor. Soften gelatin in cold water, and dissolve in hot consommé. Combine broccoli, mashed eggs, and consommé. In separate bowl, combine mayonnaise, salt, lemon juice, and Worcestershire sauce, and mix well. Fold into first mixture. Rinse 6-cup mold (or 7½x12-inch pan, or 7x11-inch baking dish) with cold water, and pour in mixture. Chill. When gelatin begins to set up, lightly stir mold with spatula using a folding motion from bottom to top to keep mayonnaise from settling to bottom. Return to refrigerator, and chill until firm. Slice remaining hardboiled eggs, wetting knife blade before each slice (keeps slices whole). Unmold salad on bed of greens and garnish with egg slices, and with optional pimiento strips for color. Serves 8-10.

Sunny Erwin Shaffer
Columbus, OH

Green Grotto Salad

Rich and glorious. Serve on a bed of lettuce, ring with cherry tomatoes, and pass a dressing made from ½ cup sour cream mixed with ½ cup mayonnaise.

3-ounce package lime gelatin
1¾ cups boiling water
dash salt
3 tablespoons vinegar
1 cup chopped celery

¼ cup stuffed Spanish olives
1 cup chopped cucumber
7-ounce can solid-pack white tuna,
    drained and flaked
¾ cup mayonnaise

Place gelatin in bowl, and pour in boiling water. Stir well to dissolve. Add salt, vinegar, chopped celery, and olives. Pour half of this mixture into 1-quart mold rinsed with cold water. Chill until firm. To remaining gelatin, add cucumber, tuna, and mayonnaise. Mix well, and keep at room temperature until first layer is firm. Spoon second layer over first in mold, and chill until firm. Serves 6.

Kay Edwards
Beckley, WV

Eggs Everglade

Serve alone on lettuce, with a sauce of cold marinated mushrooms, or with a sour cream-cucumber dressing.

2 envelopes plain gelatin
1½ cups cold chicken broth
1½ teaspoons curry powder

4 hardboiled eggs, chopped
1½ cups mayonnaise

Soften gelatin in ½ cup broth. Add remaining broth and curry powder. Heat, stirring, until gelatin and curry have dissolved. Cool. Add eggs and mayonnaise, and mix well. Pour into rinsed 6-cup ring mold, and chill until firm. Serves 6-8.

Isabelle R. Alter
Haverhill, MA

Molded Ham and Potato Salad

Attractive and filling for lunch or brunch. Serve on bed of mixed greens.

Ham Layer:
1½ cups diced cooked ham
¼ cup chili sauce
1 tablespoon finely chopped onion
2 teaspoons prepared mustard
1 teaspoon horseradish
1 envelope plain gelatin
½ cup water
½ cup mayonnaise or salad dressing

Potato Layer:
2 cups diced cooked potatoes
½ cup diced celery
1 tablespoon finely chopped onion
2 tablespoons finely chopped green pepper
2 teaspoons vinegar
1 teaspoon salt
⅛ teaspoon pepper
½ cup mayonnaise or salad dressing

Combine ham, chili sauce, onion, mustard, and horseradish. Soften gelatin in water, then heat, stirring until gelatin is dissolved. Stir ¼ cup of gelatin mixture into mayonnaise, and add to ham mixture, mixing well. (Keep remaining ¼ cup gelatin at room temperature.) Turn into rinsed 10x6-inch baking dish, and chill until almost set, when it is time to add the ham layer. (Check after 6 minutes.)

Combine all ingredients for potato layer except mayonnaise. Mix mayonnaise with remaining ¼ cup gelatin mixture, and stir into other ingredients. Mix well. Spoon atop ham layer. Chill until firm. Serves 8.

Dorothy Steller
Little Falls, NJ

Seafood Mold

Just the salad for the large fish-shape mold, but use a regular 6-cup mold if you don't happen to own a fish mold.

3-ounce package lemon gelatin
½ cup hot water
10½-ounce can tomato soup
8 ounces cream cheese
½ cup mayonnaise
½ cup diced celery

1 small onion, minced
8 ounces tiny peas
Tabasco and Worcestershire to
   taste
1½ cups shrimp or crab

Mix gelatin with hot water. Heat soup, and add cream cheese. Mash together until well blended. Remove from heat. Add mayonnaise, and stir well. Stir in gelatin mixture and all remaining ingredients. Pour into 6-cup mold greased with mayonnaise. Chill until firm. Serves 6.

Hazel D. Little
Vienna, VA

FRUITS

Avocado Cream Sherbert

Serve in between courses of a large meal to refresh the palate, or on lettuce as a salad. For best results, use freshly grated rinds. Can be kept in freezer for 2-3 weeks.

2 envelopes plain gelatin
1 cup milk
¾ cup lemon juice
¾ cup orange juice
3 cups diced and pared ripe
   avocado
½ teaspoon salt

2 tablespoons grated lemon rind
3 tablespoons grated orange rind
3 cups heavy cream, whipped
1½ cups sugar
6 drops green food coloring
4 drops yellow food coloring

In small saucepan, sprinkle gelatin over milk to soften. Combine lemon and orange juices with avocado, and whirl in electric blender until smooth. Turn into large bowl. Add salt and grated rinds. Fold in whipped cream. Add sugar to gelatin mixture, and dissolve over low heat, stirring. Add food colors. Cool slightly, then stir slowly into avocado mixture. Turn into 3-4 ice trays, dividers removed. Freeze until frozen 1 inch from edge. Turn into large, chilled bowl. Beat with electric mixer until smooth, but not melted. Turn into 2½-quart freezer container. Cover, and freeze until firm. Before serving, unmold from freezer container onto serving platter. Return to freezer until ready to serve. Garnish with chilled fruits, or place on bed of lettuce. Serves 12.

Mrs. John G. Webb
An Olde Concord Xmas

Cranberry Molded Salad

A very handsome way to serve a crowd. Unmold on large platter over bed of lettuce, or spoon out portions onto small plates with lettuce.

First Layer:

6-ounce package cherry gelatin
2 cups boiling water
1-pound can whole cranberry sauce

1-pound can crushed pineapple
  with juice
½ cup chopped nuts

Dissolve gelatin in boiling water, add cranberry sauce, pineapple, and nuts, and mix well. Rinse large glass bowl with cold water, then pour in mixture. Chill until firm.

Second Layer:

3-ounce package cherry gelatin
1 cup boiling water

1 cup cranberry juice or cold water
1 cup sour cream

For second layer, dissolve gelatin in boiling water, stir in juice or water and sour cream, and mix well. Pour on top of set first layer. Chill until firm. Serves 15-20.

Eileen Glora
Quincy, MA

Frozen Grape Salad

Another festive salad that can be made ahead of time for a special occasion. For variation, substitute canned, drained bing cherries for the grapes.

two 3-ounce packages cream
  cheese, softened
2 tablespoons mayonnaise
2 tablespoons pineapple syrup
24 marshmallows, quartered

20-ounce can pineapple tidbits,
  drained
1 cup heavy cream, whipped
2 cups Tokay grapes, halved and
  seeded

Blend cream cheese with mayonnaise, and beat in pineapple syrup. Add marshmallows and drained pineapple tidbits. Fold in whipped cream and grapes. Pour into 9x5-inch loaf pan or 7x11-inch glass baking dish, and freeze until firm. Slice or cut into squares while still frozen, but allow to soften somewhat before serving. Serves 10-12.

Elmira E. Mauger
American Legion Auxiliary, Unit 471
Boyerstown, PA

Orange Supreme Salad

A refreshing salad or dessert. For dessert, top with an additional dollop of whipped cream.

3-ounce package orange gelatin
3-ounce package lemon gelatin
2 cups boiling water
1 pint orange sherbert
4 bananas, peeled and cut into
    pieces

20-ounce can crushed pineapple,
    drained
11-ounce can mandarin oranges,
    drained
1 cup whipped cream

Dissolve gelatin in boiling water. Stir in remaining ingredients in order as given. Rinse a 13x9-inch pan with cold water. Pour in salad mixture, and chill until set. Serves 8.

Mrs. Reynolds Senior
Newburyport, MA

Zippy Pineapple Salad

A tasty luncheon salad without much fuss.

3-ounce package lemon gelatin
3-ounce package lime gelatin
2 cups boiling water
1 cup evaporated milk
1 pint cottage cheese

½ cup mayonnaise
1-3 tablespoons horseradish to
    taste
1-pound can crushed pineapple,
    drained

Dissolve gelatin in boiling water. Combine other ingredients in large bowl, and pour in gelatin. Stir to mix well, and pour into 1½- to 2-quart mold, rinsed out first with cold water. Chill until firm. Serves 6-8.

Josie Lees Powers
Laconia, NH

Jellied Strawberry Salad

Quick and easy to make — great salad to serve to a group.

two 3-ounce packages strawberry
    gelatin
¾ cup boiling water
10- or 16-ounce package frozen
    strawberries with juice, thawed

20-ounce can crushed pineapple
2 bananas, mashed
½ cup chopped nuts
1 cup sour cream

Dissolve gelatin in boiling water. Add strawberries, pineapple, bananas, and nuts. Pour half this mixture into large ring or other mold (8-10 cups), first rinsed with cold water. Chill until partly set. Spoon sour cream on top of partly set layer, then pour in remaining gelatin mixture. Chill until firm. Serves 6-8.

Janice Ryzewski
Shrewsbury, MA

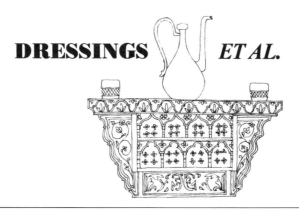

DRESSINGS *ET AL.*

Celery Seed Dressing

Serve with fruit molds or any green salad. Do not use blender.

⅓ cup sugar
1 teaspoon salt
1 teaspoon dry mustard
1 teaspoon grated onion

¼ cup red wine vinegar
1 cup salad oil
1 teaspoon celery seeds

Mix first three ingredients. Add onion and vinegar, then beat in oil, 1 tablespoon at a time. Stir in celery seeds. Makes about 1½ cups dressing.

Jane Hanson
Boulder, CO

Creamy Dressing

You really need a blender to bring this rather different dressing made with cheese, mustard, and wine to the proper consistency. Make with 1-4 tablespoons sugar, according to your taste.

2 cloves garlic, chopped
1-4 tablespoons sugar
½ teaspoon dry mustard
1 teaspoon salt
½ cup tomato catsup
1 teaspoon Worcestershire sauce

⅓ cup vinegar
⅓ cup red wine
¾ cup salad oil
½ cup Cheddar (or other) cheese,
    chopped or shredded

Put all ingredients together in blender, and whirl until creamy. Put on "liquefy" for a few seconds. Before serving, make sure all ingredients are well blended (if refrigerated before serving, bring to room temperature, and whirl in blender briefly before serving). Makes 2 cups.

Rosalee Lee
De Laud, FL

English Tea Room Dressing

A sweet dressing for fruit or greens salad. Make in a blender.

¾ cup cider vinegar
1 cup confectioner's sugar
1 teaspoon celery salt
1 teaspoon salt

1 teaspoon onion powder
¾ cup salad oil
¼ teaspoon dill weed
1 garlic clove, crushed

Mix together all ingredients, pour into blender, and whirl. Makes about 2 cups.

Jessie Bewley
The Well Tempered Kitchen

Poppy Seed Dressing

Sensational with sweet onions and/or grapefruit. Refrigerate for up to a week. Can also be made in a blender.

1½ cups sugar
2 teaspoons dry mustard
2 teaspoons salt
¼ cup poppy seeds

⅔ cup vinegar
3 tablespoons onion juice
2 cups salad oil

Combine all ingredients except oil, and beat well to blend. Add salad oil, a little at a time, beating after each addition. Makes about 2½ cups.

Kate Reed
Hanover Center Cooks

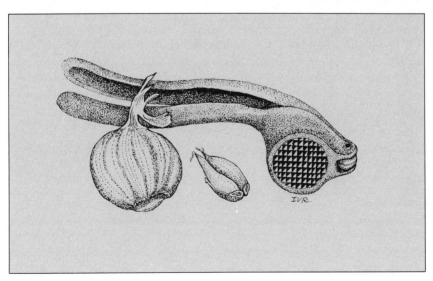

Tomato Soup Dressing

Keeps almost indefinitely in refrigerator.

10½-ounce can tomato soup
1 cup sugar
1 teaspoon salt

1 cup cider vinegar
1 teaspoon dry mustard
1 teaspoon black pepper

Combine all ingredients in saucepan, and bring to boil. Cool, then chill before using.

Martha Sharp Oyler
Anderson, IN

Raspberry Shrub

This wonderful tart-sweet raspberry syrup keeps well, and is used primarily as a beverage base. Pour a little into a glass with ice, and fill with water; or add a little gin or vodka, and then fill with water. Very cooling drink.

1 quart raspberries
cider vinegar

sugar

Place raspberries in stoneware jar and cover with vinegar. Cover jar. Let stand in cool place for 24 hours. Then strain through double layer of cheese-cloth (do not press too closely). To each cup of juice, add 1 cup sugar. Simmer gently on stove, stirring constantly, and skimming off froth. When no more froth rises to surface, take from heat, bottle, and cork well. Keep in cool place. Dip corked bottle top in paraffin to ensure seal. Makes 3-4 cups.

Abbie Murray
Mount Kisco, NY

Haymaker's Switchel

From the days when hay was cut by hand, with a scythe, this drink was designed to cool and energize the workers, without the cramping that could be caused by an iced drink. Have some after strenuous exercise on a hot day, and you'll see.

2 quarts water
1 cup sugar
½ cup molasses

½ cup vinegar
½ teaspoon ginger

Heat water, and add other ingredients, stirring until well blended. Chill. Serve at the temperature of well water. Makes 2 quarts.

Buster Charles
Brewster, NY

CHAPTER NINE

Pies and Desserts

We all have our own favorite standby desserts that our own families love. But every so often adventure calls — a need for new horizons, that overwhelming urge to do something different. Perhaps a particular fruit is in season; perhaps you are called upon to create a feast for a special group; perhaps important people are coming to dinner . . . Here are superb ideas from the Good Neighbors for such occasions.

This chapter features *ten* different pie crusts to use in all sorts of ways, wonderful pies and cheesecakes, and a fabulous array of other desserts — rich and sweet to top off a light meal, tart and light to crown a rich one — and gradations in between.

PIE CRUSTS AND PIES

Basic Pie Crust

The combination of sour milk and lard makes this crust extra flaky.

2½ cups white flour (or 1½ cups white flour and 1 cup wheat flour)
1 teaspoon salt

1 cup lard or margarine
1 tablepoon vinegar
milk added to vinegar to measure ½ cup

Combine flour and salt. Cut in shortening until mixture is of a crumbly consistency. Pour in sour milk; mix with fork to moisten. Roll dough into two balls. Wrap each in plastic wrap and refrigerate until ready to use. Bake pie shell at 450°F. for 12-15 minutes. Bake double-crusted pie as directed for filling. Makes two 9-inch crusts, or enough for a two-crust 10-inch pie.

Gertrude Richardson
Harrisville, NH

Pâte Brisée

Made in food processor, this is a rich crust for fruit tarts, quiches, or filled pies.

1¾ cups flour
½ teaspoon salt

¾ cup cold butter
⅓ cup ice water

Place flour and salt in food processor. Cut butter into pieces approximately ½ inch square. Add butter to flour. Blend in processor until of evenly crumbly consistency. While machine is running, add ice water. Stop machine when dough forms a ball. Wrap in plastic wrap, and refrigerate until ready to use. Roll out dough and place in pie pan. Leave 2 extra inches to build a high edge, allowing for shrinkage. Crimp edges in desired style, and bake at 400°F. for 10 minutes or until lightly browned. Makes one 9-inch pie shell.

Susanna Whitier
Bangor, ME

Chocolate Pie Shell

An oh-so-chocolaty crust for cream and ice-cream pies.

6 tablespoons shortening
1 cup flour
¼ cup brown sugar, packed
2 tablespoons cocoa

(⅓ cup finely chopped walnuts)
1 tablespoon water
1 tablespoon vanilla

(continued)

Cut shortening into flour. Add brown sugar, cocoa, and optional nuts. Combine liquids, and incorporate gently with rubber spatula or hands. Press into lightly greased pan. Bake at 375°F. for 15 minutes. Cool before filling. Makes one 9-inch pie shell.

Elizabeth Johanson
Providence, RI

Coconut-Walnut Pie Shell

Wonderful with ice-cream or cream filling.

½ cup flaked coconut
1 cup finely chopped walnuts

3 tablespoons sugar
2 tablespoons butter or margarine

Mix ingredients well with hands until crumbly. Press into well-greased pie pan. Bake at 400°F. for 8 minutes or until brown. Makes one 9-inch pie shell.

Mrs. David Isles
Orleans, MA

Butter-Crumb Pastry

A delicate, buttery crust for chiffon and cream pies.

¾ cup flour
6 tablespoons soft butter or
    margarine

2 tablespoons confectioner's sugar

Mix ingredients well with hands until crumbly. Press into lightly greased pie pan. Bake at 400°F. for 10-12 minutes, or until lightly browned. Cool completely before filling. Makes one 9-inch pie shell.

Carla Kardt
Harrisville, NH

Cookie-Crumb Crusts

These crusts will complement a variety of chiffon, ice-cream, and pudding pies, as well as cheesecakes and other specialty desserts. Make crumbs from gingersnaps, chocolate wafers, or vanilla wafers. Enough for one 9- or 10-inch pie shell.

¼ cup sugar
1½ cups finely crushed cookie
    crumbs

½ cup butter, melted

Blend sugar, crumbs, and butter together with fingertips until well mixed. Press into lightly buttered pie plate, and bake at 350°F. for 8-10 minutes, or refrigerate for at least 1 hour before filling so that crust will become stiff. Makes one 9- or 10-inch pie shell.

Margaret Hazelton
Rockford, IL

Graham-Cracker Crust

A good basic recipe. For variety, add the cinnamon.

1½ cups crushed graham cracker
   crumbs
4 tablespoons brown sugar, packed

6 tablespoons butter, melted (or
   shortening)
(¼ teaspoon cinnamon)

Mix ingredients well. Press into lightly greased pie pan. Bake at 350°F. for 10 minutes. Cool. Makes one 9-inch pie shell.

Carla Kardt
Harrisville, NH

Meringue Pie Shell

For a really fancy dessert. Allow pie to sit overnight after filling. This will make it easier to cut.

4 egg whites
½ teaspoon cream of tartar
⅛ teaspoon salt

½ teaspoon vanilla
1 cup sugar

Put egg whites in deep bowl; add cream of tartar, salt, and vanilla. Beat until stiff. Add sugar gradually, beating constantly. When very stiff, spread lightly in well-buttered glass pie pan. Bake at 275°F. for 1 hour. The meringue should not brown, but should be a delicate creamy tan, dry and firm. Makes one 9- or 10-inch pie shell.

Mrs. Harvey Binsfield
Spokane, WA

FRUIT PIES

Allowing fruit pies to cool completely before cutting will give the filling a chance to thicken and set. Servings will be neater and more attractive, and the juice will not be left in the pie plate.

Apple Pie

Before baking, this pie is very tall. The apples cook down into a thick filling.

¾ cup light brown sugar, packed
4 tablespoons cornstarch
1 teaspoon cinnamon
⅛ teaspoon nutmeg
⅛ teaspoon salt

6 cups thinly sliced apples
   (approximately 8 medium-size
   apples)
basic 9-inch pie crust (page 242)
3 tablespoons butter, cut into small
   pieces

(continued)

Stir together dry ingredients. Add apples, and toss together to mix thorough-ly. Pile into pie shell. Distribute pieces of butter on top. Lay top layer of crust over apples. Trim the crust, and fold in under the bottom crust. Crimp the edge, and make several decorative slits in the top. Bake at 375°F. for 55 minutes or until brown.

Elsie Somero
Springfield, MA

French Apple Tart

Very attractive, very French, and very good.

Pastry:
½ cup butter, softened
½ teaspoon salt
1 tablespoon sugar
1 small egg
2 cups flour
cold water

Filling:
20-ounce jar applesauce

4 apples, peeled, cored, and thinly
    sliced
confectioner's sugar

Glaze:
1½ cups apricot jam
2 tablespoons sugar
½ cup water
2 tablespoons Kirsch

Cream butter; add salt, sugar, and egg. Mix in flour, using pastry blender, fork, or hands. Add water gradually, using only enough to make a firm dough. Roll pastry ¼ inch thick. Place in 9-inch pie pan, and flute a rim to hold in juice.

Prick pastry and spread with applesauce. Arrange apple slices in neat overlapping circles over applesauce. Sprinkle with confectioner's sugar. Bake at 350°F. for 35-40 minutes.

For glaze, combine jam, sugar, and water in saucepan. Bring to boil, and cook for about 8 minutes. Watch carefully to avoid scorching. Put through sieve, add Kirsch, and spread over tart. Makes one 9-inch pie.

Mrs. Bradshaw Crandell
Aurora, NY
Vittles Unlimited

Apricot Tart

Flaky pastry, custard cream, and the sweet-tart taste of apricots — beautiful!

Pastry:

1¾ cups flour	¼ cup shortening
1½ teaspoons sugar	½ cup butter
pinch salt	¼ cup cold water

Combine flour, sugar, and salt, then cut in shortening and butter. Add water, and form into ball. Chill. Grease a 9-inch pie plate. Roll out dough, and place in pie plate. Bake at 300°F. for about 35 minutes. Cool completely before filling.

Filling:

½ cup sugar	1½ tablespoons flour
2 egg yolks	2 cups milk, scalded
1 egg	½ teaspoons vanilla
3 tablespoons cornstarch	

Combine sugar, eggs, cornstarch, and flour. Mix well. Gradually add hot milk, stirring constantly. Cook over medium-low heat until mixture thickens. Remove from heat, add vanilla, and cool.

Topping:

¾ cup Zweiback crumbs	1 cup apricot jam, heated and
16 canned apricots, halved	strained

Spread filling in cooled shell and sprinkle with Zweiback crumbs. Arrange apricot halves over crumbs. Pour strained apricot jam over surface. Chill. Makes one 9-inch pie.

Henry Flory
Southern Pines, NC

Chilled Blueberry Pie

A really unusual no-bake, fresh blueberry pie. Serve with whipped cream.

4 cups fresh blueberries, cleaned	2 tablespoons cornstarch
¾ cup sugar	2 tablespoons cold water
½ cup water	9-inch pie shell, baked and cooled

In a saucepan, combine 1 cup of the blueberries with sugar and ½ cup water. Bring mixture to boil, reduce heat, and cook slowly until berries are soft (about 5 minutes). Puree mixture in blender or food processor. Return to saucepan. Stir cornstarch and 2 tablespoons cold water together until smooth. Add to cooked blueberries, and continue cooking until puree has thickened. Bring to boil, remove from heat, and cool for about 10 minutes. Fold in remaining 3 cups uncooked berries, and mix gently. Turn into prepared pie shell. Chill for several hours. Makes one 9-inch pie.

Mrs. James O. Rodgers
Pelham Manor, NY
Vittles Unlimited

TO STABILIZE WHIPPED CREAM

So many of us have prepared a pie or dessert that is decorated with whipped cream, either made from scratch, or from an aerosol tube, and refrigerated it overnight or longer, only to find, when the pie or dessert is taken from the "fridge," the whipped cream decoration has fallen FLAT, and, in the case of even the best commercial product, not only fallen flat, but released the water in its content to float over the surface of the goodie in question. To prevent this calamity, either decorate with whipped cream *immediately* before serving, *or* make reinforced whipped cream, as in the recipe that follows for 2 cups of reinforced whipped cream.

½ teaspoon plain gelatin
1 tablespoon cold water
1 tablespoon heavy cream

2 tablespoons confectioner's
sugar
1 cup heavy cream

Soften gelatin in cold water. Heat over hot water to dissolve. Add 1 tablespoon heavy cream. Whip sugar with 1 cup heavy cream until thick, then add gelatin mixture, and whip until stiff. Pipe this whipped cream through pastry tube onto dessert or pie to be decorated. Cream will hold its form even when transported short distances as long as it is kept cool.

Carla Kardt
Harrisville, NH

Bob Andy Pie

Basically a cinnamon custard pie with a nice flavor. Inexpensive and quickly made.

2 teaspoons flour
½ teaspoon cinnamon
pinch salt
⅔ cup sugar

2 eggs, lightly beaten
2 teaspoons butter, melted
1 cup milk, scalded
8-inch unbaked pie shell

Combine dry ingredients. Add eggs and butter. Add milk gradually, stirring after each addition. Pour into pie shell, and bake at 400°F. for 10 minutes. Lower oven temperature to 350°F., and bake 25-30 minutes longer. Makes one 8-inch pie.

Mrs. Harvey Binsfield
Spokane, WA

Chocolate-Orange Meringue Torte

A deliciously fresh and satisfying combination of meringue, chocolate, orange custard, and whipped cream. Use freshly ground rinds and fresh juice for best results.

Meringue:

4 egg whites
¼ teaspoon cream of tartar
¼ teaspoon salt
¾ cup sugar
½ cup semisweet chocolate bits

Filling:

4 egg yolks

⅓ cup sugar
1 tablespoon lemon juice
1 tablespoon orange juice
1 teaspoon grated lemon rind
1 teaspoon grated orange rind
1 cup heavy cream
2 tablespoons sugar

Beat egg whites with cream of tartar and salt until stiff. Gradually add ¾ cup sugar, 1 tablespoonful at a time, beating after each addition. Spread in well-greased 9-inch pie pan, making edges slightly higher than center. Bake at 275°F. for 1 hour. While meringue is hot, sprinkle ¼ cup of the chocolate bits over it, and spread with the back of a teaspoon. Cool completely. Make filling.

Beat egg yolks, gradually adding ⅓ cup sugar. Add lemon and orange juice and rind. Transfer to saucepan, and cook over medium heat until thick, stirring constantly. Remove from heat, and cover with plastic wrap to prevent skin from forming. Cool. Whip cream with 2 tablespoons sugar. Spread half the whipped cream in meringue shell. Cover with cooled orange filling, gently spreading over cream. Spread remaining cream over custard. Sprinkle with remaining chocolate bits, coarsely chopped. Serves 8.

Mrs. Howard Bierkan
Madison, CT
Vittles Unlimited

Seville Chocolate Silk Pie

Silky-textured chocolate-orange filling in a chocolate crumb crust. Serve with whipped cream.

Crust:

1½ cups chocolate-wafer crumbs
⅓ cup sugar
6 tablespoons butter, melted
grated rind of 1 orange

Filling:

¾ cup butter, softened

1¼ cups superfine sugar
3 squares (ounces) unsweetened
  chocolate, melted and cooled
2 tablespoons Grand Marnier
  liqueur
grated rind of 1 orange
3 large eggs (room temperature)

(continued)

Combine ingredients for crust and press into greased 9-inch pie plate. Bake at 350°F. for 10 minutes. Cool before filling.

Cream butter and sugar until fluffy. Add chocolate, and beat until well blended. Beat in Grand Marnier and orange rind. Add eggs, one at a time, beating 5 minutes after each addition. Pour into pie plate, and chill. Remove from refrigerator 15 minutes before serving. Makes one 9-inch pie.

Bonnie Berrett
Jaffrey, NH

Fudge Bottom Pie

From bottom to top — graham crackers, fudge, custard, and whipped cream. Not for dieters!

Fudge Bottom:

1½ squares (ounces) unsweetened
  chocolate
¼ cup sugar
¼ cup plus 1 tablespoon water

pinch salt
8- or 9-inch graham-cracker crust,
  baked and cooled

Combine first four ingredients in 1-quart saucepan. Heat over medium-low heat until chocolate has melted and mixture is thick and smooth, approximately 10 minutes. Spread chocolate evenly over graham-cracker crust and place in freezer to set. Prepare filling.

Filling:

1 cup milk, scalded
1 egg, large or extra large
¼ cup sugar

1 tablespoon cornstarch
½ teaspoon vanilla
pinch salt

Cool milk slightly. Thoroughly blend egg, sugar, cornstarch, vanilla, and salt in 1-quart saucepan. Stir in milk, and mix well. Cook over medium-high heat, stirring constantly until mixture thickens and comes to a boil. Remove from heat, and cool slightly, stirring occasionally to prevent skin from forming. Pour custard over fudge bottom. Chill pie until firmly set.

Topping:

1 cup heavy cream
1 tablespoon sugar

sweet chocolate for garnish

Combine cream and sugar in small bowl and whip. Spread over the pie (or pipe through pastry bag) just before serving. Grate chocolate over pie. Makes one 8- or 9-inch pie.

Grace and James Schaefer
Milwaukee, WI

Persian Lime Pie

A northern version of Key Lime Pie, made with standard limes rather than "Key" limes of Florida. Richly refreshing.

15-ounce can sweetened condensed
  milk
3 egg yolks, beaten
⅔ cup freshly squeezed lime juice
2 teaspoons freshly grated lime
  rind

thin slices of lime for garnish
9-inch butter-crumb pie-shell (page
  243), baked and cooled

Blend first five ingredients well. Pour into prepared pie shell. Chill overnight to assure firm setting. Serve with whipped cream. Garnish with thin lime slices. Makes one 9-inch pie.

Mrs. Charles L. Quinn
New Castle, PA

Best-Ever Peach Pie

Smooth, delightful, and delovely. Easy to make, too.

two 1-pound cans sliced peaches,
  drained
15-ounce can sweetened condensed
  milk
1 teaspoon vanilla

juice of 2 lemons
1 envelope plain gelatin
9-inch graham-cracker crust (page
  244), baked and cooled

Combine peaches, condensed milk, and vanilla in bowl. Mix lemon juice and gelatin in cup, and stir until gelatin is dissolved. Quickly add to peach mixture, and stir to mix thoroughly. Pour into pie crust, and refrigerate until set, several hours or overnight. Serve well chilled with whipped cream. Serves 8.

Marie DeCapua
Montowese Woman's Club
Vittles Unlimited

Cushall Pecan Pie

Cushall is a squash similar to pumpkin that is plentiful in Kentucky. This is a superb pie in texture and flavor. Pumpkin can be substituted for cushall.

3 eggs, lightly beaten
1 cup cushall, cooked and mashed
1 cup brown sugar, packed
½ cup light corn syrup
1 teaspoon vanilla

½ teaspoon cinnamon
¼ teaspoon salt
9-inch pie shell, unbaked
1 cup chopped pecans
whipped cream   *(continued)*

Combine all ingredients except pie shell, pecans, and whipped cream. Mix well, and pour into pie crust. Top with pecans. Bake at 350°F. for 40 minutes. Cool to room temperature, then chill, and serve with whipped cream. Makes one 9-inch pie.

Mrs. Mary Stamper
Booneville, KY

Maple Pecan Pie

Maple syrup makes this a very special pecan pie. Easy and quick to make, too. You do need real maple syrup.

¼ cup butter, melted
1 cup dark brown sugar, packed
1 cup light (Grade "A") maple
    syrup
3 eggs, well beaten

¼ teaspoon salt
1 teaspoon vanilla
1 cup pecans
9-inch pie shell, unbaked

Cream butter and sugar. Add syrup, eggs, salt and vanilla. Mix thoroughly and add pecans. Pour into pie shell. Bake 5 minutes at 450°F. Reduce heat to 350°F., and bake about 40 minutes, or until firm. Makes one 9-inch pie.

Mrs. D. Charlton Gilbert
Mt. Carmel, CT
Vittles Unlimited

Frozen Pumpkin Applesauce Pie

If you can't find butter-pecan ice cream, try this with butter-almond. The original recipe called for a quart rather than a pint of ice cream, but we couldn't fit it all into the crust.

1 cup applesauce
1 cup cooked pumpkin
½ cup dark brown sugar, packed
¾ teaspoon cinnamon
¼ teaspoon nutmeg
¼ teaspoon salt

dash cloves
1 pint butter-pecan ice cream
10-inch gingersnap crust (page
    243), or other pie shell
whipped cream

Combine applesauce, pumpkin, brown sugar, cinnamon, nutmeg, salt, and cloves in saucepan. Bring to a boil. Simmer 5 minutes to blend. Cool. Mix with ice cream. Pour into crust and top with whipped cream. Freeze. Allow to stand at room temperature for 10 minutes before cutting. Makes one 10-inch pie.

Mrs. J. W. Leyerzaph
Menlo Park, CA
Vittles Unlimited

Praline Pumpkin Pie

The praline crust of this scrumptious pumpkin pie is a delightful surprise. Serve with whipped cream.

<u>Crust:</u>
⅓ cup finely chopped pecans
⅓ cup brown sugar, packed
3 tablespoons butter, softened
pastry for 10-inch pie shell

<u>Filling:</u>
3 eggs, lightly beaten
¼ cup white sugar

½ cup brown sugar, packed
2 tablespoons flour
¾ teaspoon salt
½ teaspoon cinnamon
½ teaspoon ginger
¼ teaspoon mace
20-ounce can cooked pumpkin
1½ cups light cream, scalded

Add nuts, brown sugar, and butter to pastry dough, and mix well. Press pastry into buttered 10-inch pie plate. Prick sides with fork. Bake at 450°F. for 10 minutes. Cool.

To make filling, combine eggs, sugars, flour, salt, spices, and pumpkin. Gradually add hot light cream. Pour into pie shell, and bake at 350°F. for 50-60 minutes. Cool. Makes one 10-inch pie.

Patricia Lindbo
Winchester, MA

CUSTARDS

When making custard desserts with a milk or cream base, bring milk or cream to boiling point before adding to eggs and other ingredients. Add hot milk or cream slowly, stirring constantly. This helps advance the setting of the custard, cuts down on cooking time, and creates a smoother texture in the finished product.

Rhubarb Custard Pie

The crumb topping and smooth texture give this pie such a new dimension that even people who detest rhubarb will ask for seconds.

Pie:
3 eggs, beaten
2 cups sugar
3 tablespoons milk
¼ cup flour
½ teaspoon cinnamon
¼ teaspoon nutmeg
4 cups diced rhubarb

9-inch pie shell, unbaked

Topping:
¼ cup butter, softened
½ cup brown sugar, packed
½ teaspoon cinnamon
⅓ cup flour

Combine eggs, sugar, and milk. Stir in flour, cinnamon, and nutmeg. Add rhubarb. Mix and pour into unbaked pie shell. Bake at 400°F. for 15 minutes.

Mix together all topping ingredients, sprinkle evenly over pie, and return to oven. Bake at 350°F. for 40 minutes. Makes one 9-inch pie.

Carla Kardt
Harrisville, NH

Rosé Chiffon Pie

Flavored with rosé wine, this prizewinning pie in a crushed almond crust is a show-stopper for special occasions.

6-ounce can whole almonds, ground
   (1½ cups)
2 tablespoons butter, melted
3 tablespoons sugar
1 envelope plain gelatin
¾ cup sugar

4 eggs, separated
½ cup rosé wine
¼ cup water
¼ teaspoon cream of tartar
1 cup heavy cream

Blend ground almonds, butter, and 3 tablespoons sugar in small bowl. Press mixture evenly over bottom and sides of lightly buttered 8-inch pie plate. Bake at 350°F. for 10 minutes. Remove from oven, and let cool. Mix gelatin and ½ cup of sugar in top of double boiler. Beat in egg yolks until fluffy. Blend in wine and water. Cook over simmering water, stirring constantly, until mixture just begins to boil (will coat the spoon). Pour into large bowl and chill, stirring occasionally, until as thick as unbeaten egg whites. Beat egg whites with cream of tartar until foamy. Add remaining ¼ cup of sugar a tablespoonful at a time, beating after each addition. Continue to beat until peaks form. Fold into gelatin mixture. In chilled bowl, whip cream until stiff and fold into gelatin mixture. Spoon into prepared almond crust. Chill at least 4 hours before serving. Makes one 8-inch pie.

Jacqueline T. Collimore
New Haven, CT

Sherry Cream Pie

A suave, sherried chiffon pie flavored with nutmeg and adorned with whipped cream, nutmeg, and chocolate shavings.

1 envelope plain gelatin	1 tablespoon sugar
¼ cup milk	10-inch chocolate wafer crust (page
3 eggs, separated	243), or two 8-inch crusts,
½ cup sugar	baked and cooled
1 cup milk, scalded	Garnish:
⅛ teaspoon salt	1 cup sweetened whipped cream
¼ teaspoon nutmeg	2 tablespoons sugar
½ cup sherry	nutmeg
1 cup heavy cream	unsweetened chocolate shavings

Soften gelatin in ¼ cup milk. Turn lightly beaten egg yolks into saucepan and mix with sugar. Slowly add scalded milk, stirring constantly. Heat over medium heat, stirring, until custard coats spoon. Add gelatin mixture, salt, and nutmeg. Stir well to dissolve gelatin. Slowly dribble in sherry, stirring constantly. Remove from heat, and chill until thick but not set, stirring occasionally, or place in large bowl (or sink) of ice water. Beat egg whites until stiff; in separate bowl, whip cream with 1 tablespoon sugar until stiff. Fold each into the custard, blending gently. Pour into pie shell and chill until set. When ready to serve, garnish top of pie with whipped cream, then sprinkle with nutmeg and chocolate shavings. Makes one 10-inch pie, or two 8-inch pies.

Mrs. Albert L. Larson
Avon, CT

Fresh Strawberry Pie

Like eating strawberries and cream, only better. Baked pie shell, layer of vanilla-flavored cream cheese into which you stick huge, gorgeous, hulled berries, points up. Then cover with puréed strawberries heated with a little cornstarch and sugar. Serve this bright red confection with sweetened, vanilla-flavored whipped cream. Sensational!

9- or 10-inch baked deep pie shell	½ teaspoon vanilla
(use butter-crumb crust, page	2 quarts strawberries, washed and
243, or frozen pie shell)	hulled
8-ounce package cream cheese,	½-1 teaspoon cornstarch
softened	1 tablespoon sugar
¼ cup heavy cream	*(continued)*

Line bottom of cooled pie shell with even layer of mixture of cream cheese, cream, and vanilla, beaten well together until spreadable. Choose the biggest and best strawberries, and plant them hulled end down in cream cheese mixture, arranging them close together in concentric circles. Purée remaining strawberries (an electric mixer works as well as a blender or food processor), and place in saucepan with cornstarch (the amount depends on the juices of the strawberries — you want just enough to keep the pureed layer in place), and sugar. Bring to boil, stirring, and cook over high heat for 1-2 minutes. Cool to lukewarm, and pour over pie. Chill. Makes one 9- or 10-inch pie.

Carla Kardt
Harrisville, NH

Walnut Pie

A rich custardy pie similar to a pecan pie, but less expensive. Top with meringue, whipped cream, or ice cream, or serve plain.

1½ cups chopped walnuts (put
    through food processor or
    chopper)
1½ cups sugar
1½ cups half and half, or light
    cream

1½ tablespoons flour
3 egg yolks
8- or 9-inch pie shell, unbaked

Combine first five ingredients, and pour into pie shell. Bake at 400°F. for 15 minutes, then reduce heat to 350°F., and bake 40 minutes longer. Test for doneness by inserting knife in center. When knife comes out clean, pie is done. Top with meringue (see below) if desired. Makes one 8- or 9-inch pie.

Miss Luella Eldridge
Silver Spring, MD

Meringue:
3 egg whites

5 tablespoons sugar
1 teaspoon vanilla

Beat egg whites until stiff. Add sugar, one tablespoonful at a time; add vanilla and continue beating until thick and glossy and sugar is dissolved. Mound onto pie. Bake at 425°F. for 4-5 minutes, or until lightly browned.

Carla Kardt
Harrisville, NH

Whipped Cream Pie

The contributor advises to use only real *whipped cream, and suggests a graham-cracker crust. We agree, but suggest a chocolate crust too.*

1 teaspoon plain gelatin	1 tablespoon butter
1 tablespoon cold water	½ teaspoon almond extract
½ cup sugar	1 teaspoon vanilla
3 tablespoons cornstarch	1 cup heavy cream, whipped
½ teaspoon salt	8-inch pie shell, baked and cooled
1 cup milk, scalded	maraschino cherries, grated
3 egg yolks, beaten	chocolate, or nuts for garnish

Soften gelatin in cold water. Mix sugar, cornstarch, and salt in saucepan. Add hot milk, and mix well. Place over heat and cook, stirring constantly, until mixture thickens and bubbles. Boil for 1 minute. Be careful to prevent scorching. Stir about one quarter of the mixture into beaten egg yolks. Mix thoroughly and quickly. Return yolk mixture to saucepan. Place over heat, and cook just to boiling point. Remove from heat. Add gelatin, butter, and flavorings. Cool. Fold whipped cream into custard. Pour into pie shell. Chill until set. Garnish as suggested. Makes one 8-inch pie.

Joan D. Purinton
Columbus, OH

CHEESECAKES AND CHEESECAKE DESSERTS

Champion Cheesecake

A cheesecake made in a regular square baking pan. Make at least a day ahead to give it time to mellow — does make all the difference!

Crust:

1¼ cup graham-cracker crumbs (ten 5x2¼ inch crackers)	½ cup sugar
	¼ teaspoon salt
2 tablespoons butter, melted	scant tablespoon vanilla
3 tablespoons sugar	

Filling:

Topping:

1 pound cream cheese, softened	1 cup sour cream
3 eggs (room temperature)	1 tablespoon sugar
	1 teaspoon vanilla

(continued)

Mix crust ingredients, and press into the bottom of an 8-inch square pan. Mix filling. Beat cream cheese until smooth. Add eggs, one at a time, beating well after each addition. Add the sugar, salt, and vanilla, and beat well. Pour filling over crust. Bake at 375°F. for 25-30 minutes, or until center no longer shimmies when pan is gently shaken. Remove from oven and turn oven temperature to 450°F., allowing to heat for 5 minutes. Combine topping ingredients, mix well, and spread over cheesecake. Bake 5 minutes in 450°F. oven. Cool completely on rack, then refrigerate. Cut in squares. Serves 9.

Linda Bensinger
Dublin, NH

Vermont Cheddar Cheese Cheesecake

A prizewinning cheesecake with two surprise ingredients that make a tiny, telling difference, particularly if you use sharp Cheddar.

Crust:
1½ cups sifted flour	¾ cup butter, softened
6 tablespoons sugar	½ teaspoon vanilla
1 teaspoon grated lemon rind	2 egg yolks

Combine flour, sugar, and lemon rind. Cut in butter until crumbly. Stir in vanilla and egg yolks to form dough. Chill 30 minutes. Press ⅓ of dough into bottom of 9-inch springform pan and bake at 400°F. for 8-10 minutes, or until golden brown (while baking, put a cookie sheet on oven rack below pan to catch any butter drips). Cool. Press rest of crust dough around sides of pan.

Filling:
32 ounces cream cheese, softened	4 eggs
1 cup grated Cheddar cheese	2 egg yolks
1¾ cups sugar	¼ cup beer
½ teaspoon vanilla	½ cup heavy cream
1 teaspoon grated lemon rind	

In large mixing bowl, beat cream cheese until fluffy. Gradually beat in Cheddar cheese. Combine sugar, vanilla, and lemon rind, and beat into cheese mixture. Add eggs and yolks, one at a time, beating well after each addition. Stir in beer and cream. Pour into springform pan, and bake at 500°F. for 10-12 minutes. Reduce heat to 225°F., and bake 1 hour longer. Cool on rack for 2 hours. Remove sides of pan, wrap cake in plastic wrap, and refrigerate for 3 hours before slicing. Makes one 9-inch cheesecake.

Scott J. Fruchter
Ann Arbor, MI

Cheesecake Miniatures

These are wonderful little treats, for tea or pastry tray. Use small-size vanilla wafers for miniature cupcake pans, or trim regular-size wafers to fit with small, sharp knife.

12-ounce box vanilla wafers
three 8-ounce packages cream
   cheese, softened
⅔ cup sugar

1 teaspoon vanilla
3 eggs
preserves, or fruit-pie filling

Generously grease cupcake pans. Place a vanilla wafer flat side up in each cup. Blend cream cheese, sugar, and vanilla. Add eggs, one at a time, and beat well. Fill cups almost to the top with mixture. Bake at 350°F. approximately 15 minutes, or until just firm. Do not overcook. Cool completely. Spoon preserves or filling on top of each. Makes about 17 regular or 3 dozen miniatures.

Mary F. Grover
Poquoson, VA

Cherry Cheese Crown

A spectacularly rich and festive dessert. For a higher cake, fill pan half-full of filling, add another layer of ladyfingers brushed with apricot brandy, then add remaining filling. Garnish with whipped cream and sprig of holly or mint, depending on the season.

three 3-ounce packages ladyfingers
¼ cup apricot brandy
8-ounce package cream cheese,
   softened

½ cup sugar
1 teaspoon vanilla
1 pint heavy cream
21-ounce can cherry pie filling

Separate ladyfingers, and line the bottom and sides of ungreased 9-inch springform pan with them. Brush ladyfingers with apricot brandy. Combine cream cheese with sugar and vanilla, and beat until fluffy and light, adding ½ cup of the heavy cream to lighten. Whip remaining heavy cream until stiff, and fold into cheese. Mix gently, and pile into ladyfinger crown. Cover cake with plastic wrap, and refrigerate overnight. The next morning, spread cherry filling over top. Re-cover, and return to refrigerator until just before serving. Serves 14-16.

Mrs. Gail G. Shuttleton
Port Jervis, NY

Chocolate Cheesecake

A very chocolatey chocolate cheesecake. Even a sliver will make a dedicated chocoholic shiver with delight.

8½-ounce package chocolate
    wafers
⅓ cup butter, melted
3 eggs
1 cup sugar
2 tablespoons sugar
three 8-ounce packages cream
    cheese

two 6-ounce packages chocolate
    bits, melted
1 teaspoon vanilla
⅛ teaspoon salt
1 cup sour cream

For crust: crush wafers, and mix with butter and 2 tablespoons sugar. Press over bottom and sides (to ½ inch from top) of 9-inch springform pan. Chill while you make filling. At high speed, beat eggs with 1 cup sugar until light. Beat in cream cheese. Add melted chocolate, vanilla, salt, and sour cream, and beat until perfectly smooth. Turn into crust, and bake at 350°F. for 1 hour. Cool in pan on rack. Cover, and refrigerate overnight. Serves 12-14.

Michele Verville
Peterborough, NH

Three-Cream Supreme

An easy and attractive alternative to cheesecake that your children will appreciate. Vary by making with different flavors of instant pudding.

1 pint half and half
1 pint sour cream
½ pint heavy cream
two 3-ounce packages instant
    pudding

two 3-ounce packages ladyfingers,
    or 1 pound cake, sliced
fresh or canned fruit (strawberries,
    blueberries, cherries,
    pineapple, etc.)

Combine first four ingredients in large bowl. Mix on low speed. Cover bottom of 9x13-inch pan with ladyfingers or cake slices. Top with a layer of pudding, then repeat. Top with fruit. Chill. Serves 16.

Teresa Miller
Valatie, NY

ASSORTED DESSERTS

Desserts are in a category by themselves. In contrast to those of most other foods, dessert ingredients must be measured absolutely accurately to ensure the proper consistency and rising of a dough or batter, the thickening of a pie, mousse, or molded dessert. Slipshod measurements can prevent a chemical reaction necessary to the successful creation of many kinds of desserts. Examples of such reactions are the Persian Lime Pie, where the sweetened condensed milk, egg yolks, and lime combine to set and thicken without any added gelatin, cornstarch, or other thickening; or the Holiday Cream Dessert, where not only the crumb crust, but also the mixture of eggs, sugar, and butter requires no cooking — to meld into a delicious dessert with not the slightest hint of any rawness to its taste. These are just two examples of the many actions, reactions, and interactions that can participate in producing a dessert. Do have this in mind as you measure.

This enticing collection is guaranteed to make everyone's sweet tooth (and we all have one) ache — puddings, cakes, sauces, tortes, meringues, soufflés, and fruit desserts whose very memory can make one salivate. One thing Yankee discovered during the Good Neighbor project is that America still loves desserts.

Apricot Whip

A classic children's treat — simple to make, yet elegant enough to be the perfect end-note to a substantial dinner. For prune whip, substitute prunes for apricots in the recipe below, and add 1 tablespoon lemon juice to the cooking water. Remove prune pits if necessary.

2 cups dried apricots	¾ cup sugar
1 cup water	3 egg whites
2 tablespoons sugar	1⅓ cups heavy cream

Combine apricots, water, and 2 tablespoons sugar in saucepan, and bring to boil. Turn heat down to medium, and simmer until apricots are soft, and water is almost gone — 15-20 minutes. Place in mixer bowl with ¾ cup sugar, and beat into pulp. Cool. In separate bowls, beat egg whites until stiff, and whip cream. Fold egg whites and cream alternately into cooled fruit. Chill. Serves 6.

Anna Ruffler
Tarrytown, NY

Chocolate Devil's Float

A light and moist eggless cake dessert. Best served freshly made — warm, with whipped cream or ice cream. *(continued)*

½ cup sugar
2 cups water
1 cup miniature marshmallows
2 tablespoons shortening
½ cup sugar
1 teaspoon vanilla

1 cup flour
½ teaspoon salt
1 teaspoon baking powder
2 tablespoons cocoa
½ cup milk
½ cup chopped nuts

Cook sugar and water together in a 1½-quart casserole dish, then add marshmallows. Cream together shortening and sugar. Add vanilla. Sift together flour, salt, baking powder, and cocoa. Beat dry ingredients into creamed mixture alternately with milk; then stir in nuts. Drop by spoonfuls on top of marshmallow mixture in casserole dish. Do not stir. Cover tightly. Bake at 350°F. for 45 minutes. Serves 6-8.

Patricia Lindbo
Winchester, MA

Chocolate Nut Sauce

Heavenly on vanilla ice cream — the sauce will harden when it hits the ice cream. That kind of sauce! Reheat in double-boiler top, over simmering water.

4 tablespoons unsalted butter
½ cup chopped nuts

6 ounces semisweet baking
   chocolate, or bits
1 tablespoon rum

Melt butter and sauté nuts for about 3-5 minutes. Add chocolate and rum. Cook over very low heat until chocolate is melted and sauce is smooth. Serve hot. Makes about 1 cup.

Alice Freeman
Newfane, VT

Cracker Meringue

A sweet, chewy, crunchy confection. Serve with halved, hulled fresh berries.

¼ teaspoon cream of tartar
3 egg whites
1 cup sugar
1 teaspoon vanilla

16 soda crackers, rolled fine
1 cup chopped pecans
1 cup heavy cream, whipped
½ cup flaked coconut

Add cream of tartar to egg whites, and beat until stiff. Slowly add sugar, 1 tablespoon at a time, beating after each addition. Beat in vanilla. Gently fold in cracker crumbs and pecans. Spread in buttered 8-inch square pan. Bake at 325°F. for 35 minutes. Cool. Remove from pan, place on plate, and spread top with whipped cream. Sprinkle with coconut. Serves 8.

Lucille Lyons
Indianapolis, IN

Holiday Cream Dessert

A smashing concoction of cookie crust, rich filling, and whipped cream flavored with nuts, cocoa, bananas, and cherries.

⅓ cup butter, melted
2 cups crushed vanilla wafers
½ cup butter, softened
1½ cups confectioner's sugar
2 eggs
1 cup heavy cream
¼ cup granulated sugar

2 tablespoons cocoa
1 cup chopped nuts
1 large ripe banana, mashed
¼ cup chopped maraschino
  cherries
whole maraschino cherries for
  garnish

Combine melted butter and wafer crumbs. Spread in 9x13-inch baking dish. Cream ½ cup butter with confectioner's sugar. Beat in eggs, one at a time, and continue beating until *very* smooth. Spread mixture over crumbs. Whip cream, and fold in all remaining ingredients except whole cherries. Spread over butter and sugar mixture, and chill for 24 hours. Garnish with whole cherries. Serves 8-10.

Winona Krenzer
Prairie Village, KS

Upside-Down Date Pudding

Like a crustless pecan pie. Eat warm or cold — but always with whipped cream.

Pudding:
1 cup pitted dates
1 cup boiling water
½ cup white sugar
½ cup brown sugar, packed
2 tablespoons butter
1 egg
1½ cups flour

½ teaspoon baking powder
1 teaspoon baking soda
½ teaspoon salt
1 cup chopped walnuts

Sauce:
1½ cups brown sugar, packed
1 tablespoon butter
1½ cups boiling water

Combine dates and water. In separate bowl, blend sugars, butter, and egg, and add to softened dates. Sift together dry ingredients, and mix with date/sugar mixture. Stir in nuts. Pour into greased 9x13-inch pan. Combine sauce ingredients, and pour over top. Bake at 375°F. for 40 minutes. Cut into squares, and serve. Serves 12-15.

Mrs. Laura Byler
Centerville, PA

Cold Lemon Soufflé

A light and elegant dessert to finish off a substantial meal.

1 envelope plain gelatin
¼ cup cold water
½ cup lemon juice
4 eggs, separated
1 cup sugar

½ teaspoon salt
2 teaspoons freshly grated lemon
  rind
1 cup heavy cream

Soften gelatin in water. Combine lemon juice, egg yolks, ½ cup sugar and salt in top of double boiler. Cook over boiling water, stirring constantly until thick and custardy. Remove from heat. Stir in gelatin and 1 teaspoon of the lemon rind. Cool until mixture starts to thicken. Beat egg whites until they form soft peaks. Add remaining sugar and beat until stiff. Whip cream until stiff. Fold all together lightly, and pour into serving bowl or individual dishes. Sprinkle top with remaining lemon rind. Chill for at least 3 hours before serving. Serves 6.

Mrs. Frank A. Day
The Flavour of Concord

Noodle Kugel

An old-time European dessert often served as a side dish to the main course. Ten ounces of noodles makes a firmer pudding; use eight ounces for a softer kugel. For a sweeter dish, double topping ingredients.

Pudding:
1½ pints sour cream (reserve ½
  pint)
½ cup sugar
3 large eggs, beaten
1 pound cottage cheese
½ pound cream cheese, softened
½ cup golden raisins
8-10 ounces medium egg noodles,
  cooked and drained

4 tablespoons butter

Streusel Topping:
½ cup brown sugar, packed
2 tablespoons flour
½ cup chopped walnuts
2 tablespoons cinnamon
2 tablespoons butter, softened

Mix together all pudding ingredients except reserved sour cream and butter, folding in noodles last. Pour into greased 4-quart casserole dish, or two greased 2-quart casserole dishes. Spread reserved sour cream over noodle mixture, and dot with butter. Bake at 325°F. for 45 minutes. Remove from oven. Mix topping ingredients, and sprinkle over top of pudding. Return to oven. Bake 30 minutes at 325°F. Serves 12.

Paula Rechnitz
Pepperell, MA

Grand Marnier Mousse

Subtle and fantastic for a very special occasion. Garnish with whipped cream, mandarin-orange segments, and mint leaves.

4 egg yolks	⅛ teaspoon salt
1½ cups milk	½ cup Grand Marnier
¾ cup sugar	2 egg whites
1 envelope plain gelatin	2 cups heavy cream

Combine egg yolks, milk, sugar, gelatin, and salt in saucepan. Stir to mix. Heat, stirring, until mixture becomes thick enough to coat a spoon. Do not boil. Remove from heat. Stir in Grand Marnier. Transfer to bowl, and place in sink (or larger bowl) of ice water. Stir occasionally until mixture mounds slightly. Beat egg whites until stiff. Whip cream until stiff. Fold egg whites and whipped cream into Grand Marnier mixture. Spoon into dessert cups or wine glasses. Chill at least 3 hours. Serves 6.

Carla Kardt
Harrisville, NH

Fresh Orange Pudding

Serve this pudding warm with a generous amount of the chilled fresh orange sauce over it.

Sauce:

3 medium oranges	¼ cup flaked coconut
	¼ cup sugar

Grate rind of one orange and save for pudding. Peel remaining oranges, removing as much of the white membrane as possible. Divide into segments, then cut each segment into thirds. In small bowl, mix oranges and coconut together. Add sugar, a little at a time, to taste. Allow this mixture to stand — syrup will form in bottom of bowl. Stir occasionally, and chill until serving time.

Pudding:

½ cup sugar	2 cups milk
3 tablespoons cornstarch	½ teaspoon vanilla
¼ teaspoon salt	grated rind of 1 orange
1 egg	

In medium saucepan, combine sugar, cornstarch, and salt. Mix well. Add egg, and mix again. Slowly stir in milk. Cook over low heat until thick, stirring constantly. When pudding becomes thick, remove from heat. Add vanilla and orange rind. Stir well, cool slightly, then pour into dessert cups, leaving room for orange sauce. Top with chilled sauce, and serve immediately. Serves 4-6.

Lynn Sullivan-Walsh
Peterborough, NH

GRATED RINDS AND CITRUS JUICE

The extra effort of grating *fresh* lemon and orange rinds for desserts that call for grated rinds will pay off in a taste not possible if you use the bottled orange and lemon rinds commercially available. The texture too is improved, as the dried grated rinds lend a somewhat gritty texture. The real flavor of grated rinds is in the oil, which comes through in the strength desired only with the fresh product.

Also, there is nothing like the sweetness and tartness of freshly squeezed citrus juice — lemon, orange, or grapefruit.

Peaches and Cream Cake

A cake in a pie dish — served warm or cold, a great way to usher summer into winter.

Cake:
¾ cup flour
1 teaspoon baking powder
½ teaspoon salt
3⅛-ounce package vanilla pudding
    mix (not instant)

3 tablespoons butter, softened
1 egg
½ cup milk

Combine above ingredients in mixing bowl, and beat 2 minutes at medium-high speed. Pour into deep, greased 10-inch pie plate.

Topping:
15- or 20-ounce can sliced peaches,
    drained (reserve juice)
8-ounce package cream cheese,
    softened

3 tablespoons reserved peach juice
1 cup sugar
1 tablespoon sugar
½ teaspoon cinnamon

Arrange peach slices in concentric circles to cover cake batter in pie pan. Beat together cream cheese, peach juice, and 1 cup sugar until spreadable. Then spread over peaches to within 1 inch of pan sides (this is important, otherwise the batter will not bake). Combine 1 tablespoon sugar and cinnamon, and sprinkle over top. Bake at 350°F. for 30-35 minutes, or until crust is golden brown (filling will appear soft). Serve warm or chilled. Serves 6-8.

Louise Marone
Vineland, NJ

Poached Peaches with Raspberry Puree and Crème Chantilly

Quick and easy to prepare, this makes a tangy and refreshing end to a meal. If canned peaches are used, do not cook or make syrup — just add vanilla and chill.

Poached Peaches:

6 cups water

2 cups sugar

8 large ripe peaches, peeled, halved, and stoned

3 tablespoons vanilla

In heavy 3- to 5-quart saucepan, bring water and sugar to boil over high heat, stirring until sugar dissolves. Boil briskly for 3 minutes. Turn down heat as low as possible. Add peeled peach halves and vanilla. Poach peaches at low simmer 10-20 minutes, or until barely tender. Chill.

Raspberry Puree:

two 10-ounce packages frozen raspberries, defrosted and drained

2 tablespoons sugar

1 tablespoon Kirsch

With back of spoon, puree raspberries through fine sieve into mixing bowl. Stir in sugar and Kirsch. Refrigerate, tightly covered.

Crème Chantilly:

¾ cup heavy cream

2 tablespoons sugar

1 tablespoon vanilla

Whip cream in chilled bowl until it begins to thicken. Sprinkle in sugar and vanilla. Continue beating until cream holds soft peaks.

To Serve:

Transfer peach halves with slotted spoon to individual serving dishes. Cover peaches with raspberry puree. Top with Crème Chantilly, and garnish with whole berries. Serves 8.

Lucy Ackerman
Macungie, PA

Zoe's Peach Roll

A warm and homey dessert you can whip up on a whim. Use fresh peaches or peaches canned in natural juice. Serve with cream, whipped cream, or ice cream.

1½ cups flour
2 teaspoons baking powder
¼ teaspoon salt
4 tablespoons shortening
½ cup milk

1½ cups sliced peaches
1 teaspoon cinnamon
⅓ cup granulated sugar
⅓ cup brown sugar, packed
2 tablespoons butter

Mix flour, baking powder, and salt. Cut in shortening. Add milk, and mix with fork to form soft ball of dough. Roll out on lightly floured board to ⅓ inch thick. Arrange peach slices over dough, sprinkle with cinnamon and sugars, and dot with butter. Roll up, and place in greased 9x5-inch loaf pan. Bake at 375°F. for 30 minutes. Serves 6-8.

Mrs. Robert York
Delevan, WI

Vanilla Pots de Crème

Very simple, very special. To make mocha pots de crème, simply add ½ cup semisweet chocolate pieces and 4 teaspoons instant coffee to the hot milk and cream, stir to dissolve, then proceed as described below. Serve the vanilla topped with a fresh strawberry; the mocha topped with grated chocolate — or either plain with crisp cookies.

1½ cups milk
1½ cups light cream
4 eggs
4 egg yolks
¾ cup sugar

pinch salt
1 teaspoon vanilla
whipped cream
confectioner's sugar

Combine milk and cream in saucepan, and heat to almost boiling. In bowl, beat eggs and egg yolks with sugar, salt, and vanilla. Slowly add milk and cream to egg mixture, beating constantly. Strain, skim, and pour into individual custard cups. Place cups in deep baking pan, and pour boiling water into the pan around the cups to reach a little over halfway up the sides. Cover entire pan loosely with foil, and bake at 275°F. for about 30 minutes. Remove foil, and allow custard to cool in the water. Chill, and serve topped with a dab of whipped cream. Just before serving, sprinkle each custard with a little confectioners' sugar. Serves 8.

Henry Flory
Southern Pines, NC

Strawberry Crunch

A great dessert to serve at a summer gathering. The "crunch" is in delicious contrast to the smooth, frozen strawberry mousse.

Crunch:

1 cup flour
¼ cup brown sugar, packed
½ cup butter
½ cup chopped nuts

1 cup sugar
1 teaspoon vanilla
15-ounce package frozen
    strawberries, partially thawed
2 cups heavy cream

Mousse:

2 egg whites

Combine crunch ingredients as for pie crust, and spread the crumbs on a cookie sheet. Bake at 250°F. for 40-60 minutes, until light brown. Check and stir every 10 minutes. Cool. Lightly press ⅔ of the crumbs onto bottom of a 9x13-inch pan. Combine egg whites, sugar, vanilla, and strawberries. Beat at high speed until fluffy and stiff. Whip cream, and fold into strawberry mixture. Fold in remaining crumbs. Pour over crumbs in pan. Freeze for at least 4 hours before serving. Serves 16.

Mina Foster
Corry, PA

Rhubarb Bread Pudding

This resembles a fruit crisp. The rhubarb mixture cooks to an easy-to-serve consistency. Serve with cream, ice cream, or whipped cream.

Pudding:

1 cup sugar
½ cup butter, melted
8 cups ½-inch pieces rhubarb
6 cups fresh bread crumbs,
    broken up

½ teaspoon nutmeg or cinnamon

Topping:

1½ cups flour
1 cup sugar
½ cup butter

Preheat oven to 425°F. Stir sugar into melted butter. Combine rhubarb, bread crumbs, and spice. Add butter/sugar mixture, and mix. Turn into greased 9x13-inch baking dish.

For topping, combine flour and sugar. Cut in butter until crumbly. Sprinkle mixture over top of pudding. Bake 20 minutes until top is brown. Then reduce oven temperature to 350°F., and bake 45 minutes longer. Cool. Serves 8.

Maybelle M. Scheetz
Topeka, KS

CHAPTER TEN

Cakes, Cookies and Bars, and Candy

In an age of package mixes and packaged baked goods, it is all too easy to leave the recipe box and cookbooks to gather dust. Add an egg and water, then stir — so convenient. We sacrifice a lot, however, for convenience. Made-from-scratch cookies and cakes are matchless in flavor and often in price. And all one has to do is look at the ingredients list on a package mix to see how many artificial flavors, colors, and preservatives are present.

The home baker need not use any of these. She knows exactly what goes into her products. A one-pan brownie recipe takes only a few minutes to prepare, only a few extra dishes to wash, but the flavor is incomparable. One-bowl cake recipes go together 1-2-3. With a little extra effort, a cook can have from-scratch cookies available whenever she desires.

Package mixes actually save the cook very little time. Favorite drop and refrigerator doughs can be made into freezer logs to be used at a later date as slice-and-bake cookies. Hand them over to the kids to bake. Make double batches and several different varieties. Roll the logs in foil and you'll have a bake shop in your freezer (use logs within 6 months, but they certainly won't last that long). Bake bar cookies first, then freeze, individually wrapped for lunch-box treats. If carefully wrapped, baked cookies can also be frozen. Cake layers also may be baked ahead and frozen. Such reserves can be a real boon. (If you have a problem with freezer raiders, put the treats in a package labeled *liver*.)

CAKES

Banana Pineapple Cake

An extremely moist and handsome cake — a subtle blend of pineapple and banana. Sprinkle with confectioner's sugar if desired.

3 cups flour
1 teaspoon baking soda
2 cups sugar
1 teaspoon salt
1 cup cooking oil

8-ounce can crushed pineapple
1½ teaspoons vanilla
3 eggs
2 cups diced bananas

Sift together dry ingredients. Add oil, undrained pineapple, vanilla, eggs, and bananas. Mix until blended, but *do not beat.* Pour batter into greased 8-inch tube or Bundt pan. Bake in a 350°F. oven for 1 hour and 20 minutes. Cake will crack slightly on top. Let cool 10 minutes in the pan. Very carefully remove from pan and cool on wire rack. Makes one 8-inch cake.

Virginia W. Briggs
Charleston, WV

Caramel Apple Nut Cake

An exceptionally good apple cake, moist and smooth textured. The caramel glaze is a delicious touch.

Cake:
1½ cups cooking oil
1½ cups granulated sugar
½ cup brown sugar, packed
3 eggs
2 teaspoons vanilla
3 cups flour
2 teaspoons cinnamon
1 teaspoon baking soda
½ teaspoon nutmeg
½ teaspoon salt

3½ cups peeled, coarsely diced, tart apples
1 cup very coarsely chopped nuts

Caramel Glaze:
3 tablespoons butter
3 tablespoons light brown sugar
3 tablespoons granulated sugar
3 tablespoons whipping cream
½ teaspoon vanilla

Grease and flour 10-inch tube pan. Combine oil and sugars in large bowl, and beat well. Add eggs one at a time, beating well after each addition. Add vanilla. Sift together dry ingredients, and add to batter. Fold in apples and

(continued)

nuts. Spoon into prepared pan. Bake in preheated 325°F. oven for 1 hour and 45 minutes, or until cake tests done. Let cool 20 minutes; turn out onto wire rack. Cool while preparing glaze.

Combine all ingredients in a heavy saucepan. Bring to a boil, and boil for 1 minute. Place cake on plate, and spoon or pour glaze over cake. Makes one 10-inch cake.

Jean Brownlee
Victorville, CA

Cherry Nut Cake

This lovely pink cake with pink frosting would be a fine choice for Valentine's Day.

Cake:
6-ounce bottle maraschino cherries
½ cup chopped walnuts
1-2 tablespoons flour
3 egg whites
1 cup sugar
½ cup shortening
½ cup milk
1½ cups sifted cake flour
½ teaspoon salt
2½ teaspoons baking powder
½ teaspoon vanilla

4 tablespoons maraschino-cherry juice

Frosting:
2 tablespoons butter, softened
1 cup confectioner's sugar
pinch salt
rest of reserved maraschino-cherry juice
4 whole maraschino cherries, halved
4 walnuts

Drain cherries, reserving juice. Save out 4 whole cherries, and chop the rest. Drain chopped cherries in sieve, then on paper towels to get as dry as possible. Combine cherries and walnuts, and toss with 1-2 tablespoons flour until lightly dusted. Beat egg whites until fluffy. Gradually beat in ¼ cup of the sugar, and beat until stiff. In another bowl, cream remaining sugar and shortening until light. Gradually add milk, and beat until well blended. Sift together flour, salt, and baking powder, and add gradually to batter, beating after each addition. Blend in vanilla and cherry juice. Stir in cherries and walnuts. Fold in egg whites. Pour into greased and floured 9x5-inch loaf pan or 8-inch square pan. Bake in 375°F. oven for 35 minutes, or until cake tests done. Let cool a few minutes in pan, then invert onto cake rack to cool completely. Make frosting.

Cream butter and confectioner's sugar. Add salt and blend well. Gradually add cherry juice until frosting is of desired consistency. Frost cooled cake, and decorate with cherries and nuts. Makes one 9x5-inch loaf cake or one 8-inch square cake.

Ann Drzal
Fall River, MA

CAKE AND COOKIE HELPS AND HINTS

1. Use plastic sandwich bags as mitts for greasing pans. Pull the bag off inside-out and discard.

2. Eggs beat to a better volume when at room temperature (most important when the eggs are separated). To quickly bring the eggs up to room temperature, place the whole egg in warm water for a few minutes.

3. Leftover egg yolks and egg whites can be frozen. The whites can be frozen as-is in ice trays or plastic bags, but the yolks must be mixed with a little sugar or salt depending on future use. If you've accumulated a lot of whites, bake an angel food cake. Leftover yolks can be used in custards.

4. Angel cakes slice better when they have first been frozen and then defrosted. Always use a serrated knife.

5. If you don't have the size pan that a cake recipe calls for, use a pan with the same volume, but watch carefully since a change in the thickness will change the baking time.
Pan sizes:

8x8x2 inches=6 cups	8x1½ inches=4 cups
9x9x1½ inches=8 cups	9x1½ inches=6 cups
9x9x2 inches=10 cups	8½x4½x2½ inches=6 cups (loaf)
9x13x2 inches=14 cups	9x5x3 inches=8 cups (loaf)

6. Always preheat the oven before baking cakes and cookies.

7. Always bake on the middle shelf of the oven.

8. All fats that are to be used in solid form should be softened. Using cold, hard fats will always leave some bits unblended.

9. If you have problems with cake sticking to the bottom of the pan even when greased and floured, grease the pan, line it with wax paper, and then grease and flour the wax paper.

10. If your cookies brown too quickly on the bottoms, try using one cookie sheet inside another.

11. To make rolled cookies a breeze, use a pastry cloth and rolling pin stocking. They really prevent sticking, and less excess flour gets incorporated into the dough. In a pinch, a linen napkin or clean linen dish towel can be substituted for a pastry cloth.

12. If you live in a climate with cold winters, use the garage to cool baked items more quickly or to store items that would take up refrigerator space (be sure they are in animal-proof containers). *(continued)*

13. Proper beating and folding of egg whites are critical in cakes such as angel food or sponge, leavened solely by the air incorporated in the beaten egg whites. Beating a little of the sugar called for in the recipe in with the egg whites to make a meringue will make the whites more stable and, therefore, the cake will rise higher.

14. A lopsided cake may taste out of this world but it doesn't look very nice. To level a lopsided layer, mark the desired height with toothpicks and use them as a guide for cutting with a bread knife. If the cake is too wide to be cut with a bread knife, cut around the edges of the cake with a knife, then use a length of dental floss held taut to saw through the cake.

15. Crumbs in the icing can ruin the appearance of a cake. To prevent, first spread a very thin layer of icing over the entire cake to seal the crumbs. Then, ice the cake as usual.

Bonnie Berrett
Jaffrey, NH

Oma's Graham-Cracker Cake

This flourless cake has a wonderful graham flavor. Top with the crushed pineapple and brown sugar syrup described below and whipped cream, or let the cake cool, then frost with a vanilla butter-cream icing.

Cake:

½ cup butter, softened
1 cup sugar
2 eggs, separated
2 cups crushed graham crackers
   (15 crackers)
2 teaspoons baking powder
1 cup chopped nuts

1 teaspoon vanilla
1 cup milk
¼ teaspoon salt

Topping:
8-ounce can crushed pineapple in
   heavy syrup
1 cup brown sugar, packed

Cream butter and sugar until fluffy. Beat in egg yolks. Combine graham crackers with baking powder and nuts. Add to first mixture. Add vanilla, and gradually beat in milk. Beat until well mixed. In separate bowl, beat egg whites with salt until stiff. Fold into batter. Pour into well greased 9x13-inch pan or two 8-inch square pans. Bake at 350°F. for 20-30 minutes or until cake tests done.

While cake is baking, cook pineapple with brown sugar until thick. When cake is done, remove from oven and spread pineapple mixture over the warm cake. Serve warm or cold. Makes one 9x13-inch cake or two 8-inch square cakes.

Eleanor Austin
Portsmouth, NH

Cherry-Nut Fruitcake

A very buttery white fruitcake perfect for those not partial to the standard dark, brandied fruitcake. The red and green cherries add a special Christmas touch. A fine Christmas gift.

2 cups butter, softened
2⅓ cups sugar
6 eggs
1 teaspoon butter flavoring
2 tablespoons lemon extract
½ pound red candied cherries
½ pound green candied cherries
¾-1 pound candied lemon peel
4 cups flour
1½ teaspoons baking powder
½ teaspoon salt
1 pound pecan halves

Grease three 9x5-inch loaf pans; line with brown paper, and grease again. Cream butter and sugar together until fluffy. Beat in eggs one at a time until light. Beat in butter flavoring and lemon extract. Mix candied fruit with 1 cup of the flour. Stir remainder of the flour, baking powder, and salt into the batter. Add candied fruit and pecans. Divide batter between the three pans. Bake at 275°F. for 2 to 2½ hours. Use a cake tester to check for doneness. Cool completely and wrap in aluminum foil. These fruitcakes freeze very well. Makes three 9x5-inch loaves.

Barbara Hutton
Peterborough, NH

Choco-Date Cake

An easy no-frost cake. A great cake to take to meeting or to have on hand for the family.

1 cup finely chopped dates
1 cup boiling water
1 teaspoon baking soda
1¾ cups sifted flour
2 tablespoons cocoa
½ teaspoon salt
½ cup butter, softened
½ cup shortening
1 cup sugar
2 eggs, beaten
1 teaspoon vanilla
6-ounce package chocolate bits
1 cup chopped pecans
(½ cup heavy cream, whipped)

Mix dates, boiling water, and baking soda. Set aside to cool. Sift together flour, cocoa, and salt. Cream butter, shortening, and sugar until light and fluffy. Add eggs, then vanilla and beat well. Alternately add flour and dates, mixing well after each addition. Spread in greased 9x13-inch pan. Sprinkle with chocolate chips and pecans. Bake in a 350°F. oven for 45 minutes, or until cake tests done. Cool completely in the pan. Top with optional whipped cream, if desired. Makes one 9x13-inch cake.

Mrs. Harvey Kiehl
Middleburg Heights, OH

Chocolate-Orange Yum Yum Cake

Makes an 8-inch cake with a chocolate layer sandwiched between two orange layers, or a 9-inch cake with one layer of each flavor.

Cake:

½ cup shortening
1½ cups sugar
grated rind of ½ orange
¼ cup orange juice
1 egg, separated
1 egg yolk
2½ cups flour
4 teaspoons baking powder
¼ teaspoon salt
1 cup milk

1½ squares unsweetened chocolate, melted

Filling and Icing:

3 tablespoons butter, melted
3 cups sifted confectioner's sugar
grated rind and pulp of 1 orange
3 tablespoons (or more) orange juice
3 squares unsweetened chocolate, melted

Cream shortening and sugar until light and fluffy. Add orange rind and juice. Lightly beat egg yolks, add to creamed mixture, and beat well. Sift together flour, baking powder, and salt. Add to batter alternately with milk, a little at a time, beating after each addition. Beat egg white until stiff, and fold into batter. Grease cake pans (three 8-inch or two 9-inch), line each with wax or brown paper, then grease again. Depending on the number of cake pans, divide batter into thirds or halves. Stir melted chocolate into one portion of the batter. Pour each portion of batter into prepared pan, and bake at 375°F. for 20-25 minutes, or until layers test done. Baking time will depend on size of pan. Turn out of pans and cool on wire racks.

To make filling, combine butter, sugar, orange rind, pulp, and juice, and mix well. Remove enough icing to frost top of cake, and place in separate bowl. Add chocolate to remaining icing, and beat well. Spread chocolate filling between layers. Put cake together, and ice the top with the orange icing, adding more orange juice if necessary to obtain the right consistency. Makes one 3-layer 8-inch cake, or one 2-layer 9-inch cake.

Mrs. Patricia Coffin
Laconia, NH

Mother's Fairy Fluff Ginger Cake

A light and airy lemon-ginger sponge layer baked under a coverlet of meringue.

¼ cup butter, softened
½ cup sugar
4 eggs, separated
1 teaspoon lemon extract
½ teaspoon lemon rind
1 teaspoon ginger
1 cup flour

2 teaspoons baking powder
¼ cup milk
⅛ teaspoon cream of tartar
pinch salt
1 cup sugar
½ teaspoon lemon extract
handful chopped nuts

Cream butter and sugar. Add well-beaten egg yolks, lemon extract, lemon rind, and ginger. Sift flour with baking powder, and add to the first mixture alternately with milk. Spread batter on bottom of well greased 9-inch cake pan lined with a sheet of greased wax paper (let ends of paper overlap pan to serve to lift out finished cake without disturbing frosting). Add cream of tartar and salt to egg whites. Beat until stiff and dry, adding the sugar a little at a time as you beat, and the flavoring just before you finish. Spread this meringue over the batter in the pan. Sprinkle with finely chopped nuts. Bake at 350°F. until the top is golden brown — about 40 minutes. Makes a single-layer 9-inch cake.

Mrs. Horace Newey
Hampden Highlands, ME

Kentucky Pound Cake

A crowd-sized pound cake, moist, rich, and delicious. Make just for the family, too, and freeze the extra leftover for a rainy day.

8 eggs (at room temperature)
2⅔ cups sugar
1 pound whipped butter
1 tablespoon vanilla

3½ cups flour (sifted three times
    before measuring)
½ cup half and half

Separate eggs. Beat whites until frothy; then, still beating, gradually add 6 tablespoons of the sugar, and continue to beat until stiff peaks are formed. Place in refrigerator until rest of cake is ready. Cream butter with remaining sugar and vanilla until light and fluffy. Add egg yolks two at a time, beating well after each addition. Add flour alternately with half and half, beating after each addition. Beat until very light and fluffy. Fold in egg whites. Pour into lightly greased 10-inch tube pan and bake at 300°F. for 1 hour and 30 minutes, or until cake tests done. Makes one 10-inch pound cake.

Kay Edwards
Beckley, WV

Old-Fashioned Lemon Layer Cake

Marvelously tangy lemon filling sandwiched between golden cake layers. If you don't have three 8-inch cake pans, use two 9-inch round pans, and cut each layer in half before filling.

Cake:
¾ cup butter, softened
2 cups sugar
grated rind of 1 lemon
3 eggs, separated
3½ cups sifted cake flour
4 teaspoons baking powder
¾ teaspoon salt
1¼ cups milk

Lemon Filling:
¼ cup flour
¼ cup sugar
1 beaten egg
¼ cup lemon juice
½ cup water
grated rind of ½ lemon
½ tablespoon butter
confectioner's sugar

Cream butter, sugar, and lemon rind. Beat egg yolks until thick, and add to creamed mixture. Sift dry ingredients together, and add alternately with the milk to the creamed mixture. Beat until smooth. In a separate bowl, beat the egg whites until stiff but not dry. Fold into the creamed mixture. Pour into three greased and floured 8-inch cake pans. Bake in a 375°F. oven for about 25 minutes, or until layers test done. Cool on racks.

Combine all filling ingredients except confectioner's sugar in top of double boiler and cook over boiling water until thick. Cool and spread between cake layers. Sift confectioner's sugar over top of cake. Makes one 3-layer 8-inch cake.

Mrs. Harvey Kiehl
Middleburg Heights, OH

Maplenut Upside-Down Cake

The rich combination of maple and pecan makes a nice dessert for fall and winter evenings. Serve cold — plain, or topped with vanilla ice cream or whipped cream.

1½ tablespoons butter, melted
⅓ cup brown sugar, packed
⅓ cup maple syrup
1 cup chopped pecans
¼ cup butter, softened
½ cup granulated sugar
⅓ cup brown sugar, packed

1 egg, beaten
⅛ teaspoon salt
½ teaspoon maple flavoring
1 cup flour
1½ teaspoons baking powder
½ cup milk

Combine melted butter, ⅓ cup brown sugar, maple syrup, and pecans. Pour into 9-inch cake pan. In bowl, cream ¼ cup butter with granulated sugar and ⅓ cup brown sugar, then add egg, salt, and maple flavoring. Sift flour with baking powder, and add gradually to batter, alternating with the milk. The batter will be a little stiffer than cake batter usually is. Drop by spoonfuls on top of the nut mixture. Bake in 350°F. oven for 35 minutes. Remove from pan immediately, turning upside down onto cake plate to avoid sticking. Makes one single-layer 9-inch cake.

Mrs. Mary Conover
Silver Spring, MD

Maple Walnut Chiffon Cake

A cloud-light, not-too-sweet cake. The maple glaze gives additional maple flavor and sweetness.

Cake:

2 cups flour
⅓ cup granulated sugar
3 teaspoons baking powder
1 teaspoon salt
⅔ cup brown sugar, packed
½ cup cooking oil
7 eggs, separated
⅔ cup cold water

2 teaspoons maple flavoring
1 cup chopped walnuts
½ teaspoon cream of tartar
⅓ cup granulated sugar

Glaze:

3 tablespoons butter, melted
2 cups sifted confectioner's sugar
1 teaspoon maple flavoring
milk

Measure and sift together flour, ⅓ cup granulated sugar, baking powder, and salt. Mix in brown sugar. Add oil, egg yolks, water, and maple flavoring. Beat until smooth. Stir in walnuts. In large bowl, beat egg whites with cream of tartar until foamy. Gradually add second ⅓ cup of sugar, beating until stiff.

(continued)

Gently fold maple mixture into egg whites. Pour into ungreased 10-inch tube pan. Bake in a 325°F. oven for 50-55 minutes. Cool cake in pan inverted on funnel or bottle. When cake is cool, run a thin-bladed knife around the outside of the cake and around the tube. Invert onto a plate. Sprinkle with confectioner's sugar, or make maple glaze.

For glaze, combine butter, confectioner's sugar and maple flavoring. Add enough milk to give glaze desired consistency, and pour glaze over cake. Makes one 10-inch cake.

Marge Orechia
Beverly, MA

Mississippi Mud Cake

An old-fashioned dark and moist chocolate cake. Just right with vanilla butter-cream frosting.

2 cups water	2 cups flour
4 squares unsweetened chocolate	1 teaspoon baking soda
6 tablespoons butter	1 teaspoon salt
2 cups sugar	2 eggs, lightly beaten

Boil the water, and add chocolate, stirring to melt. Boil over medium heat for 1 minute. Remove from heat and add the butter and sugar. Stir until melted. *Cool mixture completely.* Sift flour, baking soda, and salt into mixer bowl. Pour in chocolate mixture, then add eggs. Beat thoroughly, scraping the bowl several times. Pour into greased and floured 9x13-inch pan, and bake at 300°F. for 1 hour, or until cake tests done. Cool in pan. Makes one 9x13-inch cake.

Grace Hornberger
Macungie, PA

Buttercream Icing:

5 tablespoons flour	1 cup granulated sugar
1 cup milk	¼ teaspoon vanilla
½ cup butter, softened	pinch salt
½ cup shortening	

Put flour in small saucepan, and stir in milk until smooth. Place over medium heat and cook, stirring, as you would for a white sauce, until very thick and smooth. Cool slightly. Meanwhile, lightly blend remaining ingredients in medium bowl. By hand, mix slightly cooled mixture with that in bowl. With electric mixer, beat at high speed for 15 minutes. Makes about 3 cups frosting.

Mrs. Marion Johnston
Pittsburgh, PA

Orange Form Cake

A baking-powder version of Baba au Rhum. Light and attractive, pleasantly sweet, but not too rich. Serve plain, with whipped cream, or with ice cream.

Cake:
2 egg whites
½ cup sugar
4 egg yolks
1 cup sifted flour
1 teaspoon baking powder
¼ teaspoon salt
⅓ cup butter, melted
¼ teaspoon vanilla

Sauce:
2 cups sugar
2 cups water
1 tablespoon grated orange rind
1 tablespoon plus 1 teaspoon fresh
    lemon juice
½ cup rum
⅓ cup finely chopped walnuts

Grease a 9-inch* tube pan. Line bottom of pan with wax paper cut to fit, and grease again. Beat egg whites until fluffy; gradually add ¼ cup of the sugar and beat until stiff. In smaller bowl, beat egg yolks with remaining ¼ cup sugar. Fold into egg whites. Sift flour, baking powder, and salt together, and fold into batter. Gently stir in melted butter and vanilla. Bake in 375°F. oven for about 30 minutes, or until top springs back when touched lightly. Turn out onto rack and remove wax paper. Move to serving plate.

To make sauce, dissolve sugar in water in saucepan over medium heat. Add orange rind and boil for 10 minutes. Cool a bit, then add lemon juice and rum.

Pierce holes all over top of cake with a skewer. Spoon warm sauce over cake, making more holes, if necessary, right through to bottom of cake. Continue basting with any sauce that ends up on the bottom of the plate. When cake has absorbed nearly all the sauce, sprinkle the top carefully with chopped nuts. Wipe outside rim of cake plate clean. Cover cake and refrigerate. Makes one 9-inch tube cake.

Mrs. Raymond C. Cordes
Sherman Cooks!

*Any size cake pan with a capacity of 1½ quarts may be used.

Almond Torte with Mocha Filling

A really elegant grand finale.

Torte:

6 eggs, separated
½ teaspoon cream of tartar
¾ cup sugar
1 cup ground almonds
1½ teaspoons almond extract
¾ cup sifted flour
½ teaspoon baking powder

Filling and Topping:

4 ounces semisweet chocolate

2 eggs, lightly beaten
2 teaspoons powdered instant
   coffee
1 pound confectioner's sugar
1½ cups butter, cut into dots
⅔ cup apricot preserves
12 whole blanched almonds
1 square unsweetened chocolate

Beat egg whites with cream of tartar until soft peaks form. Still beating, add ¼ cup of the sugar little by little, and continue to beat until stiff but not dry. In separate bowl, beat egg yolks with remaining ½ cup sugar until fluffy and lemon-colored. In still another bowl, combine ground almonds, almond extract, flour, and baking powder, and mix well. Stir this into the egg yolks and mix well. Fold in stiffly beaten whites. Butter two 8-inch cake pans, line with wax paper, and butter wax paper. Divide batter between the two pans, and bake in preheated 350°F. oven for 25-30 minutes, until centers are firm when touched lightly. Cool on racks. Turn out of pans, and peel off wax paper. With long sharp knife, slice each layer into three thin layers, horizontally. Let rest while you make the filling and topping.

Melt chocolate in double boiler over hot water. Meanwhile, place eggs in saucepan, and beat in coffee powder and confectioner's sugar until well blended. Place saucepan on stove over medium heat, and heat, stirring, until hot (do not allow to boil!). Remove from heat, and stir in melted chocolate. Add butter, and stir until melted. Cool, then refrigerate until firm enough to spread evenly over layers.

Place bottom layer of torte on plate, and spread evenly with filling. Top with second layer. Repeat this procedure until the top layer is in place. Rub apricot preserves through sieve, then spread thinly over top layer of torte. Frost sides of torte with filling, reserving enough (about ⅓ cup) for border around top layer. Using a pastry bag, pipe reserved filling around edges of top layer. Decorate torte with whole almonds and chocolate curls, made by using a vegetable peeler or sharp knife to scale thin curls off the bitter chocolate onto the torte. Chill torte in refrigerator. Remove torte from refrigerator 20-30 minutes before serving. Makes one 6-layer, 8-inch torte, rich enough to serve 8-10 persons.

Lilly Sherman
Washington, DC

Pumpkin Cake Roll

An unusual and delectable rolled cake. The not-too-sweet cream-cheese filling is a nice contrast to the spicy cake.

Cake:
3 eggs
1 cup sugar
1 teaspoon lemon juice
⅔ cup canned pumpkin
¾ cup sifted cake flour
½ teaspoon ginger
1 teaspoon baking powder
2 teaspoons cinnamon
½ teaspoon nutmeg
½ teaspoon salt
1 cup chopped walnuts
confectioner's sugar

Filling:
1 cup confectioner's sugar
6 ounces cream cheese, softened
4 tablespoons butter, softened
½ teaspoon vanilla

Beat eggs at high speed for 5 minutes. Gradually beat in sugar. Stir in lemon juice and pumpkin. Combine dry ingredients and fold into pumpkin mixture. Grease a 10x15-inch jelly-roll pan, line with wax paper, and grease again. Spread batter in pan and sprinkle with chopped walnuts. Bake at 375°F. for 15 minutes. Turn cake out onto linen towel that has been dusted with confectioner's sugar. Starting at narrow end, roll up towel and cake together and let sit until almost cool.

Combine filling ingredients and beat together until smooth. Unroll cake and spread with filling. Reroll cake, and chill. Sprinkle with confectioner's sugar just before serving. Makes 1 large rolled cake.

Pat Begel
Exeter, NH

BUTTER MEASUREMENTS FOR QUICK REFERENCE

¼ pound=1 stick=½ cup
5¼ tablespoons=⅔ stick=⅓ cup

⅜ pound=1½ sticks=¾ cup
½ pound=2 sticks=1 cup

COOKIES AND BARS

There are far more recipes for cookies and bars than for any other type of baked goods. The varieties are endless. Just the number of recipes for chocolate-chip cookies and brownies alone staggers the imagination. Every cook has his or her favorite. Cookies and bars come in innumerable shapes, sizes, and textures; they can be cake-like, pie-like, or almost like candy — or range from gigantic to tiny. Somewhere out there, there is the perfect cookie or bar to suit every taste and occasion.

Apricot Squares

Apricot jam and rich pastry combined in a quickly prepared, quickly disappearing treat. Try it with peach jam, too.

1½ cups flour
½ cup sugar
½ teaspoon baking powder
½ cup butter, softened

½ teaspoon vanilla
1 egg, beaten
10-ounce jar apricot preserves
(ground cloves)

Sift flour, sugar, and baking powder together. Cream butter and vanilla. Add flour mixture to butter. Stir in egg, and mix well. Press three quarters of the mixture into greased 9-inch square pan. Beat apricot preserves in small bowl, then spread over bottom crust. Sprinkle sparingly with ground cloves if desired, then with the remaining crust mixture. Bake in 350°F. oven for 25-30 minutes. Makes 16 squares.

Janice Ryzewski
Shrewsbury, MA

Brown Burrs

Tasty little cookie confections. No-bake treat, too.

two 8-ounce packages dates
two 8-ounce packages shredded
    coconut
1 cup walnuts

2 tablespoons lemon juice
2 tablespoons chopped candied
    orange peel, or grated orange
    rind

Put dates, one package coconut, and walnuts through a meat grinder. Add lemon juice and orange peel or rind. Knead until well blended, and shape into small balls. Cut the remaining coconut quite fine, and toast in 300°F. oven to a delicate brown. Roll the balls immediately in the toasted coconut and set aside to dry. Makes about 50.

Marjorie Mills
Marblehead, MA

Butter Pecan Turtle Bars

Love pecan turtle candies? Then you'll love these!

Crust:

2 cups flour   ½ cup butter
1 cup brown sugar, packed

Combine crust ingredients, and mix into fine crumbs. Pat into ungreased 9x13-inch pan.

Caramel Layer:

⅔ cup butter   1 cup milk chocolate bits (half a
½ cup brown sugar, packed   12-ounce package)
1 cup pecan halves

    Melt butter for caramel layer, and add brown sugar. Sprinkle pecan halves evenly over crust, then pour butter/brown-sugar mixture over them. Bake at 350°F. for 18-22 minutes. Remove from oven, and immediately sprinkle with the chocolate bits. Allow to melt slightly (2-3 minutes), and then slightly swirl the bits, leaving some whole. Do *not* spread. Cool completely and cut into bars. Makes about 32 bars.

Dorothy Butler
Guilford, CT

Cheesecake Squares

An easy way to satisfy that cheesecake craving. Oh, so rich!

Crust:

½ cup butter   2 eggs
⅓ cup brown sugar, packed   ¼ cup sugar
1½ cups flour   1 tablespoon orange juice
½ cup finely chopped walnuts   1 tablespoon grated orange rind
                                        1 teaspoon vanilla
Filling:

8-ounce package soft cream cheese

For the crust, cream butter with sugar. Mix in flour. Reserve 1 cup of mixture for topping, and pat the rest into a greased 7x11-inch pan. Sprinkle with walnuts. Bake at 350°F. for 12-15 minutes.

    While crust is baking, combine all filling ingredients and mix well. Spoon over baked crust and sprinkle with reserved crust mixture. Bake at 350°F. for 25 minutes. Cool and cut into squares. Do not refrigerate. Use soon. Makes 1 dozen squares.

Mrs. Grant Tyte
Cuyahoga Falls, OH

Chocolate Coconut Bars

A wonderful candy-like combination of coconut and chocolate. Great for snacks or served with tea or at a "coffee."

1 cup butter
1¼ cups granulated sugar
3 eggs
1 cup flour
½ teaspoon salt
3 tablespoons cocoa
1 cup chopped pecans
15-ounce can sweetened condensed
    milk

2 cups flaked coconut
1 teaspoon vanilla
2½ cups confectioner's sugar
3 tablespoons softened butter
3 tablespoons cocoa
enough milk to make an easily
    spread frosting

Beat 1 cup butter, granulated sugar, and eggs with electric mixer until well blended. Into this mixture, stir flour, salt, cocoa, and pecans. Grease and flour a 9x13-inch pan. Spread mixture evenly in pan, and bake at 350°F. for 20 minutes. While batter bakes, mix condensed milk with coconut. Spread this on top of baked batter, and bake an additional 15 minutes. Remove from oven. Combine remaining ingredients in a smooth frosting. Spread over warm bars. Cool and cut. Makes 48 bars.
Shirley Opitz
Monroeville, PA

Mocha-Frosted Chocolate Cookies

Like the circus — for children of all ages.

Cookies:
2 eggs, beaten
2 cups brown sugar, packed
1 cup shortening
1 cup sour milk
¾ teaspoon baking soda
3⅓ cups flour
1 teaspoon salt

5 tablespoons cocoa

Icing:
1 pound confectioner's sugar
3 tablespoons cocoa
3 tablespoons butter
hot coffee
1 teaspoon vanilla

Combine all cookie ingredients in order listed, and beat well. Drop by heaping teaspoonfuls on ungreased cookie sheets. Bake at 350°F. for 10-12 minutes. Take sheets from oven and let sit a few minutes before removing cookies. Cool on rack. Frost while warm.

To make icing, combine confectioner's sugar with cocoa. Make a well, and drop in butter. Add hot coffee, one tablespoon at a time, to melt butter. As butter melts, stir all together. Add more coffee as needed to melt butter and to make frosting of spreading consistency. Add vanilla, then frost cookies. Makes about 2½ dozen.
Deb Christenson
Brookline, NH

Vermont Date Drop Cookies

Both crisp and chewy, with just the right sweetness. A Yankee prizewinner.

1 cup butter	2 cups sifted flour
1½ cups brown sugar, packed	¼ teaspoon salt
3 eggs	1 teaspoon cinnamon
1 teaspoon baking soda	2 cups finely chopped dates
1 teaspoon hot water	½ cup chopped nuts

Cream butter, add sugar, and blend well. Add eggs one at a time, beating after each addition. Dissolve soda in hot water, and add to batter. Sift flour with salt and cinnamon, and stir into batter. Then stir in dates and nuts, mixing well. Drop by teaspoonfuls 2 inches apart on buttered, floured cookie sheets. Bake at 350°F. for 10-12 minutes or until golden brown. Makes about 6 dozen.

Millie Mikkanen Baxter
Rochester, NY

Fig-Filled Butter Cookies

Scrumptiously different! Make filling at least 12 hours ahead to allow flavors to meld and ripen. The orange, figs, and almonds are terrific together.

Cousin Blanche's Fig Filling:

1 pound dried figs	7 ounces blanched and toasted almonds
1 large navel orange, peeled	honey

Put figs, orange, and almonds through meat grinder. Add enough honey to bind mixture. Refrigerate filling for at least 12 hours. Put filling between baked and cooled butter cookies (see below) to make sandwiches. Makes enough filling for 3-4 dozen sandwiches.

Elsie Stupinsky
Bernardsville, NJ

Butter Cookies:

2 cups flour	¾ cup finely chopped blanched almonds
¾ cup sugar	
1 cup butter, softened	

Mix flour and sugar and cream with butter until smooth. Mix in nuts. On lightly floured board, roll out ¼ inch thick. Cut out with small (1½-2-inch) cookie cutter. Bake on ungreased cookie sheet in 350°F. oven for 10-12 minutes. When cool, sandwich with fig filling (above). Makes 7-8 dozen cookies.

Diana Jacobs
Harrisville, NH

Harvard Squares

Rich pastry squares. Try strawberry preserves in this recipe instead of raspberry — blackberry, too. Or try Cousin Blanche's Fig Filling (page 286).

1 cup butter, softened
1 cup sugar
2 eggs, well beaten
2 cups sifted flour

1 cup chopped walnuts
¾ cup raspberry preserves
confectioner's sugar

Cream butter and sugar. Beat in eggs. Add flour and walnuts and stir well. Scatter half of this over bottom of greased 8-inch square pan and pat into place. Spread preserves over pastry to within ½ inch of edges. Cover with remaining pastry dough. Bake at 325°F. for 1 hour. Cool, and sprinkle with confectioner's sugar. Cut into squares. Makes 16 squares.

Jane Hanson
Boulder, CO

Graham-Cracker Squares

Sweet, chewy squares, great for a church supper or children's festival.

1 cup butter
1 cup sugar
2 eggs, beaten
4 tablespoons coconut
1 teaspoon vanilla

1 cup chopped walnuts
40 graham-cracker squares, finely crushed
2 cups miniature marshmallows
(red or green candied cherries)

Combine butter, sugar, eggs, coconut, and vanilla in medium saucepan and cook for 3 minutes over low heat, stirring constantly. Remove from heat and add walnuts, crushed crackers, marshmallows, and optional cherries. Press into greased 9-inch square pan. Allow to sit for an hour or so. Cut into squares. Makes 16 squares.

Mrs. Alden Slack
Bradford, VT

Honolulu Cookies

A marvelous combination of flavors in each crisp cookie.

1 cup shortening
1 cup granulated sugar
1 cup brown sugar, packed
2 eggs
2 teaspoons vanilla
½ teaspoon orange extract
⅛ teaspoon almond extract
2 cups flour

1 teaspoon baking powder
1 teaspoon baking soda
¾ teaspoon salt
2 cups rolled oats
2 cups crisp rice cereal
1 cup chopped nuts
1 cup coconut

Cream shortening and sugars. Add eggs, vanilla, and other extracts. Sift flour with baking powder, soda, and salt. Mix into batter. Add oats, rice cereal, nuts, and coconut. Dough will be stiff. Roll dough into walnut-sized balls, and place on greased cookie sheets. Cookies will not spread much, so leave only an inch in between. Flatten slightly with fingers. Bake at 350°F. for 10-12 minutes. Do not overcook. Makes about 85 cookies.

Hazel D. Little
Vienna, VA

Lemon Crunch Squares

Toasted coconut sandwiches with a lemon-tart filling. Best served on a plate and eaten with a fork.

Coconut Crust:

1¼ cups shredded coconut
¾ cups finely crushed Ritz
　crackers
½ cup sugar
½ cup flour
½ cup butter, softened

Lemon Filling:

½ cup sugar

2½ tablespoons cornstarch
¼ teaspoon salt
1⅓ cups milk
1 egg, beaten
¼ cup lemon juice
½ teaspoon grated lemon rind
1 tablespoon butter
½ teaspoon vanilla

For coconut crust, mix all ingredients until crumbly. Pat half of the mixture into 9-inch square pan. Make filling. Combine sugar, cornstarch, and salt. Stir in milk. Cook until thick, stirring constantly. Mix egg and lemon juice. Stir with a little of the hot mixture, then stir into rest of hot mixture. Cook and stir over low heat 2 minutes. Add lemon rind, butter, and vanilla. Spread filling evenly on coconut layer and top with remaining crust mixture. Bake at 400°F. for 25 minutes, or until browned. Cool and chill. Cut into squares and serve. Makes 9-16 squares.

Lola Prescott
Groveland, MA

Lemon-Oat Cookies

Lemon-flavored oatmeal cookies.!

⅔ cup butter, softened
½ cup brown sugar, packed
½ teaspoon lemon extract

⅔ cup sifted flour
1½ cups quick oats

Cream butter with sugar; mix in lemon extract, flour, and oats. Stir until well blended. Form dough into 1-inch balls and place on lightly greased cookie sheet. Flatten each ball with tines of fork. Bake at 325°F. for 13-15 minutes, or until lightly golden brown. Makes about 2 dozen cookies.

Evelyn Webber
An Artist's Cookbook

Marmalade Cookies

A crisp, golden-sweet cookie, mildly orange-flavored.

¼ cup shortening
¼ cup orange marmalade
1½ cups sugar
grated rind of 1 orange

2 eggs
1 tablespoon orange juice
3 cups flour
1½ teaspoons baking powder

Cream shortening with marmalade, sugar, and grated orange rind. Add eggs and orange juice. Sift together flour and baking powder, and add to the creamed mixture. Beat until thoroughly blended. Drop by rounded teaspoonfuls onto ungreased cookie sheets, keeping the cookies about 2 inches apart. Flatten each cookie with the bottom of a small tumbler, greased and dipped in sugar. Bake in a preheated 400°F. oven for 7-10 minutes, until barely golden. Take from oven, and let sit for 3-5 minutes before removing to cooling rack. Watch closely since the cookies will brown very quickly. Makes 3-4 dozen cookies.

Yankee *Magazine*

Mondchens

Absolutely delectable, crisp, rich cookies for special occasions. The name means little moons. If you use a food processor or blender to grind the almonds, grind them with ¼ cup of the sugar. Called almond meal, finely ground almonds are available in some stores.

Cookies:
1 cup butter, softened
1 cup sugar
½ pound almonds, finely ground
1¼ cups flour
¼ teaspoon salt

grated rind of 1 lemon

Icing:
½ cup confectioner's sugar
1 teaspoon vanilla
milk or cream

Cream butter and sugar until light. Add remaining cookie ingredients, and finish mixing by kneading lightly by hand. Roll out on floured surface to a thickness of about ¼ inch. Cut out cookies with a small half-moon or round cutter. Bake at 400°F. for 7-8 minutes. Watch closely as cookies over-brown very easily.

For icing, mix confectioner's sugar and vanilla. Add enough milk to make a thin glaze. Brush cookies with glaze while still hot. Makes about 3 dozen cookies.

Grace and James Schaefer
Milwaukee, WI

Noel Cookies

An elegant ribbon cookie. Especially good at Christmas, as the name implies.

¾ cup butter
1¼ cups sugar
1 egg, beaten
1 teaspoon vanilla
2½ cups flour
1½ teaspoons baking powder
½ teaspoon salt

1 teaspoon almond extract
¼ cup chopped candied cherries
1 square unsweetened chocolate, melted
¼ cup chopped pecans
2 tablespoons coconut

Cream butter, and add sugar, egg, and vanilla. Sift flour, baking powder, and salt, and add to creamed mixture. Add ½ teaspoon of the almond extract. Mix well. Divide dough into three parts. Add the chopped cherries to one part, the chocolate and pecans to the second part, and the remaining ½ teaspoon of almond extract and the coconut to the third part. Line a 9x5-inch loaf pan with wax paper. Put the cherry dough on the bottom, top with the chocolate dough, and make a third layer of coconut dough. Pat down

(continued)

firmly with a spatula. Cover and refrigerate overnight. Take dough out of the pan and slice in half down the middle, lengthwise. Cut each half into slices ⅛-¼ inch thick. Bake slices on ungreased cookie sheets in a 400°F. oven for 10-12 minutes. Makes about 5 dozen cookies.

Mrs. Elizabeth J. Fox
Guilford, CT

Grandmother's Oatmeal Cookies

These oatmeal cookies sparked with cinnamon and molasses and loaded with raisins and nuts won a 1983 recipe contest.

½ cup shortening
1¼ cups sugar
2 eggs
6 tablespoons molasses
1¾ cups flour
1 teaspoon baking soda

1 teaspoon salt
1 teaspoon cinnamon
2 cups rolled oats
1 cup raisins
½ cup chopped walnuts
1 teaspoon vanilla

Using electric mixer, beat together shortening, sugar, eggs, and molasses in large bowl. With wooden spoon, stir in flour, baking soda, salt, and cinnamon. Mix well. Stir in remaining ingredients and mix by hand until well blended. On greased cookie sheet, drop batter by tablespoonfuls 2 inches apart. Bake at 350°F. for 8-10 minutes. Makes 3-4 dozen cookies.

Frances R. Brautigam
Kensington, CT

Italian "Peach" Cookies (Pesce)

Pesce cookies are a specialty of the Italian province of Reggio Emilia. Like most Italian cookies, they are crisp and not too sweet, although the filling and the coating are sweet. Wrapped individually in plastic wrap and placed in a box, they freeze beautifully. To thaw, simply take from freezer, unwrap, and leave uncovered at room temperature for an hour or so.

Cookies:

4 cups flour
3 tablespoons baking powder
1 cup plus 3 tablespoons sugar
¾ cup butter, softened
3 eggs

Filling:

1 egg yolk

1½ cups instant cocoa mix
6 tablespoons butter
dash vanilla
½ cup chopped nuts
½ cup vodka
½ cup grenadine
few drops almond extract
sugar

Mix all cookie ingredients together with hands or wooden spoon to form a very stiff dough. Break off small chunks of dough and form into balls (about walnut size). Place on ungreased cookie sheet and very slightly press down tops. Bake in a preheated 325°F. oven for 18-20 minutes or until lightly golden. Remove from pan, and immediately cut out a small round hole into the flat side of each cookie with a small pointed knife. Allow to cool thoroughly.

Mix first five filling ingredients together; if too dry, add a drop or two of vodka. Fill holes in cookies with chocolate mixture, and put every two cookies together to form a "peach," being sure that the chocolate does not come out around the edges. Roll "peaches" in mixture of ½ cup vodka and ½ cup grenadine syrup flavored with a few drops of almond extract. Immediately roll in granulated sugar. Replenish sugar if it becomes too damp. Makes 30 "peaches."

Dina Thomas
Lanoka Harbor, NJ

Pecan-Almond Pastries

Sinfully rich and compellingly delicious. Serve alone or with ice cream. Golden syrup, corn syrup, or maple syrup may be used in the topping instead of honey.

Pastry Base:

1 cup butter, softened
½ cup sugar
1 egg
½ teaspoon vanilla
3 cups flour

Topping:

⅔ cup butter

¾ cup light brown sugar, packed
3 tablespoons white sugar
¼ teaspoon salt
½ cup honey
3 tablespoons heavy cream
1¾ cups chopped pecans
¾ cup chopped blanched almonds
½ teaspoon vanilla   *(continued)*

Cream butter and sugar in large bowl until light and fluffy. Beat in egg and vanilla. Add flour gradually, blending in each new addition by hand or with the electric mixer on low speed. Mix only until blended. Gather dough into a ball. Lightly grease 9x13-inch baking pan. Press dough lightly into pan to a thickness of ¼ inch, letting some of the dough go up sides of pan. Cover pan with wax paper and refrigerate 1 hour. Preheat oven to 350°F. Take dough from refrigerator, and bake for 20 minutes, or until lightly golden. Check after 10 minutes, and prick or pat down any areas that are bubbling up. When done, remove from oven and place on a wire rack, keeping oven at 350°F. while you prepare the topping.

Combine first five topping ingredients in saucepan and heat, stirring from time to time, until mixture comes to full boil. Allow to boil, uncovered, for just 3 minutes, then remove from heat. Stir in cream, pecans, almonds, and vanilla. Spread mixture evenly over pastry in pan. Return to oven and bake for about 20 minutes, or until bubbling and browned. Place pan on wire rack to cool. When cool, cut into bars or squares with a sharp knife. Makes 24 squares or bars.

Dede Merlyn
Greenwich, CT

Pumpkin Bars

Moist, cake-like bars with an attractive orange-flecked icing. The pumpkin-spice-orange combination is just great. Easily doubled.

Bars:

½ cup butter, softened
1 cup brown sugar, packed
2 eggs
1 teaspoon vanilla
⅔ cup canned pumpkin
1 cup flour
1 teaspoon cinnamon
⅛ teaspoon baking powder
½ teaspoon baking soda

¼ teaspoon ginger
¼ teaspoon nutmeg
⅓ cup chopped walnuts

Frosting:

1½ cups confectioner's sugar
3 tablespoons butter, softened
2 tablespoons orange juice, or
    orange juice concentrate
1 tablespoon grated orange rind

Cream butter and brown sugar. Beat in eggs, vanilla and pumpkin. Stir in remaining Bars ingredients. Spread in oiled 9-inch square pan. Bake in 350°F. oven for 25-minutes. Cool completely.

Beat confectioner's sugar, butter, orange juice concentrate, and grated rind to make a smooth frosting. Spread over cooled bars. Makes 9-16 bars.

Mrs. Gay Mitchell
Lake Forest, IL

Queen Bee Cookies

Thin, brown, peanutty wafers. Just the thing to have with a glass of milk.

2½ cups flour
1½ teaspoons baking powder
¼ teaspoon baking soda
½ teaspoon salt
½ cup broken peanuts
½ cup butter, softened

½ cup peanut butter
½ cup honey
½ cup brown sugar, packed
1 egg
1 teaspoon vanilla

Sift together the dry ingredients and add the peanuts. In another bowl, cream butter and peanut butter together. Add honey, and mix well. Add sugar gradually. Beat in egg, and add vanilla. Stir in dry ingredients slowly, mixing thoroughly. Shape into roll and chill for several hours. Cut into thin slices (about ⅛ inch) and bake at 400°F. for about 10 minutes. Makes about 60 cookies.

Ruth H. Enck
Otego, NY

Raisin-Filled Cookies

Filled cookies are an old-fashioned treat, happily now returning to the cookie jar.

Cookies:

2 cups sugar
1 cup shortening
2 eggs
2 teaspoons vanilla
5½ cups flour
2 tablespoons baking powder
2 teaspoons baking soda

1 cup milk

Filling:

9-ounce package raisins
1 cup sugar
1 cup water
1 tablespoon flour

Cream sugar and shortening, then beat in eggs and vanilla. Sift together flour, baking powder, and baking soda. Add to creamed mixture alternately with the milk. Chill while you make filling.

Chop raisins very fine.* Combine with other filling ingredients in small saucepan. Cook until mixture boils and thickens. (Mixture will continue to thicken after taken from stove.)

Roll out cookie dough on floured surface to thickness of about ⅛ inch. Cut with round cookie cutter. Place cookies on ungreased cookie sheet. Place a teaspoonful or so of filling on top of each cookie. Top with another cookie. Cookies will seal as they bake. Bake in a 450°F. oven for 7-10 minutes, or until lightly browned. Remove from sheet and cool on racks. Makes 2½-3 dozen cookies.

Barbara Ash
Christ Church Cathedral
Hartford, CT

*Chopping the raisins is considerably easier if a food grinder or food processor is used. If using a food processor, put ½ cup of the sugar in with the raisins.

English Raspberry Bars

An absolutely delectable creation of pastry, raspberry jam, and chewy coconut topping.

Pastry:
1½ cups flour
1½ teaspoons baking powder
pinch salt
¾ cup butter, softened
2 eggs, well beaten
2 teaspoons milk
10-ounce jar raspberry jam

Topping:
1½ cups sugar
4 cups flaked coconut
6 tablespoons butter, softened
2 eggs, lightly beaten
1 teaspoon vanilla

Sift together flour, baking powder, and salt. Cut in butter as for pie dough. Add eggs and milk. Mix until smooth. Pat onto bottom and sides of very lightly greased 10x15-inch jelly-roll pan. Spread evenly with raspberry jam.

Mix all topping ingredients in large bowl. Mixture should be moist. Drop by teaspoonfuls on top of jam, then spread over entire surface to cover jam. Bake at 350°F. for 30 minutes. Makes about 48 squares.

Anne Chambers
Cincinnati, OH

Grandma's Rum Currant Cookies

Soft, aromatic cookies similar to hermits. If dough is too soft to handle, chill in refrigerator several hours or overnight.

2 cups brown sugar, packed
1 cup lard
3 eggs
1 teaspoon nutmeg
1 teaspoon cinnamon
½ teaspoon cloves

4 cups all purpose flour
1 teaspoon cream of tartar
3 tablespoons milk
1 cup currants soaked in 3
   tablespoons rum
cinnamon sugar

Cream brown sugar and lard thoroughly. Add eggs, one at a time, and beat until mixture is light. Sift spices with the flour. Dissolve cream of tartar in milk and add with dry ingredients to creamed mixture. Add rum-soaked currants and mix well. Roll out and cut with scalloped cutter. Sprinkle tops of cookies with cinnamon sugar. Bake on greased cookie sheets at 350°F. for 10 minutes. Makes up to 7 dozen cookies.

Mrs. Harvey H. Kiehl
Middleburg Heights, OH

Scottish Shortbread

Melt-in-your-mouth, buttery delights that make wonderful gifts. Sprinkle with colored sugar crystals for a festive touch.

2 cups instant blending flour (such as Wondra)	½ cup superfine granulated sugar
	1 cup butter, softened

Sift together flour and sugar. Blend butter into flour mixture with hands (takes time) to form a ball. Turn out onto lightly floured board, and knead a few times until dough cracks. Divide dough in half. On ungreased cookie sheet pat each half into 6-inch circle. Flute edges and prick all over with a fork. (Sprinkle with colored sugar, if desired.) Bake at 275°F. for 40 minutes. Cool and leave whole or break into pieces. Makes 2 shortbreads.

Mrs. Barbara Hutton
Peterborough, NH

Sesame Seed Bars

A sweet blond brownie with the distinctive flavor and crunch of sesame seeds.

½ cup sesame seeds	½ teaspoon salt
½ cup butter	1 cup brown sugar, packed
1½ cups flour	2 eggs
1 teaspoon baking powder	1 teaspoon vanilla

In skillet, toast sesame seeds over low heat, stirring until light brown. Remove from heat and add butter, stirring until melted. Turn into mixing bowl, and cool slightly. Sift flour, baking powder, and salt together. Beat sugar, eggs, and vanilla into sesame butter until mixture is smooth. Add dry ingredients, and stir until smooth. Pour into greased 9-inch square pan, and bake in a 375°F. oven for 20-25 minutes, or until bars test done. Makes 16-18 bars.

Alice Freeman
Newfane, VT

Silver Ripple Brownies

The ultimate in fudgy brownies, with a cream-cheese mixture swirled into the batter before baking. Real chocoholics will want the chocolate chip topping, too. Mix batter right in the double-boiler top.

1 cup butter	1 cup chopped walnuts
4 squares unsweetened chocolate	½ cup sugar
2 cups sugar	1 teaspoon vanilla
¼ teaspoon salt	1 egg
4 eggs, beaten	8 ounces cream cheese, softened
1 teaspoon vanilla	(6-ounce package chocolate chips)
1 cup flour	

(continued)

In top of 2-quart double boiler, melt butter and chocolate over boiling water. Remove from heat and stir in sugar and salt until almost dissolved. Stir in eggs and 1 teaspoon vanilla, and blend well. Add flour and nuts, and stir until completely mixed in. Pour into greased 9x13-inch pan. In separate bowl, beat ½ cup sugar, 1 teaspoon vanilla, and 1 egg into softened cream cheese until smooth. Drop in globs on brownie batter in pan, and then swirl into the brownie batter with a knife until nicely marbled. Sprinkle optional chocolate chips on top if desired. Bake at 325°F. for 35-40 minutes. Remove from oven and cool on rack. Cut into squares while still warm. Makes about 2 dozen brownies.

Mary Stamper
Booneville, KY

Whoopie Pies with Best-Ever Filling

Whoopie-pie sandwiches with a wonderfully creamy, not-too-sweet filling that you can use for cakes, too. It's even stiff enough to be piped through a pastry bag.

Filling:

¾ cup milk
3 tablespoons flour
¾ cup shortening (part butter)
¾ cup sugar
1½ teaspoons vanilla

Cookies:

2 cups flour

1½ teaspoons baking soda
1 teaspoon salt
5 tablespoons cocoa
1 cup sugar
6 tablespoons shortening
1 egg
1 cup milk
1 teaspoon vanilla

To make filling, gradually stir milk into flour in small saucepan. Cook, stirring constantly, over medium heat until mixture forms thick paste. Allow to cool thoroughly. Combine shortening, sugar, and vanilla in large mixer bowl. Add milk mixture, and beat at high speed until light and fluffy and sugar is dissolved (small amount rubbed between the fingers will not feel grainy).

Mix together flour, soda, salt, and cocoa. Set aside. Cream sugar and shortening; add egg, milk, and vanilla, and mix well. Slowly stir in dry ingredients. Drop by tablespoonfuls (36) on greased cookie sheets. Bake at 425°F. for 7 minutes. Spread 18 with filling, and top with the other 18 to make 18 sandwiches.

Julie-Ann B. Scala
Strafford, NH

Surprise Cookies

A big chunk of a cookie with a surprise center.

1 cup butter, softened
½ cup sugar
1 teaspoon vanilla
2 cups flour

1 cup finely chopped walnuts or
  pecans
9-ounce bag chocolate kisses
confectioner's sugar

Beat butter, sugar, and vanilla until light and fluffy. Beat in flour and nuts until well blended. Unwrap the kisses. Divide dough into 50 pieces. Wrap each piece around a kiss to make a ball. Be sure to cover candy completely. Place on ungreased cookie sheets. Bake at 375°F. for 12 minutes, or until cookies are set but not brown. Let stand on sheets for 1 minute and then cool on wire racks. When cookies have cooled slightly, roll in confectioner's sugar. Makes 50 cookies.

Suzanne Kupher
Sherman Cooks!

CANDY

Although it has almost *no* nutritional value, candy is one of the true pleasures of life. Having a chocolate, caramel, or lollipop slowly dissolve in the mouth is a heavenly sensation to be enjoyed as long as possible. Creating these ultimate morsels of pleasure is a rewarding accomplishment for any cook, particularly since making candy can be tricky.

Recognizing the different stages of boiling syrup takes practice. Boiling candy a little too much or a little too little ends in disaster. The cold-water method of testing can be mastered with the help of a candy thermometer. Test the syrup stages with both cold water and a thermometer. And watch the bubbles. As the water evaporates during boiling, the bubbles go from tiny and numerous to large plop-plop bubbles. Follow all directions exactly.

Candy makes a marvelous gift from your kitchen, as no store-bought sweet can come close to the home-made product. Easy to store and to send, and far less expensive made at home, too.

Barley Sugar

Form candy into clear wafers, lollipops, or barley toys. The molds and lollipop sticks are available from Maid of Scandinavia (3244 Raleigh Ave. South, Minneapolis, MN 55416) or other culinary supply firms. If candy hardens in pan, place over low heat to remelt.

Barley Water:
½ cup pearl barley
3 cups boiling water

Candy:
2 cups sugar
¼ cup barley water
½ cup water

⅔ cup light corn syrup
1 teaspoon vanilla, or few drops oil of cassia (cinnamon), oil of wintergreen, or oil of peppermint
few drops food color

Place barley in boiling water, cover pot, and simmer for 50-60 minutes until barley is tender. Drain, reserving water. Use barley for something else, soup or stew. Refrigerate water. The barley water will jell somewhat when chilled. That is when it is ready to use for candy. Makes ¾ cup.

Combine sugar, barley water, and water in 2-quart double-boiler top or high-sided saucepan. Turn heat to high, and stir with wooden spoon to dissolve sugar. Affix candy thermometer to side of saucepan. Set aside wooden spoon, and allow syrup to come to boil. Keep boiling over high heat until syrup reaches 242°F. (it will be just about ready to boil over). Add corn syrup, pouring it in around the perimeter of the pan. Do not stir. Continue to boil to a temperature of 290°F. Add vanilla or other flavoring and food color. Do not stir, but keep syrup boiling until 300°F. Immediately remove from stove, and immerse bottom of pan in cool water for just a moment to stop the cooking. Set pan aside until bubbles die down. Pour syrup into oiled molds, or drop by teaspoonfuls on oiled cookie sheet or other flat, oiled surface. Add lollipop sticks if desired. When cool, wrap in plastic wrap and store in a dry place — a metal cake tin is good. Makes 6-8 barley toys, or 16 lollipop discs or wafers.

Silence Ramsay
Buffalo, NY

CANDY TABLE

How to determine the different boiling stages with thermometer and cold water tests.

Candy stage	Temperature*	Cold water test
Thread	230-234°F.	Syrup dropped from a spoon spins a 2-inch thread.
Soft ball	234-240°F.	Syrup can be shaped into a ball, but flattens when removed from water.
Firm ball	244-248°F.	Syrup can be shaped into a firm ball that will not flatten when removed from water.
Hard ball	250-266°F.	Syrup forms hard but pliable ball.
Soft crack	270-290°F.	Syrup separates into threads that are not brittle.
Hard crack	300-310°F.	Syrup separates into hard, brittle threads.

*For each 500 feet in elevation above sea level, cook syrup one degree lower.

TIPS

1. Always check the boiling point of water on your candy thermometer. If it is higher or lower than 212°F., adjust your cooking temperatures accordingly.

2. When making candies that require stirring while boiling, it is safest to use the cold water test *as well as* a candy thermometer.

3. While dissolving the sugar in a candy recipe, wash down the sugar crystals on the sides of the pan with a pastry brush dipped in cold water.

4. Too high a stove temperature while boiling syrup can cause it to scorch. Better a lower temperature that takes longer. But use high for hard candy.

5. Boiled syrup will triple in volume during cooking, so be sure to use the pan size recommended in the recipe. A heavy pan will keep a more even heart.

6. Watch candy closely. The syrup may seem to take forever to get to the desired stage, but once it nears that point, things move *very* quickly, as *you* must to avert disaster.

Bonnie Berrett
Jaffrey, NH

Five Pounds of Chocolates

You have never really tasted chocolates until you make your own. Freshly made chocolates are to even the most expensive store-boughten kind as fresh garden vegetables are to canned. Do not substitute real vanilla extract for imitation — Mrs. Perron has tried both, and she explains that the extra liquid in the imitation vanilla is vital to the texture and flavor of the fondant. Five pounds is a lot of chocolates, and you'll want the biggest bowl you can find to mix the fondant in. Get your children or neighbors in to help. You'll all have fun, and fill out your Christmas lists nicely with little boxes of your own hand-dipped chocolates. Have as many flavorings as you can find on hand, along with chopped nuts and raisins and a box of food coloring. Also, set out a lot of small bowls to mix up the different fondant flavors in. Among the myriad possibilities: rum-raisin, chocolate chip, maple walnut, lemon nut, cinnamon (use oil of cinnamon), wintergreen and peppermint (use the oils), orange, cherry, etc. Use the fondant plain for vanilla cremes.

Fondant:

six 1-pound packages
    confectioner's sugar
½ cup imitation vanilla
15-ounce can sweetened condensed
    milk

1 pound margarine, melted

Chocolate Coating:

¾ block paraffin wax
two 8-ounce packages unsweetened
    chocolate

In *large* bowl, combine all fondant ingredients and mix well, stirring or kneading with fingers until smooth. Now divide up fondant into batches in the small bowls, and flavor as desired, leaving some fondant plain vanilla. Add flavorings sparingly, a little at a time, tasting until correct. Use only a very few drops of the oils of cinnamon, wintergreen, and peppermint — their flavors are very strong. Cover bowls with plastic wrap while you make coating.

Place paraffin and chocolate in double-boiler top over boiling water, and melt over medium heat.

Meanwhile, roll fondant into little balls, or form into tiny squares, keeping each flavor separate. Spread table with wax paper. Stir chocolate when melted. Remove from heat. Pour out boiling water in double-boiler bottom, and refill with lukewarm water. Chocolate should be only slightly warm for dipping consistency. Chocolate may be rewarmed over hot water on stove if necessary. With dipping fork* or iced tea spoon (long-handled), dip each piece of fondant in chocolate just to cover. Place coated chocolates on wax paper to harden at room temperature. Reserve a different place on the table for each flavor, so that you can divide up the finished candies into the desired assortment of flavors for each box. Makes 5 pounds of chocolates.

Jeannette Perron
Dublin, NH

*Professional dipping forks are available in stores selling chocolate- and candy-making supplies. An easy version can be made at home by making a closed circle out of the tines on a long-handled, two-tine fork.

OTHER COATINGS FOR CHOCOLATES

First, if you prefer your chocolates coated with semisweet or milk chocolate instead of unsweetened, you can substitute 18 ounces (3 cups) semisweet or milk chocolate bits, and reduce the paraffin to a little less than a quarter block, then follow the recipe given above.

Or, if you really get into it, there are a number of other coatings that can be used for chocolates. They vary from being very easy to use to fairly difficult. The easiest is called summer coating — a vegetable-fat-based product usually termed "white chocolate." It comes in bars or wafers in a variety of colors and flavors (including semisweet and milk chocolate). All one has to do with this coating is to melt it over warm water. As the name implies, it is especially good for use in warm weather.

Another relatively easy coating can be made by combining semisweet or milk chocolate with tasteless vegetable oil. Shave three 7-ounce bars of chocolate into the top of a double boiler and add ¼ cup of vegetable oil. Bring water in bottom half of the double boiler to boil, and remove from the heat. Put the top half over the water and cover until the chocolate is completely melted. If necessary, cool until the chocolate is about 90°F. Reheat over warm water if chocolate gets too cool.

The most difficult coating to use, but the very best, is real chocolate without any additives. Real chocolate is temperamental. If not handled correctly, the cocoa butter will separate from the chocolate and form what is called "chocolate bloom" (greyish brown streaks). To prevent this from happening, the chocolate must be tempered. This is a process in which shaved chocolate is melted in the top of a double boiler over water and then the temperature of the chocolate is brought down to 89°F. The chocolate must be retempered if it cools too much. Using real chocolate coating definitely takes practice, *and* an accurate chocolate or microwave meat thermometer that gives temperatures below 100°F.

Bonnie Berrett
Jaffrey, NH

Coconut Swirls

Chocolate-covered coconut drops very similar to the commercial candy "Mounds." Top with a toasted whole almond for an easy variation. These candies seem to magically disappear — better make a double batch.

2 tablespoons butter	½ cup instant dry milk
3 tablespoons water	3 cups flaked coconut
1 teaspoon vanilla	6 ounces semisweet- or milk-
2 cups confectioner's sugar	chocolate bits (continued)

Melt butter in medium saucepan. Remove from heat and add water and vanilla. In bowl, stir together confectioner's sugar and dry milk. Add to butter mixture ½ cup at a time. Mix well. Stir in coconut. Drop by teaspoonfuls onto wax paper. Flatten rounds with fingers. Let stand until firm (about 10 minutes). Melt chocolate bits in top of double boiler over simmering water. Swirl a teaspoon of chocolate over each coconut drop. Chill until chocolate sets. Makes about 3 dozen.

Marguerite H. Stanas
Hopedale, MA

Fruit Loaf Candy

A colorful and mouth-watering holiday goody.

6 cups sugar	**1 slice candied pineapple**
1½ cups dark corn syrup	**¾ cup chopped candied cherries**
3 cups cream	**1½ cups walnuts**

Combine sugar, corn syrup, and cream in a large pan. Stir, and cook over medium heat until sugar is dissolved. Wash down sugar crystals on sides of pan with pastry brush dipped in cold water. Continue cooking over medium heat until mixture reaches soft-ball stage (234-240°F. on candy thermometer). Set in pan of cold water for a few minutes, then beat until stiff. Add fruit and nuts and pour into buttered 9x12-inch pan. When cool and set, cut into pieces. Makes about 4 pounds.

Winona Krenzer
Prairie Village, KS

Marshmallow-Peanut Butter Fudge

A grand gift for peanut butter lovers — so easy, too!

2¼ cups sugar	**1 cup peanut butter**
¼ cup butter	**½ cup chopped nuts**
¾ cup evaporated milk	**1 teaspoon vanilla**
6-ounce jar marshmallow creme	
(not fluff)	

Mix sugar, butter, and evaporated milk in heavy 2-quart saucepan, and stir over medium heat until sugar dissolves. Boil for 5 minutes, stirring constantly. Remove from heat; add marshmallow creme, peanut butter, nuts, and vanilla. Stir until thoroughly blended. Pour into buttered 8-inch square pan. Cool and cut into squares. Makes about 2 pounds.

Kay Edwards
Beckley, WV

Orange Balls

Creamy, mildly tart orange confections. No cooking, and super-easy.

12-ounce box vanilla wafers
½ cup margarine, softened
1-pound box confectioner's sugar
1 cup chopped nuts

6-ounce can frozen orange juice
concentrate, thawed
flaked coconut

Crush vanilla wafers into fine crumbs.* Cream margarine and confectioner's sugar. Add crumbs, nuts, and orange juice concentrate. Mix well. Form into walnut-sized balls, and roll balls in coconut. Refrigerate. The flavor will mellow after about 24 hours. Keep refrigerated. Makes about 75 balls.

Mrs. Mildred L. Hixon
Warner Robins, GA

*Using a food processor or blender will make this task easier, but a rolling pin will work just fine.

Pumpkin Fudge

A creamy fudge that tastes like pumpkin pie. A prizewinning way to use leftover canned pumpkin.

2 cups sugar
½ cup evaporated milk
2 tablespoons canned pumpkin
¼ teaspoon cornstarch

½ teaspoon pumpkin-pie spice (or
scant ½ teaspoon cinnamon
mixed with ¼ teaspoon ginger
and pinch ground cloves)
½ teaspoon vanilla

In medium saucepan, combine sugar, evaporated milk, pumpkin, cornstarch, and pumpkin-pie spice. Cook over medium heat, stirring constantly, until sugar has melted and mixture comes to a boil. Continue to cook without stirring until mixture reaches 234-238°F. on a candy thermometer (soft-ball stage). Remove from heat, add vanilla, and beat until opaque. Pour into greased 8-inch square pan. Cool until firm. Cut into squares. Makes about 2 pounds.

Ann Gergel
Olean, NY

CONTRIBUTING COOKBOOKS

Yankee is grateful to the following
organizations for giving us permission to include here
these recipes selected from their cookbooks:

The American Cancer Society, Connecticut Division, Inc., publishers of CONNECTICUT COOKS (1981, $8.95), 14 Village Lane, P.O. Box 410, Wallingford, CT 06492, for: *Breast of Chicken Sauté; Gratin Italienne; Bihon Guisado; Chicken Baked in Beer and Tomatoes.*

The American Cancer Society, New Hampshire Division, Inc., publishers of A TASTE OF NEW HAMPSHIRE (1981), 686 Mast Rd., Manchester, NH 03102, for *Chicken Crescent Squares.*

The American-French Genealogical Society, publishers of JE ME SOU-VIENS LA CUISINE DE LA GRANDMÈRE (1981, $7.50). P.O. Box 2113, Pawtucket, RI 02861, for: *Poached Eggs on Toast with Wine Sauce; Scrambled Eggs with Spinach; Sole Fillets in Creole Sauce; Fish Matelote with Red Wine; Ham Puff; Tourtière; Filets Piquants; Curried Cauliflower; Peas à la Bonne Femme; Petit Pois; Coq au Vin.*

The Concord Antiquarian Society, publishers of AN OLDE CONCORD CHRISTMAS and THE FLAVOUR OF CONCORD (1976), Concord, MA 01742, for: *Baked Bluefish with Mustard Sauce; Baked Beans; Swordfish with Wine and Sour Cream Sauce; Portsmouth Salad; Avocado Cream Sherbet;* and *Calves Liver Provençale; Glazed Corned Beef; Cold Lemon Soufflé.*

Connecticut Society for the Prevention of Blindness, Inc., publishers of VITTLES UNLIMITED (1976, $5.95), 24 Wall St., Box 20/20, Madison, CT 06443, for: *French Apple Tart; Chilled Blueberry Pie; Chocolate-Orange Meringue Torte; Best Ever Peach Pie; Maple Pecan Pie; Frozen Pumpkin Applesauce Pie; Beef Fillets Wellington with Golden Tarragon Sauce; Chicken Breasts with Apples; Chicken Tamale Pie; Ham with Champagne Sauce; Chicken Soufflé on Tomatoes.*

Hanover Center Women's Fellowship, publishers of HANOVER CENTER COOKS (1982, $6.25), c/o Ms. Lillian Bailey, Bayley Corner, Etna, NH 03750, for: *Chicken of Two Continents; Lettuce and Sweet Onion Salad; Poppy Seed Dressing.*

Ladies Visiting Committee, Massachusetts Eye and Ear Infirmary, publishers of FAVORITE FOODS (1980, $7.95), 243 Charles St., Boston, MA 02114, for: *Beef Tenderloin in Claret; Chicken in Fresh Tomato Sauce; Veal Scallopine; Sweet and Sour Brisket; Country Beef Curry; Vermont Apple Chicken.*

New Hampshire Federation of Women's Clubs, publishers of GFWC-NHFWC COMPLETE MENU COOKBOOK ($7.00), c/o Mrs. Arthur A. Brown, Jr., Box 304, Washington St., Conway, NH 03818, for: *Sukiyaki; Moussaka; Norwegian Spinach Potatoes; Coconut Butterfly Shrimp.*

The Old State House, 800 Main St., Hartford, CT 06103, publishers of the CONNECTICUT JUBILEE 1983 BREAD COOKBOOK, © 1983 United Technologies Corporation, for: *Polish Dark Rye Bread.*

The Rockport Garden Club, publishers of THE ROCKPORT HERITAGE COOKBOOK (1982), Rockport, ME 04856, for: *International Dateline Chicken; Grated Beets and Sour Cream; Baked Scallops with Sherry; Herbed Cherry Tomatoes; Fruit Cocktail Supreme; Marinated Broiled Chicken.*

The Sherman Library, publishers of SHERMAN COOKS! (1975, $5.95), RR 1, Box 146, Sherman, CT 06784, for: *Giant Popover for Two; Mozzarella Croquettes; Linguine Pepper Pond; Noodle Pie; Brown Rice, Tomato, and Cheese Casserole; Turkey Spinach Crepes; Spinach Chicken Gratin; Rice Pilaf II; Chicken with Lemon Sauce; Quenelles de Poisson; Russian Fish Pie; Italian Stuffed Peppers; Orange Form Cake; Surprise Cookies.*

The Westerly Community Chorus, publishers of THE WELL TEMPERED KITCHEN (1978, $6.95), Box 81, Westerly, RI 02891, for: *Apple-Stuffed Chicken; English Tea Room Dressing; Lettuce and Spinach Salad.*

Westerly Hospital Aid Association, publishers of BON APPÉTIT (1977, $6.00), c/o Mrs. Edward Grauel, Shelter Harbor, Westerly, RI, 02891, for: *Curried Chicken and Lobster; Chicken Breasts Archduke.*

The Westfield Women's Club, publishers of COOKING AT COURT (1975, $4.95), P.O. Box 711, Westfield, MA 01085, for: *Cottage Cheese Omelet; Poached Eggs à la Reine; Macaroni with Prosciutto-Artichoke Sauce; Braggiolotini Hélène; Chicken and Crab Valentine; Kauilani Chicken; Apricot Chicken; Rice Pilaf I; Potted Beef; Curried Beef; Phyl's Matrosen Beef; Salmon Mousse; Savory Soufflé Roll; Ham Loaf; Lamb Stew with Ginger; Cranberry Squash; Wild Rice Seafood; Onions au Gratin; Creoled Summer Squash; Chicken and Artichokes; Poulet en Cocotte; Chicken Livers Stroganoff.*

The Weston Arts and Craft Association, publishers of AN ARTIST'S COOKBOOK (1982, $4.75), P.O. Box 293, Weston, MA 02193, for: *Broccoli-Cheese Soufflé; Walnut-Cheddar Loaf; Lemon Cookies.*

INDEX

N

P